T0159175

MURDERS, MYSTERIES AND HISTORY OF CRAWFORD COUNTY, PENNSYLVANIA 1800 – 1956

DON HILTON

authorHOUSE®

AuthorHouse™
1663 Liberty Drive
Bloomington, IN 47403
www.authorhouse.com
Phone: 1-800-839-8640

Published by AuthorHouse 8/29/2012

ISBN: 978-1-4772-6616-8 (sc)
ISBN: 978-1-4772-6615-1 (e)

Library of Congress Control Number: 2012916268

TABLE OF CONTENTS

– My Brother Will –

Forever my Partner in Crime

Thanks To...

Mystery maven J.D. Sikora for encouragement and guidance. The young and bright Clare Hooper, EngD., for across-the-pond opinions. The puckish Professor Janice Broder for thoughts on the topic, edits, and always-needed assistance with pesky punctuation. Dr. Kevin Weidenbaum for his astute and careful reading, questions about structure, and enthusiasm for the subject at hand.

Artist Kat Sikora for the cover art, also made possible by Mike Sample's permission for use of the newspaper clippings—he's the present-day publisher of the *Titusville Herald*. Ms. Peggy Laley Peterson and Ms. Margie Peterson were kind enough to bring me up to speed on the life of their justice-dealing kin.

The helpful people at the Centre County Historical Society, for information on Rockview Prison and Pennsylvania's earliest electrocutions. The Conneaut Lake Area Historical Society, where this whole mess started. The Crawford County Historical Society, my second home through much of the research. The Warren County Historical Society, for information on early judges. If you don't support your local historical society, then shame on you! Those records don't get kept and microfilm readers don't get fixed all by themselves, you know.

Gratitude is owed the ever-patient women working in the Office of the Recorder in the Crawford County Courthouse. The officers and staff of the Titusville Police Department. Keith Amolsch and Meadville's WMGW. Finally, of course, my family and friends, who hardly ever complained of listening to "all that murder stuff."

PREFACE

"How in the world did you ever get interested in *that*?" Well, while researching my books *Sailing Through Time* and *Conneaut Lake Ferry Tales,* I came across a 1924 article in a local newspaper, describing how an axe-wielding, one-legged farmhand murdered a young schoolteacher. It captured my attention, but I couldn't afford to be sidetracked. I made an entry in my notebook and moved on.

I never forgot the one-legged man. He tickled my brain until, one dark and stormy night (and it really *was* a dark and stormy night), I retrieved my short notation and began digging. It was amazing to watch what I thought was an isolated incident blossom into a garden of noxious weeds.

What follows are the one hundred-plus Crawford County murders I found, along with a little history. I've detailed all crimes resulting in executions and several of the more sensational and interesting cases.

This book includes all of the deaths I could find where the initial charge was "murder." A compilation of all manslaughter cases would take a length few would read, even were I willing to write it. You'll also find crimes that would now likely be considered murder, even if they were not in past societies. A few cases don't fit any of the above characteristic but are included because they struck my fancy.

I am certain that my list of killings is incomplete. That's because information from the early part of the county's history is spotty. Court records are inaccessible. Newspapers through the mid-1800s can be dense and difficult to read. They don't always publish what we might think of as "news." Different papers present different versions of the same story, twisting the facts until they're nearly unrecognizable. You'll see plenty of question marks ("?") in the listings—indicating my inability to find those data.

I was lucky enough to meet individuals whose families were changed by some of the acts of violence I describe. For me, it helped drive home the following point: *This stuff happened to real people.* I grew uncomfortable as I moved into what I thought of as modern times; everything felt too close to home and so my list stops in 1956. That's the year I was born.

I urge you to be gentle with anyone you recognize. Remember what my Grandma Esau whispered in my six-year-old ear when she caught me staring at a man with a disfigured face: "It could just as easily be you!"

ABOUT THIS BOOK

The 156-year span covered is subdivided by the judicial terms of Crawford County's President Judges. Some of these esteemed gentlemen were on the bench for hardly a year. Others served twenty years, or more. Some presided over no murder trials. Others heard a great number. These facts give the book an uneven structure.

Population density isn't the best predictor of crime, but it's a reasonable start because fewer people commit fewer crimes. It takes a long while for the population of Crawford County to grow dense enough for murders to become frequent. The magic number is about 56,000 people, by my reckoning. In the county's two major cities, Meadville and Titusville, killings are much more commonplace once their populations reach around 7,000.

I found seven murders in the first sixty-five years of the county but nearly two dozen in the two decades that followed. *Skip to the mid-1860s to dive right into the action*, but be sure to come back to the earliest years when courts dealt no-nonsense, frontier justice to those considered guilty.

Nothing happens in a vacuum. An on-going timeline presents information that helps tie local murders back to what was happening elsewhere in the county and the rest of the world. Along those same lines, some county history is described as are a few of the social changes that controlled the reasons for crimes and changes to those involved.

"Scholarly" does not describe my style of writing, but this is a book of facts. What you'll read is based on research—nothing is "made-up." The more involved narratives were adapted from newspapers of the day. Take a look at the final chapter—*Sources and Sundries*—for a description of some of the strengths and weaknesses of the materials used.

I was lucky to have smart people proof my text and offer suggestions, but I am responsible for the content. Any sparkling insights, or woeful mistakes, belong to me.

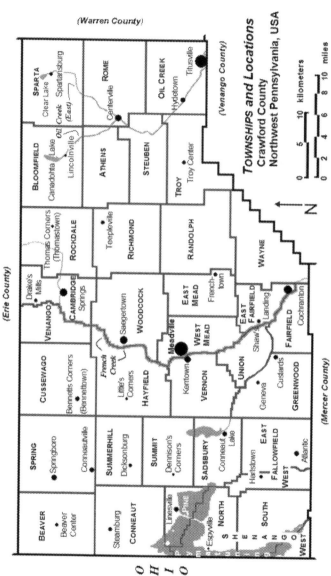

TOWNSHIPS and Locations
Crawford County
Northwest Pennsylvania, USA

N

0   5   10   kilometers
0   2   4   6   8   10   miles

(Warren County)

(Erie County)

(Venango County)

(Mercer County)

OHIO

SPARTA
Clear Lake   Spartansburg
Oil Creek (East)
ROME
Centerville
OIL CREEK
Titusville
Hydetown

BLOOMFIELD
Canadohta Lake
Lincolnville
ATHENS
STEUBEN
TROY
Troy Center

Thomas Corners
(Thomastown)
ROCKDALE
Teeplleville
RICHMOND
RANDOLPH
WAYNE

Drake's Mills
VENANGO
CAMBRIDGE Springs
Saegertown
WOODCOCK
EAST MEAD
French town
EAST FAIRFIELD
Landing
FAIRFIELD
Cochranton

CUSSEWAGO
Bennetts Corners
(Bennettown)
French Creek
Little's Corners
HAYFIELD
Meadville
WEST MEAD
Kerrtown
VERNON
UNION
Shaws
Custards
Genova
GREENWOOD

SPRING
Springboro
Conneautville
SUMMERHILL
Dicksonburg
SUMMIT
Dennison's Corners
SADSBURY
Conneaut Lake
Hartstown
EAST FALLOWFIELD
WEST
Atlantic

BEAVER
Beaver Center
Steamburg
CONNEAUT
Linesville
PINE
Espyville
NORTH
SOUTH
SHENANGO
WEST

A SHORT AND RELATIVELY PAINLESS HISTORY

The land that forms present day Crawford County, in northwest Pennsylvania, United States, was "purchased" from Native Americans in 1784. Permanent white settlers arrived shortly thereafter, mostly along a series of fortifications strung northward from Fort Pitt where the Ohio River is created by the joining of the Allegheny and Monongahela.

Fort Franklin, built in 1787 where French Creek meets the Allegheny River, was the closest safe haven to what became Crawford County. Settlers fled to Franklin as late as 1793 for safety from marauding bands of what they called (among other things) "Indians." The last fatal attack by natives on area settlers came on June 3, 1795, when James Findlay and Barnabas McCormick were shot and scalped while splitting rails a little north of where the outlet of Conneaut Lake joins French Creek. It's likely the attackers were allies of the English who influenced native populations in the wilderness to the north and west.

When the first white explorers traveled along the 117-mile long French Creek (also then known as the "In-nun-ga-ch," "Venango," or "Fleuve aux Boeufs"), they found a large, flat valley already mostly devoid of trees. It was hedged on the west by steep hills and gave way to gentler but equally high elevations to the east. It was an ideal place to put down roots, and so settlement in Meadville, Pennsylvania began in 1787.

Among the earliest to arrive was Samuel Lord, one of the men who first surveyed the area, and John and David Mead from east-central Pennsylvania who reconnoitered in 1787 and returned the following year to plant crops and winter over.

The eastern edge of what became county lands was populated somewhat more peacefully. The valley of the upper Allegheny River, that runs near that area, was dominated by the Seneca Leader Gaiänt'wakê (Cornplanter) who was mostly friendly to settlers. His influence was felt throughout that region and provided stability in the complicated relationship between the ever-growing number of newcomers and the natives they displaced.

Crawford County was legislated into existence by the Commonwealth of Pennsylvania on March 12, 1800. Like some of its surrounding sisters (Armstrong, Butler, Mercer, and Warren), Crawford was named for a hero of the American Revolution.

In June of 1782, during a raid into the great wilderness of Ohio, Colonel William Crawford had the misfortune of being captured by the British-allied Delawares who considered him a war criminal—a charge that may or may not have been true. Crawford was tortured, scalped alive, and slowly roasted to death. Considering those facts, a book on the murders that took place in his namesake county feels entirely appropriate.

Crawford County President Judges - 1800 to 1955

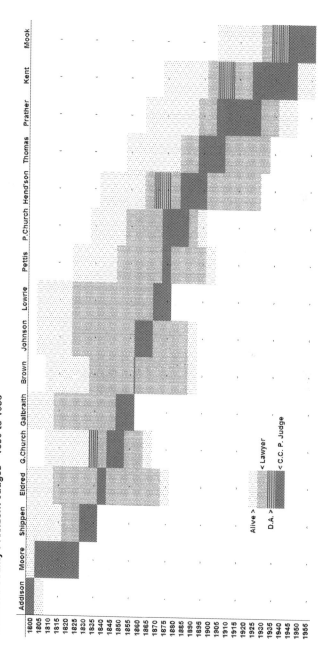

1800 — 1803

THE HONORABLE ALEXANDER ADDISON

Alexander Addison's silhouette shows him with an aristocrat's bearing: a high forehead, straight nose, prominent chin, and a heavy, substantial face. His experience in Crawford County serves as early proof of the inextricable link between the courts and politics.

Crawford County's first President Judge has a well-deserved reputation as a brilliant, if somewhat inflexible individual. A one-time Presbyterian preacher, he is happy to deliver homilies from the bench and tie the problems of those in trouble with the law to a lack of religious sincerity.

Early histories of Crawford County describe how Addison is impeached for a combination of his personality and denying an Associate Judge the opportunity to speak his mind on a case at hand. That is an inaccurate description of what really happened.

In Judge Addison's time, there are two major political parties in the United States. The Republican/Democrats who champion strong states' rights, an agriculturally-based economy, little or no central banking, few taxes, and a strict interpretation of the country's Constitution.

Opposed to them are the Federalists who believe in a strong federal government, a strong manufacturing base, strong central banks, taxes, full federal coffers, and a less strict interpretation of the Constitution.

Does any of this sound familiar?

Addison is appointed by Pennsylvania Governor McKean who is elected on a Federalist platform. That party loses ground in 1801 when Thomas Jefferson becomes President of the United States. McKean sees the writing on the wall and jumps to the Republican/Democrats. As the weakened Federalists are swept from power, Jefferson's party turns its efforts onto the Crawford County Judge who has been abandoned by McKean and is, literally, living far removed, in the frontier backwoods of the Commonwealth.

In January of 1803, the Pennsylvania State Senate impeaches Addison on the basis of an unspecified "misdemeanor." They remove him from the bench and disqualify him from holding any other judicial office.

Addison's days of sitting in legal judgment are over.

1800: John Adams is President of the United States. Future President Millard Fillmore is born. Crawford County also comes to life with 2,346 (white) people and the following townships already in place: Conneaut (west), Mead (central), and a forerunner of Oil Creek (east). From them, eight more "originals" are created in July of 1800: Beaver, Cussewago, Fairfield, Fallowfield, Sadsbury, Shenango, and Venango. (The creation of Crawford County's thirty-five townships is presented here in a straightforward manner. How the townships came to be and evolved over time is beyond the scope of this book.)

THE EARLY DAYS OF JUSTICE

Meadville was already the center of justice for the Township of Mead in 1800 when Crawford was carved from an oversized

Allegheny County. The first County Court was held in the William Dick residence on the northeast corner of Water Street and Cherry Alley, with David Mead and John Kelso as Associate Judges. By the second session, President Judge Alexander Addison was on the bench.

The county's first "real" jail was three blocks north of the court, in the rear room of a tavern owned by Henry Richard on the southwest corner of Water Street and Steer's Alley. Its first prisoner was jailed for contempt; it seems he created a disturbance by singing in the courtroom. The court asked him to be quiet. He responded with a shouted "go to hell!" In any century, that's a *bad* idea. The prisoner, left alone in the untested jail, escaped by climbing up and out the chimney—he literally "flue" the coop!

In March 1804, the Commonwealth ordered the construction of a courthouse and jail. A two-storied hewn-log building was built on the west side of Meadville's Public Square (the "Diamond"), with jail and jailor's residence on the first floor and courtroom above.

The court at Meadville met on a quarterly basis and, at first, Crawford shared its judges with all of the equally, sparsely populated counties west of the Allegheny River.

THE GRAND JURY

Through the period covered by this book, an "Indicting Grand Jury" served an entry to the rest of the criminal court system. The circumstances of a case were presented to citizen jurors from across the county who decided if there was cause or evidence to move forward into a full-blown criminal trial.

While the Commonwealth was always represented, usually by the District Attorney, the accused brought their own legal mouthpiece only if they had the money. The right to counsel in an Indicting Grand Jury was not established in the early days, and the poor were assigned lawyers only when the judge saw a need.

The Grand Jury's primary job was to determine if the facts of the case were compelling enough to justify a criminal trial for the accused. A "true bill" was returned if the jurors found reason to take the case forward into trial. The accused was then "bound over" to the next session of criminal court. "Not a true bill" indicated the facts did not warrant further action and the accused was set free—often to be re-arrested on different charges.

Judges varied in their instructions to the Grand Jury. Some wanted a gatekeeper, preventing what might be frivolous lawsuits. Others desired true bills for all but the most obviously innocent.

Crawford's Grand Jury also performed an annual inspection of the infrastructure of the county legal system: the jail, poorhouse, and courthouse itself. It was the body that decided if things were copasetic, or if purse strings were to be loosened for improvements, upgrades, or replacements.

Through the mid-1970s, the Commonwealth replaced Indicting Grand Juries with "informational procedures" of arraignments and hearings. Not everyone's happy with the change, and there have been calls, through the years, for a return to the old way of doing things.

1800, OCTOBER: The Grand Jury hands down true bills for theft of personal property, assault and battery, and forcible entry. Figure it as proof that things really haven't changed much over the centuries.

1801: There's an Electoral College tie between Thomas Jefferson and his opponent, Aaron Burr. The U.S. House of Representatives splits the difference, making Jefferson President and Burr V.P. This must've made for some interesting policy discussions. In July, Oil Creek Township is reorganized, and Rockdale is created from Mead.

1802: West Point is established. Napoleon Bonaparte causes all kinds of trouble for a lot of people across the sea in Europe. Author Lydia Child is born. She writes stories and poetry in the fight for the freedom of slaves and women's rights but ends up being best known to most of us for her poem *Over the River and Through the Woods.* Ludwig van Beethoven premieres his *Moonlight Sonata.*

1803: Ohio gains statehood—the first in the new century. The U.S. doubles its size with the Louisiana Purchase. In Scotland, William Symington shows off the first "practical" steamboat, the *Charlotte Dundas* (the name is that of his sponsor's daughter—money has always talked). Crawford's judges are shared with the counties of Erie, Mercer, Venango, Warren, and Beaver.

1803 — 1829

THE HONORABLE JESSE MOORE

Alexander Addison is impeached. Governor Thomas McKean appoints Jesse Moore. His portrait in the Crawford County Courthouse shows clear, blue-gray eyes peering directly from a full and clean-shaven face. A prominent nose over a cupid-bow mouth completes the picture of a dignified and courteous man.

A former land surveyor, Judge Moore is a short, rotund fellow who dresses in good, if old-fashioned, clothing. Partially bald, he powders what hair remains. When out and about, he favors drab, broad-brimmed, beaver hats. "He wore leather boots, well polished, and his trousers drawn down over them, a frock coat, black satin waistcoat and black satin tie which held the wings of a Henry Clay collar against his heavy chin."

Jesse Moore is a learned man but has no formal training in law. With several years experience as a "lay judge," he is fair, but is not considered brilliant by the attorneys practicing in his court. The county's longest-serving judge, he dies suddenly on December 21 1829.

1804: Future President Franklin Pierce is born—the first of the century. Lewis & Clark begin their expedition of discovery. Gas lighting is patented. New Jersey is the last northern state in the U.S. to abolish slavery (Pennsylvania was the first, sort of, in 1780). The first steam engine to propel itself on wheels, Richard Trevithick's *Pen-y-darren,* begins operation in South Wales.

BY A BLOW TO THE HEAD

The first recorded murder after the formation of Crawford County occurs in 1805, in Meadville, at Samuel Lord's store on Center Street. Lord is an original white settler, speaks the languages used by the region's Native Americans, and his store caters to them.

On the porch of the small log building, a native man, said to be under the influence of strong drink, kills his wife by a blow to the head with a hatchet or tomahawk.

It is common practice to allow for two systems of justice for serious transgressions: one for natives and the other for settlers. It is likely this crime is taken under consideration by native authorities since there is no record of the perpetrator's trial, sentence, or punishment.

1805:   Thomas Jefferson is back in office—a little more cleanly this time. Lewis and Clark reach the Pacific. In an effort to stop pirating along the African Mediterranean coast, the U.S. Marines attack the Libyan city of Derna—it's the origin of the "shores of Tripoli" in the *Marine's Hymn.*

1806:   Noah Webster publishes his first American English Dictionary. The first U.S. Federal Highway is authorized to be built between Cumberland, Pennsylvania and St. Louis, Missouri.

1807:   The first steamship in the U.S., Robert Fulton's

Clermont, sails. He owns the patent to prove it. Robert E. Lee is born. Congress passes laws forbidding the importation of slaves into any U.S. port. More than a quarter-million slaves are imported over the next five decades. Former President Judge Alexander Addison dies. Future President Judge Walter H. Lowrie is born.

1808: Future President Andrew Johnson is born. So is future President of the Confederate States of America, Jefferson Davis.

1809: James Madison is President of the United States. Future President, Abraham Lincoln is born. The U.S. Supreme Court decides that the Federal Government has more authority than the states. The electric arc lamp is invented. Wayne Township is created from Mead. Future President Judge Samuel P. Johnson is born.

1810: The tin can begins containing food. The can opener comes along a few years later. Napoleon is *still* causing lots of trouble for a lot of people. The first Oktoberfest is held in Munich to celebrate the marriage of Crown Prince Ludwig of Bavaria to Princess Therese of Saxe-Hildburghausen. He is a womanizer. She ends up the mother of nine. Crawford County's population increases 163% to 6,178. Bloomfield Township is created from Oil Creek.

1811: The New Madrid earthquake, in the Midwest United States, is so powerful it forces the Mississippi River to reverse course for a short while. Future President Judge Gaylord Church is born.

1812: Louisiana gains statehood. New Madrid rocks and rolls—again. The United States is in another dust-up with England. This time it's the U.S. that declares war. Future President Judge Rasselas Brown is born.

1813: Perry wins the Battle of Lake Erie. "We have met the enemy and they are ours!" In 1970, cartoonist Walt Kelly twists those immortal words for a poster with *Pogo the 'Possum* proclaiming the first Earth Day: "We have met the enemy and he is us!"

1814: Napoleon is exiled to St. Elba. It takes eight hours to make the first photograph via camera obscura. The British burn the White House.

1815: Meadville's Allegheny College is founded by Reverend Timothy Alden. Francis Scott Key combines his poem *The Defense of Fort McHenry* with the hard-to-sing music of the popular British song *To Anacreon in Heaven* and publishes *The Star-Spangled Banner.* Not until 1931 is Key's song adopted as the National Anthem of the United States. (An interesting side note: The Anacreon guy of the original song was an ancient Greek famed for love poems and drinking songs. "Oh, say does that star-spangled banner yet wave" was, originally, "And, besides, I'll instruct you like me, to entwine / the myrtle of Venus with Bacchus's vine." A bawdy drinking song is the tune of the U.S. National Anthem.) The U.S. and British governments sign a treaty that ends the War of 1812. One week later, Major General Andrew Jackson wins fame with a victory in a war already ended.

1816: Indiana gains statehood. The African Methodist Episcopal Church is established in Philadelphia.

1817: James Monroe is President of the United States. Mississippi gains statehood. The Rush-Bagot treaty,

14

between the British and U.S., limits the number of warships allowed on the Great Lakes. Future President Judge John Galbraith is admitted to the bar.

It's Different Than it Used to Be

At its start, Crawford County was a true wilderness. You know: cutting down old-growth forests to clear land for crops, building log structures, killing your dinner. The county was formed less than a generation after the American Revolution, and a decade past the "Whiskey Rebellion" during which Federal troops were sent to quell western Pennsylvania's violent protests against the government's taxation of booze.

The county's population grew more rapidly as the true frontier of the United States moved westward into Ohio. Crawford County's 1800 census counted slightly more than 2,300 (white) people. Twenty years later, the number had nearly quadrupled. But travel remained slow and dangerous well into the late 1800s. People of all ages carried weapons of all sorts as a matter of course, and with good reason. Robbery and other forms of personal violence were common across the sparsely populated landscape.

The Sheriff "Should do His Own Work"

On February 6, 1817, world traveler George Speth Van Holland, late of Canada and recently released from the Franklin Jail, Venango County (fornication and horse thievery) appears at the cabin of Daniel Carlin in what would become Rome Township in the far east-central portion of Crawford County. In conversation, he asks if those nearby are doing well. Carlin's wife allows that her daughter and son-in-law, the Hugh Fitzpatricks, are better off than most, considering they've been settled for only seven years.

Upon hearing this happy news, Van Holland heads north

to the Fitzpatrick homestead, near where Spartansburg would someday be. Timing his arrival for sunset, he asks the family's permission to stay the night. Not an unusual request for the time, especially during cold winter weather. He is happily taken in by the young couple who have a new baby daughter, though all they have to share is one room and a loft.

The guest is welcomed to sleep on the floor, and all say their good-nights. During the morning hours of February 7, Van Holland finds an axe and uses it to chop a large hole in the head of a sleeping Hugh Fitzpatrick.

The missus awakes with the racket and faints at the sight of her murdered husband. When she comes to, Van Holland demands not only her money but that she travel with him to Canada.

Mrs. Fitzpatrick has other ideas. She climbs to the loft and hides her silver in a barrel of maple syrup. She presents the murderer with forty dollars in bills ($500 modern) and boldly claims that's all there is.

The furious Van Holland threatens to kill the weeks-old child. The mother successfully pleads for her daughter's life. The killer then forces the woman outside to ready the horses. She releases the animals instead, returns to the house and claims she can not corral them. With Van Holland headed to the stable, Mrs. Fitzpatrick grabs her baby and makes a headlong dash for her nearest neighbor more than two miles away.

She stumbles northward, through snow, on a cold and blustery, pitch-black night. Van Holland almost overtakes her but the wind douses the lantern he carries, forcing him to abandon his hunt. The mother and child huddle most of the night in a small ravine. It isn't until the next morning that she reaches the cabin of James Winders, across the Erie County border.

On February 9, a party made up of Andrew Britton, Baszilla Shreve, Bradley Winton and a now unidentified man captures Van Holland four miles from the murder site. Lesser men might have killed him then and there. Instead, the pioneers force-march their prisoner nearly thirty miles to Meadville and a court of law.

Van Holland's trial takes place in May 1817. Judge: Jesse Moore. Deputy Attorney General (District Attorney): Ralph Martin. Jury: Thomas McMichael, Robert Story, Solomon Lord, James McConnell, John Linn, Andrew Gibson, Joseph Murtrie, David Nelson, Joseph Garwood, John Yordie, Hugh Murdock, and Jacob Kline.

Van Holland is found guilty of murder in the first degree and sentenced to be hanged.

The immensely strong prisoner almost escapes when he bends the iron bars in the hearth of his jail cell. Once convinced flight is impossible, he settles down and spends his time reading the Bible and other religious books. Like many other murderers you'll read about in this volume, he shows no remorse for his crime nor worry of execution.

His hanging takes place in Meadville on July 26, 1817—south of Chestnut and east of Grove. Sheriff Samuel Torbett has hired William Johnson to perform the hanging. Van Holland declares the Sheriff "should do his own work" and pushes Johnson from the scaffolding. It is reported that Johnson later dies of the injuries from his fall.

Standing on the scaffold, the condemned man proclaims his innocence and scorns his hanging as "judicial murder." His last words: "Oh Lord, have mercy on my soul."

~~~~~

Sometime after Van Holland's execution, letters arrive from Canadian authorities requesting a stay of his sentence. It seems they want time to interview him about his part in a New Brunswick murder. It's too late for any investigation, but it could well be that the first person legally executed in Crawford County was a serial killer.

The brave and resourceful Mrs. Fitzpatrick goes on to marry

Patrick Coyle. Nancy, the baby she carried through the snow and dark, is married at the age of 14 to Solomon Yager. They have six kids.

1818:   The U.S. flag officially becomes thirteen stripes of red and white and a field of blue containing a white star for each state. There are twenty when Illinois gains statehood. The border between the U.S. and Canada is established along the 49th parallel. *Frankenstein* is first published, anonymously, by Mary Shelly.

1819:   Alabama gains statehood. Spain cedes Florida to the United States. The U.S. pays $5 million ($70 million modern) for "property damage." A "Panic" causes bank failures, foreclosures, and high unemployment.

1820:   Crawford County's population is up 52% to 9,397. Florence Nightingale is born. Maine gains statehood. Colonel Robert Gibbon eats a tomato in public to help prove they are not poisonous. Daniel Boone goes on to the last frontier.

1821:   Missouri gains statehood. The first obscenity case in the U.S. takes place over Clelend's *Fanny Hill*. It's been on banned book lists ever since.

Murder in Degrees

The Commonwealth of Pennsylvania has classified murders since 1794. Murder in the first degree takes place during a specific set of violent crimes, or is planned, or is both. Murder in the second is not planned but takes place in the heat of the moment, or in concert with a crime not listed for murder in the first, or both. Pennsylvania eventually recognized a third degree of murder as any other that doesn't fit the first two.

And then there's manslaughter. Think of this as somebody dying because of somebody else doing something that isn't intended to be deadly.

Until 1925, those found guilty of first degree murder in a Pennsylvania court were *automatically* condemned to death. The defense lawyers then had the option of proving mitigating circumstances, like insanity, to convince the Commonwealth to commute the sentence to life in prison.

Judges would not allow a defendant to plead guilty to first degree murder because it was viewed as using the courts to commit suicide. Those charged with the crime were forced through trials where many thought the specter of execution caused juries to find for lesser charges.

Many juries did just that and placed the guilty parties into the wide gap of punishments of first (death) and lesser degrees (time in prison). Laws eventually added the option of choosing a life sentence as punishment for first degree murderers.

Plea bargaining, admitting guilt to a lesser charge with certain punishment instead of going through a trial that might produce a more severe sentence, has been around since the earliest days of Pennsylvania courts. District Attorneys in modern courts plea bargain up to 90% of their cases. Such tactics were rare for murder cases throughout the period covered. Prosecutors of old were always willing to fight for the most severe justifiable punishment. The idea of allowing a murderer to cop a plea to manslaughter doesn't enter their minds. That gung-ho attitude wasn't always the most appropriate. A trial is an unpredictable event. Suspects who seem obviously guilty to the most casual of observers are set free. Sometimes.

BETWEEN THE HEAVENS AND THE EARTH

Late May 1822. Constable Samuel W. Smith heads to the Four Corners area of the far western Conneaut Township along the

Pennsylvania and Ohio border (I was unable to place "Four Corners" on a modern map).

Smith has the unpleasant task of arresting one David Lamphier on charges of obtaining goods upon false pretenses.

In his early 30s, Lamphier is thickset and powerful, six-feet tall, with clear gray eyes and blonde hair. He knows he's about to be arrested but makes no attempt to evade the law. He is going about his business, axe slung over his shoulder as usual, when he encounters the Constable. From Lamphier's confession:

> I got along towards the end of the house and saw Mr. Smith the Constable coming out of the entry partly behind me. I turned round and spoke to him and said I understand you want to take me tonight but I don't mean that you shall. Mr. Smith then step'd up to me. I took my ax off my shoulder and I told him to stand back or I would strike him, as he came up I step'd back a few steps. Intending to run and get out of his way. As he advanced upon me I made use of my ax I hardly know how, whether with the head or how. As soon as I made the blow I turned and run...

Lamphier heads across the nearby state line to his father's house in Ohio. In short order he spies a group of armed men heading his direction. He takes his brother Andrew's rifle and escapes by the back door to hide out in the woods until evening. Lamphier returns to the house after dark but sees a person with a gun inside. The wanted man crawls back into the woods, leaving the rifle he carries at the edge of the field where it'll easily be found. He wants the men chasing him to know he's not armed.

Lamphier spends the next seventy-two hours hiding in what eventually becomes known as Pymatuning Swamp. After three days on the lam, he approaches the "John Callomy" homestead south of what is now Linesville, Pine Township, and finds him hoeing his garden. Asked about Constable Smith, Callomy replies that he won't answer questions unless Lamphier allows himself to be taken prisoner.

The wanted man surrenders and is shocked to learn that Smith is dead. Upon arrest, and after being fed, he makes a full statement to lawyer Sheldon Sherwood.

The June trial doesn't take long. Judge: Jesse Moore. Deputy Attorney General: George Selden. Jury: James Baker, Obed Garwood, Nelson Smith, George W. King, George Davis, Joseph Hide, Cooper Ray, John Kline, Elder Hutchinson, William Walker, John Daniels, and James O. Johnson.

Lamphier is found guilty of murder in the first degree. He might've avoided the death penalty except that he gave Constable Smith fair warning before striking. That's considered premeditation. Judge Moore sentences the prisoner to be hanged by the neck at 2:00 in the afternoon on the first of November, 1822.

~~~~~

The hanging of David Lamphier is an event. Papers estimate the crowd at 4,000—nearly half the population of the county. It's likely the biggest group of people most of those attending have ever seen. A guard composed of the Meadville Light Artillery and a detachment of the militia assembles at the courthouse at noon the day of the execution. The prisoner appears soon after, clothed in his shroud, his noose and rope draped around his neck. This is standard practice for the time.

Accompanied by Sheriff Withrow and the Reverends Alden and Jackson, Lamphier could ride, but chooses to walk the mile north to the gallows located along a ravine on Baldwin Street. Two horse-drawn carts precede the party: one carries a coffin to accept the killer's mortal remains, the other travels empty but is intended to carry the condemned should he falter. Lamphier does fade about halfway into his next-to-last journey, but "takes a little wine," recovers, and continues on his own.

They arrive an hour early. The military guard surrounds the gallows. Lamphier, the Sheriff, and the Reverends mount the platform. The Sheriff strings the rope. At the request of the condemned, Reverend Alden tells of the prisoner's life, his fall from and eventual reacceptance of Grace. No doubt energized by this huge, captive audience, Alden goes on for almost the next hour during which Lamphier interrupts to deny meaning to hurt his victim. It was Constable Smith's sudden appearance and actions, the murderer claims, that kept him from thinking clearly.

Four minutes to the hour. Sheriff Withrow tells Lamphier his time has come. As Reverend Alden asks for the Mercy of the Almighty, Lamphier helps to place the cover over his own head. Prayers cease. Authorities, legal and religious, leave the platform.

At 1:59:30 in the afternoon, half-a-minute ahead of schedule, the death trap is sprung and, in the words of the *Crawford Messenger*, "the wretched being hung suspended between the heavens and the earth."

The press expresses relief that local authorities completed the work since it would have been "highly improper" to hire a hooded executioner. The papers praise all parties for their good and solemn work. Equal measures of credit are doled to both the good Sheriff Withrow and the very brave but now very dead David Lamphier.

1822: Future Presidents U.S. Grant and Rutherford B. Hayes are born.

1823: Randolph Township is created from Mead.

1824: A new Crawford County Courthouse is constructed on the east side of the Diamond. It is described as "a long brick building with a Doric temple front consisting of four pillars, and is surmounted by a circular copula or belfry." The old log building that has housed both the court and jail for the last twenty years is given over entirely to keeping prisoners.

1825: John Quincy Adams is President of the United States after election by the House of Representatives because the Electoral College failed to find a majority for any candidate. Adams also lost the popular vote by a substantial amount. The election is disputed. Andrew Jackson charges "corrupt bargains." Crawford's judges are shared with the counties of Erie, Mercer, and Venango.

1826: Past Presidents Thomas Jefferson and John Adams die of old age on the same day—July 4. The internal combustion engine is patented by the U.S. inventor Samuel Morey.

1827: Beethoven dies and begins de-composing. Modern matches are a striking idea. Future President Judge S. Newton Pettis is born.

WHERE TO PUT THEM?

Even before the formation of the United States, colonial Pennsylvania had abolished the use of corporal punishment (torture) as retribution for crimes. Replacing it was hoped-for rehabilitation through incarceration. Early prisons were county- or city-based and sometimes operated by often-corrupt private companies.

In 1827, eight years after it was authorized by the Pennsylvania legislature, the first Western State Penitentiary began receiving prisoners. Like Eastern Penitentiary in

Philadelphia, West Pen's inmates were intended to live and work in complete isolation. That turned out to be impossible due to the dark and dank conditions in the extremely small cells of 20 (!) square feet. Western quickly abandoned solitary confinement and built common areas for its general population.

The original West Pen operated until the early 1880s. It was replaced by a fortress-like and still-standing facility of the same name. This "new prison" is located a short distance away from where the old one stood: along the north bank of the Ohio River in what was then known as Allegheny City (now part of Pittsburgh in Allegheny County).

1828: Jules Verne, one of the fathers of Science Fiction, is born in Nantes, France, arriving ahead of Englishman, H.G. Wells, by nearly 40 years. Hungarian Ányos István Jedlik demonstrates his latest invention, "the lightning-magnetic self-rotor." You can see the original device, still in perfect working order, at the Museum of Applied Arts in Budapest. You'd probably recognize it as an electric motor.

1829: Andrew Jackson is President of the United States. His opponents refer to him as a "jackass" which Jackson adopts for use on his own election banners; it's the birth of the Democratic Donkey. A major adjustment realigns all existing Crawford County townships except Mead and Oil Creek. The following townships are created: Athens, Sparta, Rome, and Troy (eastern part of the county), Snowhill and Summerhill (northwest), Greenwood and North and South Shenango (south, south-west), Richmond, Woodcock, Vernon and Hayfield (center). Snowhill is renamed "Spring" later in the year. The first passenger train in the U.S., the Baltimore and Ohio Railroad. It's the *B&O* you find in Monopoly®. Future President Chester A. Arthur is born. Future President Judge Walter H. Lowrie is admitted to the bar.

1829 – 1839

The Honorable Henry Shippen

Judge Jesse Moore dies in office. Governor George Wolf appoints Henry Shippen. His silhouette, cut a few years before his appointment to Crawford County's bench, shows him with soft, nearly feminine features: a round head with a small, turned-up nose, full mouth, and a gentle, soft chin. This might not be what you'd expect given his background and career.

Born in Lancaster, Pennsylvania, in 1788, Shippen's great-grandfather was the first mayor of Philadelphia. His father was with Braddock in 1755 and at the taking of Fort Duquesne. His uncle served as Pennsylvania's Chief Justice.

Our future judge, Captain Henry Shippen, organizes a volunteer company of heavily armed cavalrymen for the War of 1812. The some-day United States President James Buchanan was a lowly private in "Shippen's Dragoons."

In 1817 Shippen marries Elizabeth Wallis Evans, a granddaughter of a battalion commander at the battle at Trenton, New Jersey. In 1819 the couple moves to Huntingdon County in central Pennsylvania where Henry practices law before his election to the state legislature.

On the bench, Judge Shippen is known for common sense and sound judgment. He displays contempt for trickery or fraud to the point of growing angry in court when presented with dishonesty. Attorneys find him an able and conscientious judge, an upright and kind man. He is forgiving of mistakes rookie lawyers make in courtroom protocol, taking care to instruct in private instead of embarrass in public.

Judge Henry Shippen serves until his death in 1839.

Shippen's daughter, Frances, marries Edgar, one of the fairly well-known Huidekoper clan. Their son, Henry Shippen Huidekoper, carries on his namesake's military tradition. He rises to the rank of Colonel in the Civil War, losing his right arm in the process. He later serves as Senior Brigadier-General of the Pennsylvania National Guard.

Judge Henry Shippen's grandson does something that directly affects all of us. While serving as the postmaster of Philadelphia, in the 1880s, he institutes the practice of charging for postage by the ounce.

1830: Crawford County's population is up 70% to 16,030. Emily Dickinson is born. The Indian Removal Act becomes law. Native Americans of the southeast U.S. will soon start their way along their Trail of Tears.

1831: Future President James A. Garfield is born. Past President James Monroe dies of tuberculosis (probably). Charles Darwin sets sail on the H.M.S. Beagle. We have Cyrus McCormick to thank for the mechanical reaper. Ed Smith is the country's first bank robber, netting almost a quarter-million bucks from the City Bank of New York ($11 million, modern). Smith also nets five years in Sing-Sing. The song *My County 'Tis of Thee* (lyrics by Samuel Francis Smith) with its "sweet land of liberty" makes its public debut on July 4th. A month-and-a-half later, a slave revolt near Jerusalem, Virginia, is led by Nat Turner, slave and preacher. Fifty-seven white citizens, including women and children, are killed. Turner is hung and skinned. Hundred of blacks are killed by white vigilantes. New laws are passed to severely restrict the activities and education of slaves.

1832: The "Black Hawk Indian War" from Illinois to Wisconsin. South Carolina threatens to leave the union after permanent tariffs on imported goods are put in place by the U.S. Congress. President Andy Jackson gains official authorization to use Federal troops against South Carolina should it make good on the threat.

1833: Future President Benjamin Harrison is born. The U.S. overseas slave trade is abolished—again. The sale of native-born human beings continues for another three decades. Oberlin College is founded—eventually becoming one of the first such institutions in the United States to welcome those of different races and the first to offer higher education to women. Future President Judge Samuel P. Johnson is admitted to the bar.

1833, JULY 23: Location: Fairfield Township, "near the canal aqueduct" near present day Shaw's Landing in East Fairfield Township. Victim: Charles Hickenbottom (Higgenbottom). Suspects: ___ McCauley, James Foley, Edward Tobin, Edward Canty, Nandy Gilleland, George Gosnell, John Mallone, Jas. Kenny, and others numbering eleven in total ("all Drunken Irishmen"). Act: Beaten / drowned in canal. Notes: While working on the canal, the victim is killed by suspects after they were discharged from their own canal jobs. Witnesses for the Commonwealth are harassed and attacked on the highways to discourage them from testifying. Outcome: Of the eight tried for murder, five are acquitted. George Gosnell is found guilty of murder in the second degree and given twelve years imprisonment. John Mallone and Jas. Kenny both receive six years in jail for manslaughter.

1834: Pennsylvania leads the United States in its move away from public hangings. Executions are now held within the Commonwealth's county jails and state prisons. Future President Judge Gaylord Church is admitted to the bar.

1835: In the first assassination attempt on a U.S. President, unemployed, and perhaps lead-crazed house painter Richard Lewis tries to kill President Andrew Jackson. The attempt fails when the pistols Lewis is using misfire at point-blank range. Old Hickory's response? He gives Lewis several whacks with a walking stick. Halley's Comet comes calling.

1836: Texas War of Independence. Samuel Colt's revolver. Arkansas gains statehood. Past President James Madison dies of heart failure. Native leader Gaiänt'wakê dies. In 1965, the Kinzua (Place of Many Fishes) Dam on the Allegheny River above Warren, Pennsylvania, permanently floods the Cornplanter Tract. Local papers make sport of his descendant's reluctance to leave the land that the Federal Government promised to his people "forever."

1837: Martin Van Buren is President of the United States. Future President Grover Cleveland is born. Michigan gains statehood. Samuel Morse gives us the telegraph. The next year Sam graces us with the dots and dashes of his famous code: --. ---, ...- --! Failures of large banks in New York City kick off the Panic of 1837. This forces the U.S. to stop building its first Federal Highway (started in 1806) in Vandalia, Illinois instead of finishing in St. Louis, Missouri. It also eventually causes a world-wide economic depression. U.S. banks begin issuing their own paper currency. By the time this practice ends in 1863, fully one-third of all U.S. paper money is fake.

1838:   Charles Dickens publishes *Oliver Twist*. Laws pertaining to judgeships change. The Governor still makes judicial appointments, but "for life" is no longer part of the deal. Supreme Court Judges serve fifteen years. Common Pleas Court Judges serve ten years. Both can be re-appointed an unlimited number of terms. Future President Judge Pearson Church is born. So is John Wilkes Booth.

1839:   Future President Judge Rasselas Brown is admitted to the bar.

1839 – 1843

The Honorable Nathaniel B. Eldred

Henry Shippen dies in office. Governor Joseph Ritner appoints Nathaniel Bailey Eldred. Portraits show him of medium build. His heavy, square, and plain face is by no means handsome with close-set eyes, large nose, and wide, thin mouth. His very-much-receding, dark hair is combed back but drops to cover what looks like a pair of unusually large ears.

Crawford County's new President Judge is born in Orange County, New York in 1795. Admitted to the bar in 1816, he subsequently serves four terms in the Commonwealth's Legislature.

In contrast to his plain looks, he is known for sparkling conversation and excellent story-telling. Eldred is admired by the community and considered a straightforward gentleman full of honor, honesty, and sympathy.

He is quick to understand the arguments at hand and approaches the law from an unfailingly practical angle. He displays sound judgment and stern impartiality. He has little legal training, yet his decisions, often based in common sense, are seldom appealed.

Judge Eldred is Crawford County's judge until he resigns to accept the post of the Naval Appraiser at Philadelphia. He is later appointed, and elected judge to several districts, including

Dauphin, which holds Pennsylvania's capitol, Harrisburg. He dies in 1867.

1839: Goodyear vulcanizes rubber. The Daguerreotype is developed. Mississippi becomes the first state of the U.S. to give married women the right to own (but not control) private property. Pennsylvania's married women have a fairly long wait before permanently gaining that same right in 1887.

1840: Crawford County's population is up 98% to 31,724. Painter Claude Monet is born.

1841: William Henry Harrison is President of the United States—for a month before he dies of pneumonia. Vice President John Tyler takes over. Sam Slocum fastens himself to history when he patents the paper stapler. The first long filibuster in U.S. Senate lasts from February to March. Hot air, it seems, has never been in short supply.

1842: Harmonsburg Township is created from portions of Sadsbury and Summerhill.

1843: Future President William McKinley is born. Look up "dead" in the American English Dictionary and maybe you'll see a picture of Noah Webster. In March, Summit Township is created from all of Harmonsburg and parts of Sadsbury and Summerhill. Future President Judge John J. Henderson is born.

1843 – 1851

The Honorable Gaylord Church

Judge Nathaniel B. Eldred resigns. Governor David R. Porter appoints Gaylord Church. Full-faced Judge Church gazes coolly from his portrait through small, oval, wire-rimmed glasses sitting upon what appears to be a perfectly straight nose. His combed, but somehow windswept, dark hair lifts from his high, round forehead. His mouth plays with the beginnings of a smile. He looks as if he is the most confident man in the world.

Former farm-boy Church is born in Oswego, New York, in the year 1811 (the first Crawford County judge from that century). He is "ardent, ambitious, industrious, painstaking, and prompt." Admitted to the bar in Mercer County in 1834, he is the county's Deputy Attorney General from 1837 to 1840 when he is elected to the first of two consecutive terms in the Pennsylvania Legislature.

Judge Church possesses much ability and no sympathy. He demands a rigid enforcement of criminal law and an exacting interpretation of the civil codes. He is "a terror to evil-doers."

Unlike his charming predecessor, Church is awkward in social settings. He is not entirely well-liked by some members of the bar who consider him promoted too fast and too young. They'll admit Judge Church is well-balanced in his decisions and has a thorough understanding of the law, but many are happy to agree the judge is something of a know-it-all.

After his term, attorney Church practices law in the Crawford and Venango County courts. In 1858 he is appointed to fill a short-term vacancy on the Commonwealth's Supreme Court. He dies in Meadville in 1869. His eldest child is Pearson Church, who will be elected to his father's old job as President Judge some thirty-five years later.

1844: High-speed, long-distance communication becomes a reality when Samuel Morse sends the first telegraph message from Washington D.C. to Baltimore, Maryland: *What God hath wrought.* The Y.M.C.A. is founded. East and West Fallowfield are formed by splitting Fallowfield Township along Crooked Creek.

1845: James K. Polk is President of the United States. Florida and Texas gain statehood. Baseball rules are formalized by Alexander Cartwright and the New York Knickerbockers (the *basketball* team with the same name doesn't come along until June of 1946). Past President Andrew Jackson dies of tuberculosis, among other things.

1846: Massachusetts dentist Dr. William Morton is the first to use anesthesia when extracting a tooth. It takes a while for the practice to catch on. Ouch. Pine Township is created from Shenango. Iowa gains statehood. The Mexican War fires up.

1847: The first adhesive-back U.S. postage stamps go on sale. They're a Franklin 5-center and a Washington dime.

1848: Wisconsin gains statehood. Gold is discovered in what becomes California. The Mexican War ends. That country gives up everything above the Rio Grande. The U.S. pays $15 million in return ($373 million modern). Past President John Quincy Adams dies of stroke. Work begins in the U.S. Capitol on the Washington Monument.

1849: Zachary Taylor is President of the United States. Babies everywhere giggle and coo with joy when the safety pin is invented. After forty-six years, the old log jailhouse is razed when the new Crawford County Jail is constructed behind the courthouse. This stone structure is used until 1912 and eventually becomes known as "the worst county jail in the state." Elizabeth Blackwell becomes the first woman doctor in the United States. Crazy Horse of the Lakota is born (his real name translates to "His-Horse-Is-Crazy"). Past President James K. Polk dies of cholera.

THE PUBLIC PROSECUTOR

Many think the courts of the United States are tied directly to their roots in England and, except for those weird robes and funny, little wigs the English wear, things are pretty much the same. The gist of the courts may be similar, but there are startling differences. One of the most basic is the American idea that a criminal act against an individual translates into a criminal act against the public as a whole and that it is the *responsibility of the government* to hold the criminal responsible.

Early legal processes in England's North America were copied directly from Britain. Grievances were brought to a central court by private individuals to face the summary judgment of the colony's governor and council. As populations grew and became widespread, a more elaborate, two-tiered system developed. A Governor-appointed Attorney General ran a central court of appeals. This was fed disputed cases from local courts that decided matters with the help of an appointed Deputy Attorney General. This DAG, responsible for interpreting and enforcing the laws of the land at a local level, was unique to the United States.

Like the appointed judges, deputy attorneys general were big frogs in little ponds. Their roles continued to grow, both because of the influence they wielded "up the food chain" and the desire to settle as many disputes as possible in the local courts. Travel to the central courts was both time-consuming and dangerous, but the biggest problem with the Governor's Court was that it fed personal matters to a large and capricious political machine—something many pre-revolutionary colonists did not like.

Public prosecutors were entrenched in American lower courts well before the War of Independence which did nothing to change the system. In Pennsylvania, both judges and district attorneys were appointed from the state capitol until 1850, when they became locally-elected officials.

Crawford County's first Deputy Attorney General (1800) was Henry Baldwin, born in Connecticut and graduated from Yale at the age of 17. Following his stint in Crawford, he won election to Congress as a Democrat-Republican. After strongly supporting Andrew Jackson's successful bid for President, Baldwin received an appointment to the U.S. Supreme Court. He served from 1830 until his death in 1844 and, often finding himself in the minority, began the court's practice of publishing dissenting opinions.

Gaylord Church had the distinction of being appointed both Deputy Attorney General (1837) and President Judge (1843). Ruddy-faced David Derickson was appointed Deputy Attorney General (1823 & 1826), and later served as "Law Judge" (1856).

Crawford County's first *elected* District Attorney was Almon Benson Richmond. Born in Indiana in 1825, he moved with his family to Meadville in 1834. He entered Allegheny College in

1839, where he studied the sciences. He practiced medicine and surgery while reading law and continued after gaining the bar in 1849. Richmond specialized in criminal defense before and after his stint as D.A. He died, in Meadville, at the age of 81.

Through the period covered by this book, several District Attorneys ran for President Judge. Only three won election: John J. Henderson, O. Clare Kent, and Herbert A. Mook.

1850:   Zachary Taylor, the last head of state to own slaves while in office, dies of causes unknown, but after eating a bowl of milk and cherries (which is why some of us kids were told the combination is deadly). Vice President Millard Fillmore takes over. The Fugitive Slave Law is passed *requiring* U.S. Marshals either to assist in the capture of slaves escaping to northern states or face $1,000 fines ($43,000 modern). The law is so unpopular that Fillmore threatens enforcement by use of Federal Troops. California gains statehood. Crawford County's population is up 19% to 37,849. Steuben Township is created from Athens and Troy.

Commonwealth Judges are now elected by popular vote; Supreme Court Justices to an unlimited number of fifteen year terms, and Common Pleas Court Judges to an unlimited number of ten year terms. District Attorneys (up 'til now called "Deputy Attorneys General") also become elected officials, serving, at first 3-year terms. Governors still make appointments in the case of an uncompleted term.

Future President Judge S. Newton Pettis is admitted to the bar.

1851 — 1860

The Honorable John Galbraith

The term of Gaylord Church ends when judgeships become elected offices. John Galbraith is Crawford County's first judge chosen by popular vote. His looks are strongly reminiscent of Andrew Jackson's picture on the U.S. twenty-dollar bill. His most striking feature is a full head of almost wild, white hair; bushy eyebrows of the same color, with gray eyes over a long, straight nose and wide, thin mouth. He presents a stiffly formal visage, no doubt in part because his portrait was painted from a photograph that required him to "hold still and don't move" for what we would think was an unreasonable amount of time.

Galbraith is born in Huntingdon, Pennsylvania on August 2, 1794. In 1802 his family moves to Centre Township, in Butler County, where he attends school and serves as a printer's apprentice. He puts in a stint as a school teacher, then studies law and is admitted to the bar in 1817. He begins his practice in Butler, Pennsylvania.

He is elected to the Pennsylvania House of Representatives in 1829 but is not re-nominated in 1836. A year later, Galbraith moves to Erie, Pennsylvania and resumes his law practice. From there he wins the county's first election for President Judge.

Judge Galbraith brings age, learning, and experience to the bench. He is known for being honest and forthright. Despite his stern portrait, he displays a great deal of sympathy to both victims and perpetrators of crimes and is, perhaps, too well able to see both sides of a situation. He tends towards mercy so strong that it sometimes weakens his judgment and tempers his decisions "to the point of dilution." The judge is criticized for being too forgiving to those who break the law.

Still, a newspaper story of the time presents this anecdote of an exchange between Galbraith and a vocal prospective voter: The candidate "did not believe in capital punishment, but replied to a voter who objected to his candidacy for judge on that ground that when his (the voter's) case came up he would waive his objections."

Galbraith serves until his death on June 15, 1860.

1851: Cambridge Township is created from Venango. The "trine," a small, three-dollar silver coin is placed into circulation and remains in use until 1873. Singer and his sewing machine. *Moby Dick* is published. So is *The House of Seven Gables.* Crawford's judges are shared with the counties of Erie and Warren.

1852: Giffard combines a balloon with an engine. It's a good thing he's persistent because his first design doesn't take off. The anti-slavery weekly newspaper, *National Era,* publishes the final installment of *Life Among the Lowly*—a story inspired by the Fugitive Slave Law of 1850 and written by Harriet Beecher Stowe. Better known as the book, *Uncle Tom's Cabin,* hundreds of thousands of copies are sold over the next few years, outraging the South, arousing the North and according to President Abraham Lincoln helping to start the Civil War.

Modern Americans of all colors continue to employ the stereotypes presented so vividly in Stowe's book: the accepting slave Uncle Tom, the black cook Dinah, and the evil slave-driver Simon Legree. Probl'm is, mos' 'em 'r' fit-up t'be ign'r'nt o' dere or'g'ns.

Don't be ign'r'nt. Read the book!

1853: Franklin Pierce is President of the United States and is so disliked by his own party that they refuse to nominate him for another term. A successful manned glider is built. Commodore Matthew Perry begins prying open Japanese ports. The Gadsden Purchase sets the southwest border between the U.S. and Mexico.

1853, FEB 14 (TRIAL DATE): Location: ? Victim: ? Suspect: Simeone Brecoev. Act: ? Notes: Newspapers refer to him as "the Frenchman." Outcome: Found not guilty.

Remember, now, a " ? " simply means I didn't find the information.

1853, APRIL 5 (TRIAL DATE): Location: ? Victim: ? Suspect Anna Breeder. Act: ? Outcome: Acquittal. Grand Jury finds no true bill.

1854: The modern Republican Party is founded in protest against the Kansas-Nebraska Act that enables voters in those territories to decide for themselves if they desire to allow slavery. The Act is supposed to be a compromise between opposing points of view. It doesn't work out that way. Annapolis graduates it first students.

1855: Rock Island, Illinois sees the first railroad bridge to span the Mississippi River.

1856: Future President Woodrow Wilson is born. Louis

Pasteur figures out how to kill the cooties that can grow in raw milk.

1857: James Buchanan is President of the United States. Future President William Howard Taft is born. George Pullman designs a railway sleeping car and gives it his own name. Otis invents a safe elevator. The U.S. Supreme Court's "Dred Scot decision" says a slave does not become free by transport to a free state and that Congress cannot ban slavery. Also, by the way, blacks are not eligible for citizenship.

1858: The non-citizen, semi-free Dred Scot is set completely free when he becomes a citizen of the afterlife by dying of tuberculosis while working as a reporter in St. Louis, Missouri. Future President Theodore Roosevelt is born. Minnesota gains statehood. In March, a bill passes both houses of the Pennsylvania Legislature to create a new county named "Marion" from parts of Erie, Crawford, and Warren Counties with Titusville as the seat. The reason? To eliminate the long and dangerous journey far-flung citizens must make to their respective county courts. Titusvillians seem surprised when the idea fails to generate enthusiasm. Recent changes to the Commonwealth's constitution forces the measure to a vote in the named counties in the upcoming November elections. Newspapers predict a sound defeat and it does fail due to heavy disagreement in Warren County. Titusville will not give up so easily. Future President Judge Pearson Church is admitted to the bar.

1858, MARCH 24: Location: Hugh Shellito farm in ? Township. Victim: Hugh Shellito Sr. (father). Suspect: Hugh Shellito Jr. (son). Act: Struck on head during a heated argument. Notes: Arrest reported April 20, 1858. Outcome: Not guilty.

1859:   Oregon gains statehood. The petroleum age truly begins in Titusville, eastern Crawford County, when driller Billy Smith finds oil in a well Edwin Drake is overseeing for the Seneca Oil Company. Prominent citizens of Titusville renew their campaign for the creation of a new county with their city as the seat. The *Tioga County Agitator* notes "in the last four years there have been six murders in Crawford County without a single conviction." (I was able to find only one—that doesn't mean they didn't happen.) Future President Judge Frank J. Thomas is born.

1860:   Abraham Lincoln is elected President. South Carolina secedes from the Union. The United States are disunited. Crawford County's population is up 29% to 48,755. Crawford's judges are shared with the counties of Erie, Warren, and Elk.

1860 — 1860

The Honorable Rasselas Brown

Judge John Galbraith dies in office. Governor William F. Packer appoints Rasselas Brown to complete his term. Photos of him show a stern man with a no-nonsense, patriarchal look. Nearly bald, with a thin, lined face, he has no mustache, but possesses a full, neatly trimmed, shovel-shaped, white beard; piercing eyes; a large, full nose; and ears that look as if they sit a smidgen too low.

Born in Brownsville, Jefferson County, New York on September 10, 1812, Rasselas Brown studies law in the office of Judge Lansing Wetmore, and then Struthers and Johnson in Warren, Pennsylvania. He is admitted to the bar in the spring of 1839, is a State Supreme Attorney in 1845 (what we call an "Attorney General"), and then becomes a member of Struthers, Johnson, and Brown.

Officially a Democrat, his politics are compliant enough to allow him to partner with the rabid Republican, Samuel P. Johnson (the man elected to replace him). The two remain partners until 1860 when Brown is appointed to the county bench.

After his short term as President Judge, Brown returns to Warren County and private practice, first by himself and then with his son, H.E. Brown. He is a director and legal representative for a number of firms including the Lake Shore and Michigan Southern Railway, and the Dunkirk, Allegheny Valley and Pittsburgh Railroad (which figures in one of the stories that follows). Attorney Brown is the first Director of the First National Bank of Warren when it opens for business in 1864. His clients are many of the most wealthy and powerful in his part of the country.

In 1880, Rasselas Brown is elected judge of Warren County. Some think him "too old" for the position. But he stays sharp through advancing age. Spending days in his law office, well after his second judgeship ends, he is praised as "a living example of a long and useful life of upright and noble industry."

Brown's health slowly declines in the last years of his life. He passes away in August 1895.

You'll Send Me to The Poor House

In the early days of the Commonwealth, there was no such thing as "the public welfare." The counties auctioned the destitute to agents who paid the debts owed by the poor in exchange for their work. A typical payment was a few cents a week, though a skilled worker, such as a wheelwright, cooper, or cobbler could command nearly $4.00 a month.

It wasn't slavery, exactly, but the temporarily-indentured servant enjoyed few rights. There was little in the way of recourse in case of mistreatment. Still, all in all, it was better than debtor's prison.

In the first quarter of the 1800s, county governments began establishing "homes" where the poor could be sent by the courts, or the poor themselves could petition for entry to avoid starvation, or worse. The Crawford County Poor House (also rarely called the "Almshouse") was in Woodcock Township, near Saegertown. More than just a house, it was a farm operated by the county where inmates worked for their place to eat and sleep.

Like the courthouse and the county jail, the poor house received an annual review by members of the Grand Jury. It was they who decided if the facility was adequate for the task at hand. The jurors could, and did, require the county to perform tasks large and small, from building a new structure to repainting a single room.

The Grand Jurors almost always took the point of view that, while the unfortunate poor should not be coddled, neither should they live in hunger or squalor. The newspapers always printed the Poor House Report which was scathing when the Superintendent of the place was found to be skimping on food, safety, or sanitation.

The poor house system didn't consider *why* a person had no money. Those with outmoded skills, families abandoned by husbands, the mentally or physically unable to work; all types were tossed together with sometimes tragic results.

Once radical, but now familiar government programs such as unemployment insurance, worker's compensation, welfare, and public housing eventually rendered poor houses antique. But such services didn't vanish completely. The Crawford County Almshouse slowly morphed into the "Quality Living Center," a nursing home and assisted-living facility. It remains in Saegertown.

"Secured With Some Difficulty"

The summer of 1860 has been a long one at the poor house. Work on the farm has been heavy. The unrelenting heat makes it hard to sleep. There seems to be a lack of good food.

Tempers erupt during the noon-time meal on August 4. An argument breaks out between inmates Lewis Hope and James Garvey. Angry words lead to a scuffle and fisticuffs that are broken up by the poor house Superintendent, Mr. Long.

Long, never one to put up with nonsense, orders the men to

different locations on the farm with instructions to remain apart until they're able to behave in a civilized manner.

The superintendent's not worried about Hope. He can be a hot-head, but is a good fellow. Garvey, though, is another matter. He's subject to fits and, Mr. Long will concede, does not seem of sound mind. The Superintendent threatens the unstable man with jail should he continue with violence. He tells his staff members to watch Garvey closely for more signs of trouble. They observe none.

Later that same day, a neighbor, Mr. Hunter, is riding past the farm and hears sounds of a struggle coming from behind a barn. Hunter investigates and finds Garvey whacking Hope in the head with a fence rail.

Hunter raises the alarm. Garvey flees the scene. A group of men, staff and inmates alike, give chase. In short order Garvey is caught, subdued, and "secured with some difficulty."

Hope, who never lost consciousness through his ordeal, is badly bruised on his head, neck, and shoulders. Superintendent Long and Mr. Hunter help the injured man to the main house. Dr. Best is summoned. The good doctor is of the opinion that his patient will recover from the beating. Despite the physician's optimism, Hope fades rapidly and dies on August 5.

At his murder trial, Garvey is ably defended by future judge Solomon Newton Pettis in front of Law Judge Derickson. The defendant is found "not guilty; on the ground of insanity," and remanded to the county jail.

Crazy Like M'Naughten

In 1843, Daniel M'Naughten (also spelled "McNaughton") attempted to assassinate British Prime Minister Robert Peel. Edward Drummond, Peel's secretary, took a bullet in the back and died five days later. With so many witnesses, the case was thought to be water-tight, but a clever lawyer was able to win an acquittal for M'Naughten by convincing the court the man was insane and, so, not responsible for his crime.

In response to the public outcry, the British House of Lords formulated what became known as the "M'Naughten Rules" that say, in part: A.) Jurors must assume a defendant is sane and reasonable. B.) Insanity must be clearly proved. C.) Defense by reason of insanity must establish that: 1.) the defendant was operating under insanity at the time of the illegal act and, 2.) because of that insanity, the defendant did not know the illegal act was wrong. We've pretty much stuck with these simple rules.

In the United States, complete forgiveness because of insanity, especially for a murder, has always been rare enough to produce the same sort of outrage that M'Naughten's lawyers stirred up in 1843. Today, most often, the best insanity can do is reduce a sentence, or win time in a hospital instead of a prison. The sentence is usually open-ended, depending on the doctors in charge to decide when things have returned to "normal."

Likewise, in 1860, being considered of unsound mind didn't get James Garvey off the hook for the poor house murder of Lewis Hope, it only kept his neck out of the noose. Garvey was sent to jail until that time he was deemed by his keepers as no longer a danger to others.

I found no record of a release.

1860 — 1870

The Honorable Samuel P. Johnson

Rasselas Brown does not run for office. His former law partner, Samuel P. Johnson is elected President Judge. His portrait is one of a pioneer: sparse, rough featured, no nonsense; a strong chin, wide, thin mouth, large nose, well-combed, iron-gray hair. He is not smiling—at all. His light-colored eyes have seen much of life.

Born in Venango County on January 31, 1809, Johnson graduates from Jefferson College at a young age and is twenty-four years old when admitted to the bar. In 1834, he moves to the city of Warren, in Warren County. It remains his home for the rest of his life.

In 1837 he marries Martha Hazeltine of Jamestown, New York. By 1840, he's formed a partnership with Rasselas Brown, the man he replaces on the bench.

Johnson's first wife dies in 1858, leaving him four children. One year later, he marries the widow, Mrs. Martha L. Parmlee, sister of Rasselas Brown and mother of one of his future partners.

President Judge Johnson is considered learned, faithful, honest and fearless in the discharge of his duties. He shows mercy only to those deserving of it. Sure in his rulings and noted for impartiality, he is a life-long advocate of temperance and gives no quarter to those guilty of violations of the liquor laws.

In 1867 he designates $600 in liquor fines to help fund local schools (about $9,000 modern).

His long experience as a trial lawyer serves him well as judge, giving him the ability to hear and understand both sides of an argument. Judge Johnson sets high standards for attorneys in his court. He is disdainful of sophistry or chicanery. This strikes sparks against some members of the bar. Not everyone likes the judge. He doesn't really seem to care.

Judge Johnson does not run for re-election and chooses to resume his legal practice which he will continue for another 15 years. Off the bench he is a "Republican of the most radical sort." He remains prominent in Warren County and his advice carries great weight. Attorney Johnson gradually withdraws from active practice but remains an advisor and assistant member of Johnson, Lindsey & Parmlee.

In the fall of 1892 Samuel Johnson visits Chicago to see work being done on the World's Columbian Exposition. He is of the opinion that he will not live to see the fair itself. He is correct. Johnson becomes ill on New Year's Day, 1893 and dies a month later, three days after his 83rd birthday.

1860, JULY 7: Location: Bloomfield Township. Victim: Mrs. Thomas Mosier (wife). Suspect: Mr. Thomas Mosier (husband). Act: Axed. Notes: Married only a few months. Separated twice for unknown reasons. Wife leaves him in Greenfield, Erie County and travels to her father's in Bloomfield. Suspect follows and tries to persuade her to return home. Wife refuses. As he is leaving, husband spies wife at a window, sewing. Suspect picks up an axe from the woodpile, goes to the back door, enters the room. Victim tries to escape. Suspect knocks her down and inflicts fatal wounds to her neck, face and head. Outcome: *Hold on a second*, Mrs. Mosier *does not* die as previously reported. She survives to testify against her brutal husband who is locked up for attempted murder.

1861: Kansas gains statehood. Abraham Lincoln is President of the United States. Jefferson Davis resigns his post as State Senator of Mississippi. The U.S. Civil war begins with the Union surrender of Fort Sumter. In the early morning hours of November 18, and in a matter of minutes, Julia Ward Howe composes the poem *Battle Hymn of the Republic* which is published in the *Atlantic Monthly*. The tune it's mated with was written some five years earlier by William Steffe as part of a spiritual named Canaan's Happy Shore. This same year, Earnest Halphin (nom de plume of George H. Miles of Maryland) writes and publishes what was considered by many in the Confederate States as their anthem. No, it's not *Dixie*, it's *God Save the South*. Combined with stately and fervent music by Charles Wolfgang Amadeus Ellerbrock that sounds a little like *My Country, 'Tis of Thee*. The first stanza: God save the South, God save the South / Her altars and firesides, God save the South! / Now that the war is nigh, now that we arm to die / Chanting our battle cry, "Freedom or death!" / Chanting our battle cry, "Freedom or death!"

1862: President Lincoln tells the Confederate States of America that, unless they rejoin the Union, he will issue a proclamation freeing all slaves. "Rat-a-tat-tat" says Richard Gatlin's gun. Ironclads! Past President John Tyler dies of stroke and respiratory failure. Past President Martin Van Buren dies of asthma.

1863: The Confederate States prove stubborn. President Lincoln issues the Emancipation Proclamation. Trouble is, it doesn't include southern slaves because, technically, the Confederacy isn't part of the United States. Henry Ford is born. West Virginia gains statehood. West

Shenango Township is created from South Shenango. "Four score and seven years ago..."

1864: During the U.S. Civil War Battle of Spotsylvania, in Virginia, Union Army General John Sedgwick says of Confederate troops: "They couldn't hit an elephant from this distance!" He is shot dead almost before he can draw his next breath. Nevada gains statehood.

1864, APRIL 3 OR 10: Location: Randolph Township. Victim: John Shoemaker. Suspect: J. Rouchlander. Act: Hit on head with wood. Notes: Suspect married the day of the murder. In the evening, a group has gathered outside his house to engage in a "serenade" where all kinds of hideous noises are made. It's a custom in some communities. Shoemaker, a good friend of the suspect, is inside the house. At 11:00 pm, several revelers enter the building. Rouchlander grows angry, grabs a piece of firewood, and throws it at the group. The intended target evades the blow and it strikes Shoemaker on the head. He dies that same night. Outcome: ?

1865: Abraham Lincoln is President of the United States— again. U.S. Civil War comes to an effective end with over 200,000 dead from combat (*and* 375,000 wounded *and* 413,000 dead from disease). Five days later, Lincoln is assassinated by John Wilkes Booth, the arguably insane actor. Andrew Johnson replaces Lincoln. Jefferson Davis is captured, charged with treason and imprisoned for two years, but never tried. Later in the year, the 13th Amendment to the Constitution of the United States takes effect to abolish slavery. In July, prominent citizens of Titusville once more hope to form a new county with their city as the seat. The reason remains the excessive distance those in the area must travel to Meadville courts. Future President Warren G. Harding is born.

1866: The Klu Klux Klan. Alfred Nobel's dynamite. Do you remember those rectangular sardine cans with the key? Thank J. Osterhoudt for that memory. The 5-cent nickel coin goes into circulation replacing a very small silver coin called a "half dime." Future President Judge Thomas J. Prather is born. Lemuel Cook, the "last official veteran" of the winning side of the Revolutionary War passes away at the age of 106. Two years later, John Gray dies. He is the "last verifiable veteran" of the same war. The difference between "official" and "verifiable" you might ask? Lemuel receives a pension. John's service is too brief to qualify.

1866, JUNE 19: Location: Oil Creek Township, on the road from Titusville to Thompson Corners. Victim: John Doyle. Suspects: Several, but Zebulon B. Burdick is charged. Act: Gunshot. Notes: Doyle is found along the roadside in a pool of his own blood. This case is held by the Titusville District Judge and never makes it to the county courts. Assumption is Doyle was on his way to visit Mary Curry as her accepted suitor, but that he was being watched and threatened by a disappointed rival. Burdick shows "uncommon knowledge" of the crime which he attributes to his research on the topic. He is described in newspapers as "a little, old, dried up man, with ferret eyes peering through his silver 'specs,' with army pants on with one leg tied up, he bobbles around on crutches with a pile of mysterious documents protruding from his pockets." Abandoning their original motive, authorities arrest Burdick because of his insider's view on the crime. He is shortly released without being charged. Charles Chase a.k.a. George

Chase a.k.a. Charles Winton a.k.a. George Winton is suspected of the crime but proof sufficient for arrest cannot be produced. He is pursued and escapes. No matter, since he is convicted and hung for the murder of a Mrs. McDonald in Jefferson County, Pennsylvania. Outcome of the Doyle murder: Unsolved.

1866, DECEMBER 19: Location: Titusville. Victim: Mrs. John Hickey (wife). Suspect: John Peter Hickey (husband). Act: beat to death with a large piece of firewood. Notes: Suspect is known to be a kind and gentle man unless drinking, but is a habitual drunkard. After work, the night of the murder, he stops at Lahey's Saloon on Mechanic Street and downs two glasses of whisky and one glass of hard cider. That night, during a pitched battle with his wife, he is heard to shout "Annie, what makes you make such a d____d [*sic*] beast of yourself!" Then, silence. The next morning, Hickey knocks on the window of Lahey's and says he had killed his wife. Outcome: Guilty of murder in second degree. Judge Johnson's sentence is $100 fine and seven years solitary confinement in Western Penitentiary. In April of the next year, the papers publish a letter from the convicted man. In it, he bemoans his plight saying that he'll never survive, criticizes his lawyers as ineffectual, requests help in securing a pardon, tries to stir pity for himself and "aged parents." The editorial and general response to his missive is the 1867 version of "too d____d bad! "

1867: Nebraska and Colorado gain statehood. Laying of the first Trans-Atlantic cable. Meadville lawyers petition Harrisburg to prevent Titusville from having its own court. Union Township is created from Fairfield, Greenwood, and Vernon. The "Victorian Courthouse" is built on the site of the previous building. Its large dome contains a clock and is capped by a figure of Justice holding her scales. Seward's Folly, Alaska, is purchased from the Russians for $7.2 million ($111 million modern). Future President Judge John J. Henderson is admitted to the bar.

1867, JANUARY 1: Location: Titusville, John S. Bevan's Grocery Store, east side of Franklin Street, just below Arch. Victim: John Devinger (12, "colored boy"). Suspect: Simeon Clark a.k.a. Simeon Brown a.k.a. Simeon Scott, (18, "vagrant Negro," on the run from the law of Buffalo, New York). Act: Victim struck in head with an axe during a robbery of Bevan's store (for $5.05). Notes: Blow severe enough to expose the brain. Charge is murder since there is no hope of recovery for the youngster. He's becoming paralyzed as he passes the days with his parents and half-dozen siblings at their home on Breed Street. Family is "exceedingly poor." Suspect is a "hard looking customer for one of his years... A little hanging would probably do him more good than a life of prison discipline, but unfortunately he will not get either." *Hold on!* The boy does not die as expected and goes on to survive. Outcome: Time in Western Penitentiary. *Note: This is the first major crime I found where either the victim or suspect (in this case, both) were identified as something other than "white" or "foreign."*

1868: East Fairfield Township is created from Fairfield. The 14th Amendment to the Constitution is ratified. In theory, this grants citizenship to "all persons born or naturalized in the United States," including recently freed slaves. It also forbids states from denying "life, liberty or property, without due process of law" or denying "to any person within its jurisdiction the equal protection of the laws." It sounds good, but some argue it's never really applied as written. The 14th Amendment replaces the United States Naturalization Law of 1790 that limited naturalized citizenship to immigrants who were "free, white" and of "good moral character." Past President James Buchanan dies of respiratory failure.

1868, June 13: Location: ? Victim: ? Suspects: William Mook and Esther Work. Act: Murder. Outcome: Not guilty.

1869: Ulysses S. Grant is President of the United States. U.S. transcontinental railroad is completed. The Suez Canal opens for business. The first group to take a trip down the Colorado and through the Grand Canyon is led by the one-armed Major John Wesley Powell. Past President Franklin Pierce dies of stomach inflammation. Former President Judge Gaylord Church dies.

He Could Whip Them Both Together

Everyone in Beaver Township knows the Varnes and Curtis boys don't get along. They've been on bad terms for years, though nobody is quite sure why. It's true that Clarence Curtis, bigger than any of the Varnes brothers, is a bit of a bully because of his size, but that doesn't seem a reasonable cause of trouble since Clarence is almost unfailingly kind to everyone else he knows.

On December 2, 1869 some of Clarence's geese wander onto the Varnes' property. When George Varnes sees them picking their way along, he gathers up a younger brother and the two set out to drive them off their land. Well, it's more like they set out to kill them, if they can. On the way past the woodpile, George picks up a two-foot-long hard maple stick to help with the task.

As they give chase to the geese, Clarence Curtis appears. An altercation erupts among the three young men. Clarence, 22, expresses his opinion that he could whip them both together and dares the brothers to attack. The Varnes boys refuse. When

Clarence stumbles to his hands and knees while chasing his geese, George Varnes takes advantage and smacks the kneeling man on the head with the stick brought to kill the geese.

Clarence drops like a sack of potatoes. Frightened, George and his brother do the first smart thing of the day; they run to get help. Clarence is carried to his home where he's tended to by Doctor Greene. Turns out the blow with the stick landed behind and a little above Clarence's left ear. There's no break in the skin, but the skull is fractured.

Clarence Curtis never comes to his senses. He lingers a few days and dies on Saturday, December 4.

A sorrowful George Varnes is arrested the day he strikes Clarence in the back of the head. His trial isn't until April of 1870. It's found the death was completely unintentional—a matter of high spirits and nothing more.

George is found not guilty and released.

A WEEK GOES BY. THEN, ANOTHER

Well-to-do Mead Township farmer and Frenchman, Christian Richards bids farewell to his family as he leaves his home in February 1870 on a trip to buy some cattle. He has five miles to travel, west to Meadville, and then another five in that same direction before he reaches his destination.

He tells his wife he plans to stop for lunch in town and, despite the winter-shortened day, expects to finish his travels by sundown. He will spend a night or two and return by the end of the week.

Richards makes it to Meadville and stops for lunch at a roadhouse at the corner of Mercer and West Streets. Vaucher, the proprietor, is a fellow Frenchman whose cooking reminds the traveler of home. With a full belly and half his journey behind him, Richards steps out and onto the road. He turns west, crosses the creek, and continues on his way.

A week goes by. Then, another. Richards' wife contacts

the authorities. It's unlike her husband to be gone so long on business. At her behest, a constable makes a trip to the cattle seller's farm and is told Richards never arrived to close the deal.

On April 30, 1870 it becomes apparent why Christian Richards has gone missing; his robbed, dead body is found in French Creek some two miles south of Meadville. There's a gag in his mouth. His hands are tied behind his back.

The Powers That Be are outraged by the murder. The County Commissioners and Meadville City Council pool their money to offer a $2,000 reward for information leading to the capture and conviction of those responsible for the farmer's death. Almost $50,000 in modern funds, the huge sum of money generates incredible activity toward finding the perpetrators. But, in the end, it does no good. The case is never solved.

1870, APRIL 13: Location: Titusville. Victim: Viable infant. Suspect: None. Notes: Body found on the wall of the cemetery at the top of Franklin Street (near the present day "Pioneer Park"). Coroner's investigation elicits no important facts. Jury returns a verdict of "death from causes unknown." Outcome: Unsolved.

1870: Crawford County's population is up 31% to 63,832. Standard Oil is incorporated. Georgia is officially readmitted to the Union and the Confederate States of America are no more. Two weeks after suffering a stroke, Robert E. Lee dies after serving a five-year stint as President of Washington College (now Washington and Lee). Vladimir Lenin is born eight years before his political partner in crime, Joseph Stalin. Crawford's judges are no longer shared.

1870 – 1876

The Honorable Walter H. Lowrie

Samuel P. Johnson does not run for re-election. Walter H. Lowrie is elected President Judge. In his portrait, Lowrie's eyes are shaded by a furrowed brow. He stares as if he sees something he can't quite understand. The judge has an aristocratic countenance with a high forehead, full face, a large, slightly hooked nose and a surprisingly narrow mouth. He sports somewhat unruly sideburns that travel well below his generous ears.

Born March 31, 1807 while his family is traveling from Butler County to Pittsburgh, Lowrie receives his education in the best schools that city has to offer. Graduating from Western University (University of Pittsburgh) in the mid-1820s, he studies law in the Pittsburgh office of Allegheny County's former District Judge Walter Forward and is admitted to the bar in 1829.

By 1848 he has been appointed President Judge of Allegheny County. Three years later, he is elected to the Pennsylvania Supreme Court where he serves as Chief Justice from 1851 to 1863.

After a stint practicing law in Philadelphia, and at the age of sixty-three, Lowrie is elected President Judge of Crawford. He is one of the most experienced, well-qualified, and scholarly judges the county will ever have.

He is described as just, upright, honest, and conscientious with a quiet understanding of the world and great personal dignity. He is, it seems, a kind, generous, and sincere gentleman with an even-handed but stern and unbending sense of justice.

Judge Lowrie serves Crawford County until he suffers a stroke on November 12, 1876. He passes away two days later at the age of sixty-nine.

1870, DECEMBER DAY ?: Location: Oil Creek Township, Hydetown. Victim: Rowland Kightlinger. Suspects: George Turner, and Francis (Frank) Brown (as an accessory). Act: Shooting. Notes: Bad blood between victim and Turner. Drinking is done. Threats are made. A weapon discharges either purposefully, out of fear of threats by victim, or accidentally during a "tussle." Outcome: Turner and Brown are acquitted. Six years later Turner is arrested, tried, and convicted of larceny. Judge Lowrie sends him to Western Penitentiary for a term of nineteen months.

1871: The National Association, the world's first professional baseball league, debuts with a game between Cleveland and Fort Wayne. Cleveland loses. The Chicago Fire—that stupid cow! The National Rifle Association comes to life.

1871, JANUARY 28: Location: Titusville. Victim: J.S. Wisner (Wisnor). Suspect: Charles Gross of Tidioute, Warren County. Act: Stabbing. Notes: Suspect charged with murder but released when alibi is supplied. Outcome: Unsolved.

1872: Mr. Ward sends out the first mail-order catalog. Yellowstone Park is established. Susan B. Anthony breaks the law by voting in the presidential election.

Ulysses Grant is back as President. It helps that his opponent, Horace Greeley, has died (look up Horace if you have any interest in how twisted U.S. politics can grow). Future President Calvin Coolidge is born.

1873:   First U.S. "silver dollar" is minted. Barbed wire. Jesse James becomes famous for, among other things, pulling off the first successful train robbery in the U.S. He gets away with a few hundred dollars (several thousand, modern). The New York Stock Market crashes, ringing in a five-year economic depression.

1873, DECEMBER 26: Location: Titusville. Victim: Charles Nileson (Nilsson). Suspect: Edward Hallingreen. Act: Fractured skull from fight in a fall or push to brick sidewalk outside a bar. Outcome: ?

1874:   Future President Herbert Hoover is born. Pennsylvania laws pertaining to judgeships change. Supreme Court Justices are now elected to serve a single, twenty-one year term. The rules for Common Pleas Court Judges remained the same; an unlimited number of elected, ten-year terms. The Philadelphia Zoo, the first in the country, opens. The elephant starts to its journey to symbolizing the U.S. Republican Party, thanks to Harper's Thomas Nast using it to show the large Republican vote cringing in fear from a braying Democratic jackass. That liberal press! Harry Houdini escapes his mother's womb. Past President Millard Fillmore dies of a stroke.

1875:   Past President Andrew Johnson dies of paralysis.

1875, JULY 30: Location: Venango Township. Victim: Male child. Suspect: None. Act: Drowning. Notes: Baby is found, tied up in a sack, in a pond at the residence of Philip Blystone. Outcome: Unsolved.

1876: Alexander Graham Bell takes credit for inventing the telephone, but that's okay because the following year he invents the phonograph and Thomas Edison gets most of the credit for that. Nicolaus Otto invents his four-stroke engine. Melville Bissell and—what else—the carpet sweeper. All Native Americans are ordered onto reservations in the western United States. George Custer loses the Battle of Little Big Horn in a hair-raising manner. Future President Judge O. Clare Kent is born.

1876 – 1878

The Honorable S. Newton Pettis

Judge Walter H. Lowrie dies in office. Governor John F. Hartranft appoints Solomon Newton Pettis. His U.S. Congressional photo shows him with a wide mouth, a long, straight nose and the most startling pale eyes. From his strong chin, to the top of his long face capped by a head of dark, unruly hair covering his ears, he looks as if he's ready to burst into smiles.

Solomon Pettis is born October 10, 1827 in Lennox, Ashtabula County, Ohio. By his late teens, he's studying law a few miles away in Jefferson at the office of Joshua R. Giddings (teacher, lawyer, state and federal representative). Pettis arrives in 1848 Meadville where he continues in law at the office of H.L. Richmond, Sr. The young man is admitted to the Pennsylvania bar in 1850.

Pettis is interested in politics and is a member of the 1860 Republican National Convention that elects Lincoln and Hamlin. Crawford's future judge is considered the guiding hand that swings the Pennsylvania delegates to Lincoln and, in doing so, wins him the nomination. In his own way, Pettis helps start the U.S. Civil War.

President Lincoln, whom Pettis considers a close personal friend, appoints him Justice of the United States Court for Colorado in 1861. A devoted abolitionist, he resigns his post during the Civil War to apply his full efforts to building the ranks of the Union Army.

Pettis is elected as a representative to the 40th Congress to complete the term of D.A. Finney who dies in 1868. After an unsuccessful run at re-election, Pettis begins his practice of law.

As President Judge, he strives to look past prejudice and anger to find justice. He encourages jurors to be brave in applying the law and to do so in the knowledge that they are doing what is right. Pettis views Grand Juries as conservative bodies, instructing them to find a true bill and allow a full trial to sort out the matter if there is any chance of guilt.

Judge Pettis is well-liked by local newspapers, and they sing praises for his skill on the bench, though the cynic might note his term is so brief that he doesn't have the time to make any big mistakes. He remains well-connected in legal and political circles and is a good friend of U.S. President James Garfield (who, like Lincoln, is assassinated). Kind-hearted and generous, sometimes to the detriment of his own financial good, Pettis wins many friends.

He is defeated in 1878 for a spot as judge on the Crawford County Republican ticket. That same year, U.S. President Rutherford Hayes appoints attorney Pettis for a year's service as Minister Resident (ambassador) and Consul General to Bolivia.

Pettis returns to Meadville late in 1879 and once again establishes his practice of law. Later in life, he becomes an ardent Spiritualist. He dies in Meadville's Spencer Hospital on September 18, 1900 after an illness of several months.

1877: Rutherford B. Hayes loses the popular vote but is President of the United States on a one-vote margin in the Electoral College. He is declared the winner when contested states, including Florida and South Carolina, swing his way after the Republicans, Lincoln's party, promise to stop the liberalization of racial roles imposed by post-Civil War southern reconstruction. That's the way the world works.

Edison invents the cylinder phonograph and Muybridge, the first moving picture. The Irish gang, the Molly Maguires, is broken when eleven of them are hung for the murder of police and mine officials in and around Scranton, Lackawanna County, in northeast Pennsylvania. His-Horse-Is-Crazy dies after being bayoneted by a guard during an escape attempt at Camp Robinson in what would become northwest Nebraska.

1878 – 1888

The Honorable Pearson Church

Pearson Church wins the election for President Judge by a margin of 43 votes. A portrait of the man shows a nattily dressed, fairly young and balding fellow with sharp features. He wears a dark, bushy moustache, and a long, pointed goatee extending several inches off the end of his chin. He has his father's, former Judge Gaylord Church's nose, but unlike his dad, who looks right at you, the younger Church gazes down and to his left. He appears to be a substantial, lively, and active sort of man and must have cut a dapper figure, peering from the bench through his pince-nez spectacles. I'm not sure he'd appreciate the fact his official courthouse portrait lists his first name as a misspelled "Pierson."

Born on March 13, 1838, Church arrives in 1843 Meadville with his family when his father, Gaylord, is appointed President Judge. The first of many Crawford County judges to graduate Allegheny College (class of 1856, at the age of 18), Pearson reads law with his father and is admitted to the bar two years later.

Citizen Church is elected to serve on the Meadville School Board in 1870, and in 1872, is Board President. It's appropriate that Judge Church becomes well-known for his first-of-a-kind 1881 decision in favor of Elias Allen, a black man who wants to send his kids to a nearby neighborhood school in Meadville instead of a more distant one the city has constructed especially for children of color. Church establishes the illegality of school districts to distinguish between students on the basis of race or color.

The judge isn't so famous for holding Crawford County Courts together when serious efforts are made to split them apart.

He takes office a few months before the passage of Pennsylvania's "New Court Bill." The end-result of wrangling by Titusville power-brokers, the law is seen as an alternative to setting up a separate county with that city as its seat. It specifies the creation of a parallel court system in Titusville. It forces the court to travel to the eastern edge of the county instead of making citizens take the long journey to the west.

Titusville is pleased. Meadville is appalled. As for Judge Church, his position is clear: the original statute creating Crawford County and setting up a 27-mile travel limit to its courts still stands as valid. He is certain the bill will be found unconstitutional. It is a waste of time, effort, and money to establish a court in Titusville only to have the law struck down. Better to wait, he argues, and be sure of your actions.

On June 30, 1878, Crawford County Commissioners resolve to meet in Titusville for the purpose of procuring suitable rooms for the holding of courts. Prominent Meadvillians obtain a preliminary injunction against the commissioners and stop the process dead in its tracks.

Judge Church allows the injunction to stand and sets off a firestorm in Titusville. "Vilification" is not a strong enough word for what happens to him in that city's newspapers. But His Honor holds firm and is eventually proven correct.

In November 1878 the matter is argued before the Commonwealth's Supreme Court, and the law is found to be unconstitutional. The legislature resurrects the bill, and the re-worked version is, once again, passed into law. Judge Church holds fast. The Pennsylvania Supreme Court again finds it invalid. State Legislators try one last time in January of 1881, and fail. Titusville loses the chance to have its own courts and never again tries, in any serious way, to wrest legal control from the county seat.

Pearson Church dies June 13, 1898 at the age of 60.

1878, APRIL 4 (2ND TRIAL): Location: Sparta Township, Spartansburg. Victim: ? Suspect: Charles Snyder. Act: Murder. Outcome: ?

CORONER'S JURY

In the past, a group of several local men would be called to consider any death that was deemed unusual. The findings of the Coroner would be heard, along with the testimony of any witnesses. The formality varied. Attorneys were almost never present unless the case was notorious or involved the rich and powerful.

Upon hearing the facts, the jury decided the cause of death. This could be something general ("a visitation from God," also known as natural causes), to the odd, ("eel thing," a bacterial infection of the skin), to specific, ("a blow to the head by Milo Peer," who was acquitted, by the way). Any responsible party might be arrested and held for the Grand Jury.

There was a single Coroner for the county—for years the post was held by one of the Byhams, of Meadville undertaking fame—with several "Assistant Coroners" scattered throughout the townships. It seemed, sometimes, that any person familiar with death could act as an unofficial Assistant Coroner. This is understandable when you figure the nature of a dead body in the days prior to refrigeration.

As time went on, the numerous Assistant Coroners gradually became fewer and the jury was dropped from the process.

Deaths Of Innocents

It hasn't been all that long ago since nearly a quarter of all (white) babies born in the United States died—despite the best of care. This, along with a general belief that even an unwed mother was incapable of killing her own child, meant that a woman was almost always given the benefit of the doubt in the questionable death of her infant. Legal action against the mother was rare and, if brought, the result was more likely treatment for lunacy than criminal punishment.

Up until the 1930s, the Crawford County Coroner routinely documented the remains of unknown infants found in creeks, ponds, and ditches. This despite the fact that many hospitals and churches would take a newborn "no questions asked." Without a recently pregnant woman, little could be done to solve such cases and they were closed. This would cause an uproar in today's world, but because of the reasons spelled out above, and a lack of forensic science, past societies tended to be much more forgiving.

Consider the following, taken verbatim from the May 10, 1878 edition of the *Titusville Morning Herald*...

A Shocking Discovery

A Tale of Shame and Possible Crime

About 9 o'clock yesterday morning the police were notified that the body of a newly born infant was lying in the vault of an outhouse in rear of Broas' Row, on Franklin Street. Chief Rouse and Officer Hardenburg went there and removed the body to the office of Dr. Young. Coroner Strouse was summoned and proceeded to empanel the following jury: J.J.

Marsh, Foreman; William Lowrie, H. Hazard, D. Gray, L.W. Brown and H.W. Potter.

Drs. Barr and Young made a thorough examination and removed the heart and lungs, which floated in water, showing that the infant must have been born alive.

Chief Rouse upon investigation discovered that a young woman named Lizzie Fairchild had that morning been delivered of a child. She claimed that she was all alone in a room in Broas' Row, and that the child was unexpectedly born about 2 o'clock in the morning. She waited in bed for about three hours, but the child allowed no signs of life, and having neither money nor friends she took the body down stairs and threw it into the vault. Upon being further questioned she asserted that a young man named Edward Bartholomew was the father of the child and expressed a desire to see him. Mr. Rouse at once complied with her request, and when brought before the girl, Bartholomew did not deny being the father, Mr. Rouse also telegraphed for the mother of the unfortunate girl. There are many rumors regarding the cause of death, some claiming that being left alone at so critical a moment the inexperienced mother unknowingly permitted the child to smother, while others believe that she may have strangled it, which allegation can never be proved unless she should confess her guilt. There are so many mishaps which occur after childbirth, even in the hands of skillful nurses and physicians, that the death of the child under such trying and adverse circumstances is not at all extraordinary. Lizzie Fairchild is only twenty-two years of age and is respectably connected. Rumor says that at one time she was engaged to be married to a wealthy operator in Edenburg (now named "Knox," Clarion County, Pennsylvania), but that he had deserted her, and since that time she had been reckless and fallen prey to the wiles of the seducer. She is said to be a person of very comely and attractive appearance, and the discovery of her shame has produced a very distracted state of mind, requiring medical attendance.

The Coroner's jury met at the office of Coroner Strouse at 4 o'clock, and the following evidence was elicited:

Dr. Theodore Young sworn: The child was fully developed, weighing about ten pounds, and was apparently born at full time; there were no marks of violence visible, and the healthy cord and afterbirth were still attached; the surface of the body was generally ecchymosed (discoloration caused by bleeding into the skin, sometimes a sign of difficult delivery); all the vital organs were in a healthy and normal condition; the lungs upon being removed, with the heart attached thereto, floated freely in the water, and therefore of our professional opinion (is) that the said child was born alive and subsequently died of asphyxia; there were no marks of violence; smothered by a pillow would have the same effect; child when examined had been born not over twenty-four hours and probably not over eighteen hours; can't form an opinion as to whether the child died of its own accord or was artificially smothered; a child born so strong and healthy must have struggled in death; I don't know where the child was when it was found; when a man is hung and his neck broken the struggle is but a short time; if air only is stopped the struggle is violent; the child might have had its throat constricted or have been drowned in the mire of the vault; it could not have been some organic disease or it would not have been so fat; death could not have been caused by disease of the heart; it had a full, healthy color; the child might have been smothered under the clothes, but under such circumstances it would have screamed; the child might have been smothered by the bed clothes and the mother might have fainted, but I never knew this to occur in my experience.

Mrs. J. Miller, sworn—I don't know anything about Lizzie Fairchild, but she came into my house last Tuesday; my house is on Franklin Street in Broas' building; I hired her in my rooms; that is the first time I ever saw her; she came there on Tuesday morning and worked all day, and she went out to Mrs. Brice's in the evening and staid [sic] till half-past 11 o'clock; yesterday morning she got up and said she had eaten cucumbers and was sick; she felt very miserable all day, and I did not suspect anything but helped her all I could; I went to bed about half-past 9 o'clock, and we all went to bed at that hour, and that is the last I saw of her till this morning; after breakfast I went into her bed-room to see how she was; saw for myself what the trouble was, and said what have you been doing? She said, not anything, only I was sick all night; the bed bore evidence of what had happened; went to search for the slop bucket and found it down stairs turned bottom side up; then I went to see where it had been emptied; looked down the vault and saw the child there; went up stairs and said to Lizzie what have you done? She looked worried and said not anything, and I said I think you have; she was inclined to deny it, but finally she up and told me all about it: she claimed that she had the child all alone; I told her that I thought it was perfectly awful for her to do such a thing; I meant to presume abortion and murder, and I guess she knew what I meant; asked her why she came to my house to deceive me so, and she said she did not know it was going to happen so quick; I said what shall be done? Just think of that poor little innocent thing being down there; she said that if she had some paper she would write a note to Ed Bartholomew for some money to get the baby removed away; she did not claim that she murdered the child; heard her go down stairs in the morning which woke me up; I said how could you ever have done alone in this way, and she said she did not know how she got along so well; she did not have any help as they would have done it more particular than she did; there was nothing in the slop bucket on the previous evening; when I got up this morning she was sitting on the bed with her shoes on; she appeared to be a stout, healthy girl; I should think it was 5 o'clock when I heard her go down stairs; don't know where her people live or how old she is; she claimed that Ed Bartholomew was the father of the child; I don't know Mr. Bartholomew; I saw him today with Mr. Rouse; the child lying in the vault was not bloody but clear and white; I was about seven feet away when I saw it.

Mr. Rouse sworn : Before 10 o'clock this morning I was called in and found the child laying in the vault; I went to the tool-house, got an implement and pulled it out; Mr. Hardenburg got some water and washed it off and I went after Dr. Barr; I have seen this girl; she said that the child was not alive when it was born, and she stuck to it; she thought that the child was born at 2 o'clock, and she carried it out to the vault at 5 o'clock; she said that she did not strangle it, but that it had been born dead; she said the father of the child was Bartholomew and wanted that I should go and get him which I did; also sent for her mother in Pithole (a rough-and-tumble oil town a short distance away in Venango County); think she is from twenty to twenty-two years of age, and for many years she has had no home to speak of.

The jury then retired and in a few minutes rendered a verdict in accordance with the above evidence.

Outcome: No charges against Lizzie Fairchild in the death of her newborn daughter.

1878, AUGUST 19 (TRIAL DATE): Location: ? Victim: Lydia Miller (Apps). Suspect: Gaylord Minium. Act: Murder. Outcome: Case thrown out by Judge Church at the end of the testimony for the Commonwealth because "the evidence was altogether insufficient to justify a conviction." He directs the jury to find a verdict of not guilty without even hearing the testimony of the defense.

1878, OCTOBER DAY ?: Location: Cambridge Township, Drake's Mills. Victim: Suspect's brother. Suspect: Andrew Miller. Act: Murdered during a family argument. Outcome: ?

1879, APRIL 13: Location: Troy Township, 2.5 miles south of Troy Centre. Victim: Mary (Polly) Winters (wife). Suspect: George M. Winters (husband, a butcher). Act: Beaten to death by husband's fists. Outcome: ?

1879: On November 15 there is an attempted murder in Meadville when 35 year-old John Hood hides beneath a set of stairs and ambushes Samuel Dearment *inside the Crawford County Courthouse!* Hood fires—and misses. The would-be victim hightails it out the door at the north end of the building and turns left onto Center Street. Hood, in pursuit, fires—and misses—again. Dearment continues around to the front of the building with Hood firing—and missing—twice more. Dearment runs in the front door of the courthouse with the would-be assassin close on his heels. Hood again takes aim. Before he can fire, the crowd chasing him knocks him to the ground with the aid of ex-Sheriff Ryan and present-Sheriff Apple. As might be expected, the building is placed into an uproar, the courtroom abandoned by all but Judge Pearson Church who is "left the sole occupant of the seat of justice."

The cause of the attack? The shooter, Hood, claims the two grew up as fast friends in Greenwood Township but that Dearment tried to steal his wife. In response, Hood moved his family to Armstrong County in west-central Pennsylvania. The men had avoided contact until both were called as witnesses in a larceny case involving the brothers of Hood's wife (the former Elizabeth Riley).

Dearment contends that Hood's explanation is a complete fabrication. He and Hood were childhood friends, that much is true, but Hood's anger and move was caused by him having to sell his property to pay off a loan owed to Dearment. Dearment speculates that his own testimony, which sent the Riley boys to jail, was the final trigger that caused Hood to open fire. No matter which story is true, the unrepentant attempted murderer, John Hood, gets to spend time in jail with his brothers-in-law.

In contrast to all of this, the world grows a little smarter when Albert Einstein is born.

1880: Crawford County's population is up 8% to 68,607. Crawford's northern border with Erie is redrawn. Many families go to sleep in one county and awake in the other. Toilet paper is invented.

1880, December 24. Location: Cussewago Township, Bennettown. Victim: "Hattie." Suspect: None. Act: Improperly performed abortion. Outcome: Unsolved.

1881: Chester Arthur becomes President of the United States when James A. Garfield is shot by an insane lawyer, Charles Guiteau, in early July and dies from massive infection in mid-September. Garfield's killer literally dances his way to his own hanging. The player piano is patented. The Gunfight at the O.K. Corral.

Have Another

Inebriation increases stupidity and decreases judgment, and that's always a dangerous combination. Crawford County's most brutal acts tend to take place when both the perpetrator and victim are under the influence, and everyone involved lacks control.

Booze is a known factor in almost a third of all killings listed herein. Drunkenness is no excuse, but it is a fact. It's easy to see why many judges were, and are, strong on moderation—if not outright temperance.

Shout Loudly For Minnie

Late night on Saturday, July 2, 1881. Ed Howard has spent the last day traveling from his work in Youngstown, Ohio to his hometown of Meadville to celebrate the Fourth of July.

He and Charlie Knorr fell in together earlier in the evening and, of course, have enjoyed sharing a few drinks along with some lively conversation. Ed gets it in his head that he wants visit this girl, "Minnie," who works at the Bork house on the corner of Willow and Canal. Charlie isn't quite so enthusiastic; that neighborhood can be rough late at night. But Ed convinces him that some young thing'll catch his eye. Really, isn't that exactly the reason Mother Bork always has plenty of talent on hand?

The two men arrive at the 300-block of Willow a little after 11:00. The house is dark. Ed is not deterred. He begins to pound on the window glass and shout loudly for Minnie.

Mrs. Bork opens the door. The strident and lumpy woman recognizes the two gentlemen but tells them to go away. Ed isn't listening. He jams his foot in the door and hollers around the madam for his girl to come out and play. Mother Bork tries again to close the door. Ed forces his way inside, Charlie tagging along. The woman calls for her husband, Ferdinand. His effort to wrestle the two younger men out the door is unsuccessful.

Mrs. Bork runs to the parlor, returns with a revolver, and comes out blasting. Her first shot hits Charlie Knorr high in the considerable muscles of his left arm. Her second strikes Ed Howard square in his chest. He staggers back, out onto the porch. He takes a few steps, and drops, dead.

The police arrive. The Borks are arrested. Ferdinand is released. His wife remains in her cell.

District Attorney John J. Henderson charges Mrs. Bork with murder. The ensuing trial reveals the only regret the red-headed woman carries is that she was unable to kill both of the drunken young men who barged so rudely into what she claims is a house of good repute. Defense lawyer A.B. Richmond works hard enough to see her found guilty of the lesser charge of manslaughter. Even in 1881 there are legal repercussions for shooting somebody dead when they're forcing their way into your home.

Surgeons probe several times for the slug in Charlie Knorr's arm before they decide that, maybe, it's best to leave it in place. As *Meadville's Democrat Messenger* puts it: "It is probable he will wear it all his life as a reminder that it don't pay to stay out late nights."

1881, DECEMBER DAY ?: Location: Titusville. Victim: Ella Childs. Suspect: None. Act: Improper abortion. Outcome: Unsolved. "Ella's silence prior to her death allowed the guilty parties to escape."

1882: Remember the first successful train robber Jesse James? He's shot dead by Robert Ford, a member of his own gang, for the $5,000 reward ($143,000 modern). Is there no honor among thieves? The "New" Western Penitentiary opens. Located a few blocks west of the prison it replaces, five miles below Pittsburgh on the north bank of the Ohio River, the facility eventually encompasses 21 acres of land with approximately 12 acres inside a fortress-like brown, sandstone-block-wall perimeter. The penitentiary operates for 123 years. It is closed in early 2005 but reopens in June 2007 as SCI Pittsburgh to house male inmates in need of treatment for the abuse of alcohol and other drugs. Future President Franklin D. Roosevelt is born.

1883: The Brooklyn Bridge opens for business. Local time gives way to "Railroad" or Standard Time, created so trains can run without crashing into each other.

1884: Future President Harry S Truman is born. *Adventures of Huckleberry Finn.* The Washington Monument is finished in D.C. after more than 35 years of work.

1884, MARCH 13, 10:00am: Location: Meadville. Victim: Frank Campbell. Suspect: Albert Schultz (about 20). Act: Blow to the head during an argument. Outcome: Charged with murder. Convicted of involuntary manslaughter.

1884, MAY 23: Location: Titusville. Victim: Viable infant girl. Suspect: None. Act: Drowning. Notes: Baby is about four-hours old. Found in a basket floating in Oil Creek at the foot of Martin Street. Outcome: Unsolved.

1885: Grover Cleveland is President of the United States. Daimler invents the first motorcycle run by a gasoline engine. Benz builds the first practical automobile. Past President Ulysses S. Grant dies of tongue and throat cancer. Ferdinand Joseph LaMothe is born. You should know him as "Jelly Roll Morton."

1885, AUGUST 6: Location: Titusville. Victim: Walter Kepler. Suspect: George Keck. Act: Shot. Outcome: ?

INFAMOUS TRAFFIC

Bawdy house, beauty parlor, bird cage, bordello, brothel, call house, cat flat, cat house, chippy house, crooked house, den of infamy, den of iniquity, disorderly house, fast house, flat joint, goosing ranch, hook shop, hot house, house of call, house of ill fame, house of ill repute, house of joy, ice palace, man trap, resort, service station, sin spot, sporting house, steer joint, and, more recently, the *House of the Rising Sun*. The list is nearly endless—even moreso if you're brave enough to include the naughty words!

Prostitution was once legal in much of the United States. It was common for brothels to be located with other businesses, especially hotels, theaters, and bars where "sporting men" congregated.

In the mid-1800s, middle- and upper-class citizenry began agitating against prostitution. With an eye toward licensing and control, many large cities forced houses of call away from the general mix of businesses, concentrating them, and creating what became known as "red-light districts." The origin of that name is shrouded: Some think it came from the red lights prostitutes used to disguise imperfections of their skin. Others assert it's from railroad workers hanging their red, signal lanterns in front of the bawdy houses they visited so that they might be located in case of emergency or changes in schedule.

It wasn't until the late 1800s that municipalities in Pennsylvania began trying to ban "the trade." Such laws were often dropped or ignored because they were considered against the public good: It was believed prostitution prevented rape while protecting pure women from the unthinkable demands of pre-marital relations or unnatural acts. In the days when a good girl wouldn't, bordellos were considered a necessary evil for satisfying the base desires of poorly controlled men. To many wives of the Victorian era, a husband's visit to a fallen angel was distasteful, but it was *not* infidelity.

The 1860s brought ties between the abolition of slavery and the elimination of prostitution. The early 1900s saw the association of prostitution and the evils of strong drink. The ever-more powerful Women's Christian Temperance Union joined the fray, calling for an end to all prostitution. By 1915, selling sex was illegal in almost all of the United States and remains so, except (when this was written) in parts of Nevada.

The 1920s found middle-class suffragettes holding venomous opposition to the world's oldest profession. Much of illegal prostitution moved out of easily targeted cat houses and onto sidewalks, giving birth to the "streetwalker." This was made possible, in part, by the rise of the automobile.

Dens of iniquity also moved themselves to locations near where immigrants worked and lived since a great majority of them were unattached men. There, in the lower-class neighborhoods, prostitution continued unabated, safely out of the sight and minds of the mid- to upper-crust.

Almost all Crawford County towns of any size had at least one brothel that was, as long as there was no trouble, left alone. Everyone knew of the existence of such "pits of sin," including judges, district attorneys, lawyers, police, and jurors.

The prostitute has always been viewed in popular culture with a curious mix of pity, cruelty, and pathos. It is a dangerous way to live. The women (and they are mostly women) are not treated gently by their overseers and customers. They are victimized at a rate far exceeding that of the rest of the population. Disease and addiction are rampant.

It is also common for them to be mishandled by the courts, but that isn't always the case. Particularly in Crawford County.

"Soiled Doves" of Bradford

It's late November, near Thanksgiving in 1886 when Maude Shannon and Grace Brooks Fairchild arrive in Meadville. These two "soiled doves" of Bradford, McKean County, don't take long to discover the city's hotspots and settle into their usual notorious business (it's not known if Grace Fairchild is related to the 1878 Lizzie Fairchild mentioned earlier).

Miss Fairchild makes the acquaintance of 28 year-old John Powers, a boilermaker at the Phoenix Iron Works. The only man and sole breadwinner in a fatherless family of women, he seems nice, at first, but soon displays a violently jealous temper.

Early Wednesday evening, December 1, Fairchild and Shannon are well into several drinks with a couple of men in a "private stall" of the Office Restaurant, a saloon in the more questionable part of town. Powers, who has also been drinking, barges into the small room and berates the two women. Words beget shoves that leads to violence.

The angry man strikes Fairchild a severe blow to the head. She falls to the floor. As the rest of the group stands by, Powers kicks her in the guts and then, pulling her to her feet, puts his hands around her throat and begins to choke the life from her.

Fairchild, "inflamed by strong drink," pulls a blade from somewhere in her clothing and slashes her attacker, cutting him on his face and chest. The crowd comes alive at the sight of blood and pulls the man from the smaller woman.

Fairchild is thrown in the clink. Powers is hauled off to the doctor where his wounds are cleansed and stitched. He prefers not to press charges, and it looks like the woman will be released once she serves her time for public drunkenness.

Things grow much more complicated when the man she sliced dies on December 20 due to an uncontrollable infection of his chest wound. The Coroner's Jury decides Fairchild, "seduced by the devil," is the cause of his death. Court-watchers expect the worst for the sinful young woman. But, with A.B. Richmond and George L. Davenport defending her, the Grand Jury refuses a true bill for murder and drops the charge to manslaughter.

Once they hear of the brutality visited upon Fairchild by John Powers, the all-male jury at her criminal trial refuses even this. With the verdict of not guilty, the gallery bursts into long and loud applause amid which the acquitted receives the congratulations of her counsel and those seated near.

In its description of the facts at hand, the *Argus* of Greenville, Pennsylvania, 30 miles south in Mercer County says, "the verdict does not give general satisfaction."

Perhaps you had to be there.

1886: Coca Cola! Riots and bombings take place in Chicago as workers protest for an 8-hour day, something that business itself eventually accepts as the best for all involved. The American Federation of Labor (AFL) is formed. The Statue of Liberty is dedicated by President Grover Cleveland, who is the first and only president to get hitched while in office. Past President Chester A. Arthur dies of kidney disease and stroke.

1887: Pearl Harbor Naval Base is leased by the U.S. Navy from the government of Hawaii and Queen Lilioukalani. The first "official" Groundhog Day in Punxsutawney, Pennsylvania. How'd they know when winter would be over before Phil's prognostications?

1888: "Jack the Ripper" prowls the streets of London. Former Edison inventor Nikola Tesla shocks the world with the AC transformer. George Westinghouse puts his name to this form of electricity that, two years later, is used to execute New York murderer William Kemmler.

1888 – 1898

The Honorable John J. Henderson

Pearson Church loses the election to John J. Henderson. Judge Henderson's portrait shows an old man nearly overwhelmed by his black judicial robes. He carries thin, somewhat combed-over white hair and a similarly-colored but much thicker moustache. His mild, sad blue eyes look off to his right and are deeply set into an old, handsome, care-worn face. The image is misleading.

Born in Allegheny County on September 23, 1843, he moves with his parents to Meadville when he is thirteen-years old. A graduate of Meadville's Allegheny College, he serves under Henry Shippen Huidekoper in the U.S. Civil War.

Henderson is honorably discharged as a private. He begins the study of law after his armed service and is admitted to the bar in August 1867. In five year's time he is elected as the county's District Attorney, often working without a partner or clerk. In 1887, much younger than his courtroom portrait shows, he wins his election to President Judge.

He is the recognized head of Crawford County's Democrats but stays out of politics while serving his term. On the bench, he is noted for his concern for the victims of crime, often asking after their well-being once court is adjourned. He wrestles with licensing businesses to sell liquor in a time when even the definition of what constitutes an intoxicant is in question. "Fresh cider is fine. Hard or adulterated is not."

The judge is in his mid-fifties when he loses the next county contest to a lawyer he helped educate. Henderson is then elected to Pennsylvania's Superior Court in November of 1903, 1913, and again in 1923. Throughout his travels, he maintains Meadville as his residence. When in town, he stays with his brother, Edward H., in the 300-block of Chestnut Street.

While on court business in Philadelphia, Pennsylvania, in December of 1928, Henderson comes down with a bad cold. On the 12th, at the age of 85, he is dead of pneumonia in the City of Brotherly Love.

A side-note: Henderson, and an equally young friend, attended Ford's Theater the evening of April 14, 1865 and witnessed President Lincoln's assassination. The judge always maintained that John Wilkes Booth *never* shouted "Sic semper tyrannis!" ("Thus always to tyrants"—the official motto of the state of Virginia).

1889: Benjamin Harrison is President of the United States. He loses the popular vote but wins the Electoral College. North Dakota, South Dakota, Montana, and Washington gain statehood. The Johnstown, Pennsylvania flood kills 2,200 when the rain-tested South Fork Dam fails its exam. Jefferson Davis, ex-President of the ex-Confederate States of America, dies. Future President Judge Frank J. Thomas is admitted to the bar.

A PACK OF LIES

On December 29, 1889, Mrs. Olive Turner died of a skull fracture while at her farm in Conneaut Township. Of that much, we're sure. The night of her death, Mrs. Turner remained at home while her husband John attended a Grange Meeting about a mile north in Conneaut Center. Mr. Turner left the meeting early. When others came by his home, they found him missing and his wife in the woodshed, dead of a broken head.

There's a heavy, blood-stained fencepost next to the body. Mr. Turner maintains that, as high-strung as his wife was, she'd probably suffered apoplexy and struck her head after falling down the steps into the woodshed. But the Civil War Vet can't be sure. He was with his son and not even at home when Olive died.

Turner and his son are believed, and the body is buried. Then, upon suspicion of foul play, Meadville Constable Shaefknocker interviews those who had prepared Olive Turner's body for burial. Three weeks later, and upon receiving the constable's report, Coroner J.W. Hannen orders the body exhumed. A graveside autopsy is performed by Dr. C.O. Woodring of Meadville and Dr. Greenfield of Penn Line (Conneaut Township).

Their report, in part:

We found the body well preserved and a great deal of hemorrhage in the tissues above the shoulders and neck. We removed the hair from the scalp and found three scalp wounds in the back part of the head; severed the scalp and under that found a great mass of clotted blood; under one of the larger scalp wounds found an apparent fracture of the middle part of occipital bone (the back of the head), and on removing that part of the skull found considerable hemorrhage and traces hemorrhaged into the partly decomposed brain underlying this locality, and under the meninges [sic] found considerable clotted blood and traces of hemorrhage which could not have come there without considerable external violence. Found no broken bones in the arms. The injury of the skull and brain with its resulting hemorrhage and pressure on the brain was the cause of death in our opinion.

The skull was comparatively thick and it would have been very difficult to produce these injuries unless the person had fallen from a considerable height on a very hard and resisting substance, and the person had been of considerable weight. A fall down three or four steps would hardly be sufficient to cause the injuries found there.

The Coroner's Jury decides Mrs. Turner came to her death at the hands of some person or persons unknown to the jury. Mr. Turner, the Commonwealth's only suspect, is arraigned. Turner's son testifies and convinces the court that his father was not home on the day of the murder, and the older man is released. The general belief of nearly everyone involved is that John Turner murdered his wife but the statements of the son, and lack of other evidence makes it impossible to proceed to trial.

A short time later, Constable W.J. McMillin of Conneaut Township is given a warrant for the arrest of Mr. Turner, sworn out by an I.B. Miner. Turner is "alienating the affection" of Miner's wife. In modern parlance, Mrs. Miner and Mr. Turner are lovers.

Bail is set at $600. Turner pays up. He then gathers his remaining funds and skips "for the west," taking along Mrs. Miner, who divorces her first husband and becomes the second Mrs. Turner.

That Mrs. Turner dies, of natural causes, sometime around 1908. Shortly after, Mr. Turner marries his second wife's sister.

Mr. Turner and his third wife eventually settle in Girard, Ohio, about 60 miles to the southwest of the Turner family farm.

~~~~~

From page 6 of the February 2, 1916 *Titusville Herald*, this article about the Turner Homestead:

Linesville House is Said to be Haunted:

Forest Bean and family recently moved from Ashtabula O., to a house in Linesville, offered them rent free, because it was said to be haunted, the result of a murder committed several years ago in the building.

All went well for a time and the Bean family began to laugh at the stories. Then strange things began to happen. According to reports, doors left locked at night were found open in the morning. Windows left open when the family went to bed were found closed in the morning, and windows left closed were found open.

Unearthly noises and cries as of someone in agony made night hideous. James Bean, father of Forest Bean came on to investigate and nailed up a door of the house, using long wire nails. He asserts that they heard more ghostly noises than ever that night and when they investigated found the door open, the nails having been pulled out.

The family moved out of the house the next day.

~~~~~

In March of 1917 the now 83-year old and ill John Turner calls the Methodist Reverend J.B. Cook to his home and confesses to killing his first wife.

He says he returned home from the Grange meeting that night, twenty-eight years ago. That Olive and he argued. That she slashed at him several times with a horsewhip he was using to break a colt. That she turned her back on him and walked into the woodshed.

Infuriated, he picked up a piece of fencepost, stole up behind her, and clubbed her several times about her shoulders, neck, and head. Once she was dead, the old man says, he arranged Olive's body to look like she'd fallen and struck her head.

He ran away with Miner's wife to escape further trouble

with the law. But none of that mattered, not anymore. He was guilty of murdering his first wife. The story his son told to the courts to get him off the hook? It was nothing but a pack of lies.

Reverend Cook contacts the police, who inform Crawford County District Attorney Albert Thomas. It's Thomas' opinion that, even if the old man's story is true, he's protected by double jeopardy—he couldn't be tried again since he was already acquitted. The son may have committed perjury, but any worry over that is long gone, taken care of by the statute of limitations.

But, a careful search of county records, and an interview with a surviving member of the 1889 coroner's jury, K.O. McLans, reveal that Turner was never actually charged with a crime. There is no double jeopardy.

The Reverend Cook states that the confession seems genuine, that the old boy isn't hallucinating. Turner's doctor, J.K. Taunchill, says his patient might be indisposed, but that he's suffering from nothing more serious than advancing age.

In contrast, Turner's relatives say he has been acting mighty peculiar of late, spending much time pacing his room. Turner's son, the one who might've lied to the courts, claims his father's confession is a fake, a delusion. Then, wisely enough, he clams up and refuses to be interviewed by anybody.

The present Mrs. Turner goes to the courts to take charge of her husband's estate and have him declared incompetent. If Turner is a lunatic, then no action can be taken against him and, as the papers say, "the authorities will probably be glad of it."

The confessed murderer of Olive Turner is, in fact, judged legally insane in early April of 1917. The case remains "unsolved."

Do you suppose that satisfies the restless spirit of Mrs. Turner?

1890: Future President Dwight D. Eisenhower is born. Battle

of Wounded Knee. Idaho and Wyoming gain statehood. Crawford County's population declines for the first time ever, dropping 5% to 65,324. This trend continues for the next 40 years.

1891: Ever want to play Carnegie Hall? Well, now you can! It opens in New York. Something similar to modern basketball is played by James Naismith's P.E. classes at the Springfield Massachusetts YMCA.

1891, March day ?: Location: Hayfield Township, Little's Corners. Victim: Norton J. Hotchkiss. Suspects: Edward S. Skeel, Jr., Albert L. Peelman, and J. Leonard Hites. Act: Blow to head during a fight. Outcome: Suspects tried for murder and acquitted. Re-arrested for involuntary manslaughter.

1892, June 4: After days of heavy rain, Crawford County's northern townships are deluged by a storm that dumps more than 10 inches of rain in 24 hours. Downstream communities are severely flooded.

Just past midnight, Sunday, June 5, the Thompson and Eldred sawmill dam at Spartansburg fails. A wall of water containing hundreds of logs is released into the east branch of the already rain-swollen Oil Creek. Bridges, rails, roads, and houses along the stream are swept away.

Titusville, from Spring Street to the hills across the creek, is destroyed in minutes with substantial loss of life. Refineries fall apart. Huge oil-fires illuminate the dark, still-rainy night. Those somewhat safe in flooded buildings or on floating debris are incinerated. Entire families are lost. Millions of dollars in damage is done.

As bad as things are in Titusville, the City of Oil Creek, several miles downstream, has it worse. When the water hits, tanks of extremely volatile naphtha burst open. The liquid spreads and partially evaporates before its ignition. The explosion and fire wipes out a large chunk of the city and kills hundreds—many of them immigrant children whose bodies are never found.

The telegraph spreads news of the calamity throughout the English-speaking world. Donations arrive from around the globe. The cities begin to recover.

1892: In New York Harbor, Ellis Island begins taking in the first of 12-million immigrants over the next 62 years. Francis Bellamy, Baptist minister and socialist, publishes the original U.S. *Pledge of Allegiance*: "I pledge allegiance to my Flag and the Republic for which it stands, one nation indivisible, with liberty and justice for all." It takes several edits and 50 years for it to become the nation's "official" pledge. Steelworkers strike in Homestead, Allegheny County, Pennsylvania. Guess what Rudolf Diesel invents. On August 4, Lizzie Borden takes an axe...

1893: Grover Cleveland is President of the United States (again). Henry Ford builds his first car. In New Zealand and the state of Colorado women can vote. It's a big day for Meadville when Judson invents what will become the zipper. The "Universal Fastener Company" is founded in Chicago, Illinois, moves to Hoboken, New Jersey, and then on to Meadville. The company eventually grows into Hookless Fastener and, in 1937, Talon Zipper. The government of Hawaii and Queen Lilioukalani are overthrown by the United States. That's what happens when you don't check the lease agreement! The New York Stock Exchange collapses and starts the Panic of 1893. Past President Rutherford B. Hayes dies of heart disease. Former President Judge Samuel P. Johnson dies.

1893, month ? day ?: Location: Titusville. Victim: John Crecraft. Suspects: Emma Crecraft (wife) and Marvin Newton (friend/boarder). Act: Strychnine poisoning. Notes: Main witness against them is arrested and charged with perjury. Outcome: Acquittal.

1894, July 4: Location: Titusville, Spruce Alley. Victim: John (Johnnie) McAndrew (17-18). Suspect: Frederick McDonnel (about same age). Act: Victim's skull "beaten to jelly by an iron coupling pin." Outcome: Convicted and sentenced to death by hanging. Sentence commuted to life in prison by the State Pardon Board. McDonnell is paroled 20 years later.

Make the Punishment Fit the Crime

The Governor's power to pardon criminal wrongdoing in the Commonwealth can be traced to the 1681 Charter of Pennsylvania. In it, England's King Charles II gave to William Penn the ability to forgive any crime or offense except treason and murder. Even in those cases, Penn could grant reprieves until the pleasure of His Highness might be known.

Pennsylvania's 1776 constitution transferred that power to its highest elected official. The constitutions of 1790 and 1838 continued to give the Governor exclusive and unlimited power to forgive fines, abolish forfeitures, and grant both reprieves and pardons for anything except cases of impeachment.

It's *always* a bad idea to place that much authority in the hands of any individual. There were constant allegations of abuse, some imagined, others real. Governor William Findley, for example, granted 530 pardons and 774 remissions of fines during his three years in office (1817-1820)!

Pennsylvania's Constitutional Convention of 1872 created the "Board of Pardons" to limit the Governor's power of forgiveness. The Board, made up of a number of elected and appointed officials, remained in place throughout the period covered in this book. It took only a simple majority of votes to commute a sentence and force the Governor's action.

At first, the Board of Pardons only considered the sentences of death or life in prison. Everyone else served their time, or died trying.

1895: Japanese troops land in Taiwan. Former President Judge Rasselas Brown dies.

1896: Utah gains statehood. Despite what former Crawford County Judge Pearson Church might've thought about the matter in 1881, the U.S. Supreme Court rules racially "separate but equal" facilities as legal. First modern Olympic Games held in Athens, Greece. Future President Judge Thomas J. Prather is admitted to the bar.

1896, APRIL 23: Location: Meadville. Victim: Mrs. Edward Karleskind (25, wife). Suspect: Mr. Edward Karleskind (40, husband). Act: Shooting. Notes: Third marriage for suspect. Second wife died from broken neck falling from porch. Many thought suspect was responsible for the fall, but there was no proof. Outcome: Suspect commits suicide by cutting own throat with razor.

1897: William McKinley is President of the United States. John Philip Sousa composes the *Stars and Stripes Forever.* Ragtime, one of the first American forms of music, becomes popular. Who's buried in Grant's Tomb? You can ask at its dedication in New York. The Klondike gold rush. Amelia Earhart lands—on earth. Bram Stoker's novel, *Dracula.*

1898: Mead is split to create the last of Crawford County's present townships: East and West Mead. New York is the first state to mandate public school students recite *The Pledge of Allegiance,* creating fodder for law suits that continue for almost the next century. Remember the Maine? How about the short Spanish-American War? How about H.G. Wells' *War of The Worlds?* Former President Judge Pearson Church dies.

1898 – 1908

The Honorable Frank J. Thomas

John J. Henderson loses reelection to a lawyer he helped educate. Frank J. Thomas looks straight at you from his photograph. He is dressed in a snappy, pin-striped suit, and you can see his watch chain strung on the left side of his vest. His ears look a little large, but they're offset by clear features and a white, bristle-brush moustache. He has a pretty good head of silver hair. His merry eyes peer through round, rimless glasses. Were he smiling any deeper, dimples would appear. He is almost cherubic. Do not be fooled.

Born in Woodcock Township, October 13, 1859, Thomas is Crawford's first President Judge born within the county's borders. He spends his youth on the family farm, graduates from the Cambridgeboro (Cambridge Springs) high school, and moves to Tuscola, Illinois, where he teaches school and serves as principal.

Thomas returns from the west to graduate from Allegheny College in 1885 and study law in the office of future judge John J. Henderson. Admitted to the bar in 1889, Thomas does not immediately begin practice, returning instead to Illinois to work a number of years as a school superintendent.

He is the 1896 chair of the Crawford County Democratic Committee. Thomas has never held public office, unless you count him being a member of the Cambridgeboro School Board. But he is nominated to the "Fusion Ticket" for President Judge and, at the age of 38, wins the election by no more than 110 ballots. There are ugly accusations that purchased votes were used to oust Henderson. There is talk of contesting the election, but that never happens.

It is apparent from the start that this new judge is different from his more amiable predecessor. Always the school teacher, Thomas is an excellent and forceful speaker. He is not afraid to lecture lawyers, witnesses, and juries when they stray from the facts at hand.

Like Henderson, Thomas struggles with controlling the sale of liquor from un-licensed locations. In his first session he is called out for "punishing" several business that supported his opponent by denying them liquor licenses. That the businesses are in the Titusville area serves to increase tension between the courts and the eastern part of the county.

Through the newspapers, Judge Thomas peevishly tells the public to stop sending recommendations to the court suggesting who should be granted a license to sell alcohol. Not only do such petitions have no bearing on his decisions, he warns testily, but such attempts to influence the court could result in charges of contempt.

In September of 1907, Thomas makes national news by consigning serial rapist Henry Lehna, who confesses to robbery and three assaults on a fourteen year-old girl, to fifty-five years of solitary confinement in Western Penitentiary. It is the maximum sentence allowed by law.

Thomas is best known for his civil rather than his criminal decisions, but in the end even his doubters deem him a first-rate judge. He presides over more than a thousand cases with few appeals.

Thomas, now in his late forties, declines to run in the 1908 election and turns his attention to the practice of law. With his son, Paul E., he forms the partnership Thomas & Thomas. The former judge becomes well-known for helping younger lawyers find their way.

At the same time, attorney Frank J. Thomas uses his knowledge of the courts to bring the county's legal wrangling to a new level. Well-known for twists and turns, courtroom surprises, an encyclopedic knowledge of case law, and always with his school-master's demeanor, he is not reluctant to appeal convictions or sentences.

At the age of sixty, he survives being struck a severe blow from a falling bookcase in a law library (there's irony for you). He practices law until December of 1934 when he contracts a severe cold and dies unexpectedly at the age of seventy-five.

1899, SEPTEMBER 19, MIDNIGHT: Location: ? Victim: *Viable infant Kelly*. Suspects: Dr. H.G. Chamberlain and Mrs. L.L. Havaty. Act: Illegal abortion. Outcome: No charges.

1899, SEPTEMBER 19, MIDNIGHT: Location: ? Victim: *Anna Kelly*. Suspects: Dr. H.G. Chamberlain and Mrs. L.L. Havaty. Act: Illegal abortion. Outcome: No charges.

THE QUEEN CITY

Meadville, Crawford County's central seat, on the way between Pittsburgh and Lake Erie, grew steadily as modes of transportation developed: foot, horses, rafting on French Creek, the overland stage, canals, railroads, and highways. Each change brought its own flavor of trade and economic growth.

Titusville, Crawford County's "Queen City," in the far southeastern corner of the far southeastern township of Oil Creek, was as distant and different from the county seat as it could be.

Founded by surveyors John Titus and his uncle, Samuel Kerr, along the inside of a large bend of the fast-flowing, 50-mile long Oil Creek, the village was permanently settled in 1796 and struggled to find its place.

Through the years, Titusville city fathers tried, more than once, to establish a separate county with their town as the seat. The distance of travel to Meadville's courts was the usual reason. The twenty-some miles up and down steep hills on foot, horseback, carriage, or stage were a real hardship before rail lines were established in the mid-to-late 1800s. This was true no matter what the time of year, but particularly in the cold winters and wet, muddy springs. Add the ever-present danger of highway-robbery and you ventured forth at your own risk!

People living in other parts of Crawford County weren't always willing to lend a sympathetic ear to the travails of far-eastern citizens. It's true that others had just as far to travel, but a trip from the western townships to the centrally-located courthouse was a different and relatively easy experience when compared to one coming in from the east.

Colonel Edwin Drake, working for the Seneca Oil company, drilled his first petroleum well near Titusville in 1859. Over the next decade, the production of crude oil in the United States jumped from thousands of barrels a year to millions. Much of that was coming out of the ground within a few miles of the Queen City.

The world's first oil-boom caused Titusville to swell from barely four hundred souls to well over 8,000. It's true that the city spilled across Oil Creek, but the main part of town was hemmed to the south by water and to the north by scary-steep hills. Much of the flat land was consumed by businesses involved with the production, storage, refining, and transportation of petroleum. Titusville proper was barely fifteen blocks wide and just over half that deep. With everyone living in such a small geographic space, the city was graced with a cocky, bustling, full-speed-ahead crowdedness that was unmatched in Crawford County.

Who needed Meadville's staid lawyers and stuffy judges?

Titusville's oil trade gave it sufficient muscle to be an economic powerhouse known all over the world. The Queen City wasn't merely "on the way"; it was a destination for those with cash and, unfortunately, for those wanting more than their fair share.

"You'll See I'm Not Forgotten"

In November of 1899, Daniel J. Kelly, M. P. Maloney, and William F. Snider of Brooklyn, New York, register for rooms at the United States Hotel on the corner of Spring and Franklin, downtown Titusville. The three men, working for a company that repairs safes, spend the next few days visiting local businesses.

In the very rainy early morning hours of November 11, Ed Derby, night watchman for the Dunkirk, Allegheny Valley and Pittsburgh Railroad (D.A.V.&P.), is spending a quiet shift in the curtained cab of a warm steam engine that sits along-side the railroad's Victorian-style depot located on Martin, between Spring and Arch, a short distance south of the United States Hotel. Derby thinks nothing of the sounds of those passing by. The area around the station is full of industry. Men walk past the depot at all times of day and night.

The curtain lifts in the window closest to the building. Three men stand outside. One, with a blue kerchief wrapped around his face, points a revolver at Derby.

"Don't move," says the masked man. "Stay right where you are!"

He orders the other two men to go ahead with their task. They easily kick aside the door to the depot and use a pickaxe to smash their way into the ticket office, where they attempt to blow the safe.

From start to finish, the job takes a quarter hour. It would've taken less, but the first charge of nitroglycerin (purchased from a local hardware store) is not powerful enough. Almost like a movie's plot, the second explosion wrecks both the safe and office, blows out the windows, and drops the plaster ceiling.

They make such a mess of things that they miss money held within different compartments of the ruined safe. They also fail to notice a bag of cash buried under fallen plaster. Their haul is less than fifty bucks.

The three hurry a few blocks east on Spring Street and invade the "Slate Roof," a well-established and popular house of ill repute—a business they'd cased earlier in the week. There, after trashing the place, they threaten to torture proprietress Bertha Bloom by burning the soles of her feet unless she gives up the goods. The robbers gather cash, gold, and diamonds from the fallen angels and their customers. The take is $800 ($21,000 modern). The experience frightens Miss Bloom so badly that, within the week, she's under treatment for nervous exhaustion in a private hospital on the corner of Spruce and Petroleum Streets.

Patrolman Michael Moran hears the second explosion while standing one block north and west, on the corner of Spring and Franklin. He arrives at the ruined depot minutes after the safe-crackers have fled the scene. Moran uses the telephone there to call Officer William Sheehy, who is on duty at the Western New York and Pennsylvania station, on Mechanic Street, between Washington and Franklin, less than two blocks away.

Sheehy rushes to 163 South Franklin, home of the Titusville Police Chief Daniel McGrath (pronounced "McGraw"). The Chief is well-liked in his city and possesses a well-deserved reputation for being tough on crime, holding his job as Titusville's top cop for more than a decade across changing elected officials. McGrath possesses sharp, alert and even features, a good head of dark hair and a full, slightly drooping moustache. With an athletic six-foot build, the 43-year-old man is enormously strong, fearless, and brave—too brave, sometimes.

McGrath and Sheehy begin at the ruined depot and track the criminals along their muddy trail to Miss Bloom's. Sheehy sneaks in through a side entrance. McGrath bursts through the front door, disarms and subdues one of the trio.

One of the other two men takes shots at both officers. Sheehy is knocked to the floor when a bullet strikes him in the face. McGrath takes a round in the left arm with no apparent effect. The robbers rush outside. McGrath follows, dragging his captured thief. Another bullet strikes the chief in the abdomen before he draws his weapon and blasts his now-escaping prisoner.

All three criminals vanish into the dark.

The wounded Sheehy exits the house through the same door he entered. Bloody and falling into shock, he cannot find McGrath. Sheehy starts uptown, meeting Patrolman Moran, who's headed toward the gun battle. They eventually locate their injured chief a few blocks away at the United States Hotel— where the three safe-crackers had roomed.

McGrath is attended by nearly every doctor in town: Steele, Johnston, Jameson, Preston, Burchfield, and Waid. The bullet that entered his arm is found below the skin of his chest and is easily removed.

The shot to his gut is much more severe. An incision is made to stitch the chief's twice-perforated colon. The bullet is left behind, embedded inside the muscles at the back of his abdomen. Buoyed by the spiritual assistance of Rev. Jos. M. Dunn, McGrath pulls through the surgery.

The chief seems to have a reasonable chance of surviving, until peritonitis sets in. His condition degrades. Conscious until the end of his life, he dies a few days later on the morning of November 15, surrounded by family and friends. He leaves behind two brothers; two sisters; his wife of five years, Anna (Leo); and teenaged boys, Frank and James from a previous marriage to the deceased Lillian (Graham). McGrath is buried in Calvary Cemetery after services at St. Titus. City flags are flown half-mast.

Patrolman Sheehy's ongoing survival is considered something of a miracle. The projectile that struck him entered his mouth, grazed his tongue, broke several teeth, and lodged itself in the side of his throat, less than an inch from his jugular vein. The decision is made to leave the slug in place. Doctors are certain it will remain there for the rest of his life, but Sheehy "coughs up the bullet" about a week later. It's from a .32 caliber revolver but it's a non-standard "short round," like the ones removed from McGrath.

The death of Chief McGrath is, at first, kept from Patrolman Sheehy as he begins a slow recovery. Within a month he's up and out of his bed. He resumes his duties as a police officer at the start of the new year.

~~~~~

At 7:00 the evening of the shooting, a night watchman named Swanders finds a dead body near the American Oil Works. It's the man McGrath wounded during the battle at Miss Bertha's, a block distant. The corpse is dressed in a dark suit, a striped blue and white cotton shirt. Two blue kerchiefs around the throat identify him as the man who held Ed Derby at gunpoint while the depot's safe was blown. The chief's parting shot pierced the dead man's chest and tore through his pulmonary arteries.

After autopsy, the body is prepared by the McNett Funeral Home and put on public display in hopes of someone making an identification. Hundreds throng the viewing over the course of the next two days. So many continue to stop by that the funeral director can finish no other work. The body is removed to the Titusville City Hall and locked away. The dead man is eventually donated to the Philadelphia Dental College, where he turns up on the table of student Lynn Wallace who hails from Oil City, Venango County, a few miles downstream from the scene of the crime.

Nobody knows the dead man's name, but he is recognized as one of three men who stopped at several businesses and government offices throughout the county, posing as safe inspectors and repairmen.

He has size 9 feet, is of average height but more muscular

than might be expected. He looks to be about 45 years old, has a fair complexion, blue eyes, dark red hair and a sandy moustache. His body is "wonderfully tattooed," arms covered by crucifixes and other religious symbols. His identity remains a mystery.

The robbery and murder stops the city in its tracks. News spreads far and wide via the wires of Titusville's Central District Printing and Telegraph Company. It's their quick work in alerting authorities to the northeast in Grand Valley, Warren County, that leads to the nearly immediate capture of one of the two surviving burglars.

Miss Bertha Bloom and Miss Mary Hites of the resort on East Spring are positive the captured man is one of those wanted. He goes by the alias "Daniel J. Kelly," but is identified as "Frank Major" by an older gentleman who claims to have raised him as a child. Once jailed, the suspect refuses to talk, or even allow others to see him, using his hands to cover his face when anyone comes nearby.

Major looks to be in his mid-20s, is about 5 feet 8 inches tall, and weighs just over 150 pounds. He has a dark complexion with a full head of straight, dark, chestnut hair that's parted down the middle. His light blue eyes and round face give him a youthful appearance that contrasts with his slightly hawkish nose. He is also tattooed on his arms. On the left, a weeping willow marked "Sailor Boy at the Tomb"; a ballet dancer poses on the right, and there are dots between the thumb and index finger. These last marks are often associated with convicts in prison.

County police pour into Titusville to search for the last man of the trio. Many extra hands are deputized. There are reports of a running gun battle in the vicinity of Grand Valley between Special Officers George Preston, Billy McKenzie, and the remaining wanted man. Several shots are exchanged at a distance of about 200 feet before the trackers lose their quarry in a swamp.

The burglar later shows up at the back door of a Grand Valley hotel, asking for, and receiving, a bite to eat. After his brief repast, the man heads up over the hill into Dunderhead Hollow.

The chase goes on—and on. Even though they're unable to spot him, his pursuers know their man is only slightly ahead of them. They continue to find farm houses at which he has stopped and begged for food. They fully expect to overtake him, possibly near Marienville, in the wild and increasingly mountainous landscape of Forest County located to the east, across the Allegheny River. Papers report that crack shots are waiting and any criminal wandering the area "might as well surrender or make lightning preparations to meet his Maker."

The last of the trio eludes capture. One by one, his pursuers return to their regular lives. Within a few weeks, the chase is abandoned. Sporadic reports of the escapee's whereabouts don't pan out. There are hopeful stories of arrest, but they are either false or cases of mistaken identity. Emotions in the region run so high that a tramp found in a boxcar eighty miles west in Youngstown, Ohio, is suspected of being the wanted man and nearly lynched by a mob before he can prove his identity and gain freedom.

Then, there's a break in the case. Following a tip from an anonymous young lady who knew something of the wanted man's "previous character," lawyer C.W. Benedict travels to Little Valley, the seat of Cattaraugus County, New York and then to the Erie County Penitentiary in New York. He returns with photographs that are immediately recognized by Miss Marguerite Garnett, another of the ladies in Bloom's disorderly house.

Police now have a name to go with their wanted man: "Frank Woodard." Mr. Woodard has a harrowing history. Reported to be born "Frank Farrell" in Richburg, south-central New York (in the direction he fled), he was the only one of several children to escape being killed by an insane mother who then killed herself.

Disowned by his father and raised by an uncle, Woodard was considered a bad boy who grew into an even worse and violent man. Suspected of one murder, he served a term in the Little Valley jail for the killing of a Native American woman. He followed this with three recent terms in the County Pen at Buffalo, New York: for larceny, for shooting at a streetcar, and the last for firing a weapon at the feet of small boys to make them jump!

Woodard goes by the alias "Frederick Adams" and is described as about 5 feet 8 inches tall with a medium-heavy build. He's balding with thin, brown hair and a chestnut brown moustache that curls slightly at the ends. His eyes are brown and small "with a peculiar squint." His nose turns up slightly at the end. He has a florid complexion and is tattooed with a woman's figure on his left forearm. Copies of the photos and description are circulated first throughout the region and then the nation in hopes of spurring the capture of the badly wanted man.

~~~~~

In the meantime, the young fellow known as Frank Major makes his way through the county courts. He's indicted by the Grand Jury and held for trial in the February term of 1900. He still refuses to divulge his real name, he says, to protect his mother's feeble health. He tells reporters that he's from a good home and family, and enjoyed a good upbringing. He's deemed a model prisoner, a well educated and non-profane man who fell into the wrong crowd and was unable to pull himself out of his downward spiral. Denying anything to do with the crimes, all he admits to is having been with those who were probably the guilty ones.

He says he has a trade, a way of making money, but keeps it a secret because it will give away his identity. It does, because the way he makes money is *to make* money—he's a counterfeiter.

During an unrelated prisoner transport, Sheriff Wilcox of Meadville takes photos of "Frank Major" to Western Penitentiary. The warden recognizes the man as "Joe Kennedy" of Brooklyn, New York, who served three years for making his own money.

He was also convicted in May, 1894, for robbing post offices in the towns of Alden and Wanamie in Luzerne County, northeast Pennsylvania. He was released two and a half months before the crimes in Titusville with a train ticket to Brooklyn.

But Kennedy didn't return home. He disembarked in Harrisburg, Pennsylvania and, after tramping around, landed in Kane, McKean County, in the north-central portion of the Commonwealth. It was there he hooked up with Woodard, whom Kennedy knew as "William Snider" and the unidentified dead man he called "Maloney." There was also a fourth man, their leader, "Joe Sullivan."

They split up and then met in Titusville, a few days before their crimes. Their leader was late, so the other three checked into the United States Hotel and started drinking—heavily. This worried Boss Sullivan who found them blitzed and wisely abandoned them, leaving on one of the early trains as his erstwhile gang began their botched robbery of the D.A.V.&P.

Heading into Kennedy's trial, it's noted that there have been a number of murders in Crawford County in the past few years and all have resulted in either acquittals or prison terms. One "prominent Meadville lawyer" tells the papers that nobody will pay the ultimate price for murdering McGrath because Crawford County jurors "haven't got the backbone to stand up and convict a man of murder." What's more, he continues, Judge Frank J. Thomas will use any excuse to avoid passing the death penalty. Therefore, the general consensus is that even if Kennedy is found guilty, the worst that will happen to him is more time spent in Western Penitentiary.

Kennedy is kept on his own in the county lockup with little or no contact with other prisoners. He's frequently found in tears as his February trial grows near. Attorney Thomas J. Prather, who had consented to defend him, withdraws "for reasons I do not care to state at this time." Kennedy cannot be tried without counsel and Judge Thomas is forced to postpone the proceedings until the May term of court.

More money suddenly becomes available for Kennedy's defense. By early April of 1900 the defendant is "a mere shadow of his former self" due to his close confinement. But Prather is back as his counsel, with Attorney Frank P. Ray. The prosecution is District Attorney Willis R. Vance, Titusville lawyers C.W. Benedict and George Frank Brown, and former D.A. Philip Willet.

Hopes are that the still at-large Woodard will turn up in time for the trial. He does not oblige.

Jury selection begins on May 16. The trial is a lop-sided affair with the prosecution gaining and holding the upper hand from the start. The ladies of Miss Bertha's house of ill repute provide damning and unshakeable testimony. They identify Kennedy as the shooter and quote him as saying he'd "fill McGrath's head with lead" if he came near. For one of the first times in county history, the prosecution is helped by ballistics. The pistol Kennedy carried when arrested takes short rounds like the bullets found in McGrath and Sheehy. Dr. William G. Johnston testifies that the slug taken from the dead Chief "fit perfectly" in the barrel grooves of Kennedy's pistol.

Within six days, the accused is found guilty of both burglary and murder in the first degree.

Shortly after the trial, it's learned that Kennedy's "real name" is Daniel J. Kehoe and that money for his defense was provided by his family, most notably his sister, Miss Margaret Kehoe from Brooklyn, New York.

Kehoe's lawyers file an appeal for a new trial. It is denied. In mid-July, 1900, with Miss Margaret on hand, and despite defense attorney Prather's plea for leniency, Judge Thomas sentences the convicted man to death by hanging with the date to be set by Pennsylvania Governor Stone.

An early November, 1900, appeal is planned for the Pennsylvania Supreme Court with C.W. Benedict arguing for the prosecution and Homer J. Homes for the defense. Kehoe is quiet in his cell with little apparent hope. The Supreme Court refuses a new trial. The State Pardon Board refuses to commute Kehoe's death sentence to life in prison. Governor Stone sets the date of execution for April 16, 1901, a year and a half after the crime.

It may be a hanging, but it will not be public, taking place, instead, inside the Meadville jail. Allowed to witness are the jail's physician, twelve citizens, the immediate male relatives of the prisoner, if any, two ministers, if desired, and such law enforcement as deemed required.

The weeks leading to the execution throw both Meadville and Titusville into turmoil, but for different reasons. As the site of the hanging, and removed nearly thirty miles from the scene of the crime, many at the county seat are convinced the hanging smacks of revenge. Meadville churches fill to capacity as religious leaders preach against the sentence.

Titusville responds with ridicule and derision. How could any other city understand the impact of the murder of their beloved Chief McGrath?

Crowds begin forming at the courthouse and jail well before dawn on the day of the execution. To satisfy the curious and give them something to do, as many people as possible are shepherded through Sheriff Scott's office to view the scaffolding and gallows inside the jail.

Admission for witnesses begins promptly at 1:00 in the afternoon, an hour before the execution. Each person shows a ticket issued to them by the sheriff in the preceding weeks. The press is allowed on the upper floor of the building where they can look down upon the scaffolding some eight feet below. The crowd of spectators, including the reporters, comes to one hundred. The Widow McGrath is the only woman to possess a ticket. She does not attend.

Kehoe, for his part, is shaved by a barber at ten the previous night and sleeps well. He eats his usual breakfast. His last meal is lunch: four crackers and a cup of tea. He meets to bid farewell to his sister, Miss Margaret. Though sad, he never shows an iota of fear.

A jury of twelve spectators, mostly physicians, sits close to oversee the proceedings and attest to their solemnity. All invited law enforcement stand near and around the scaffold.

Titusville Deputy Sheriff Hall announces the prisoner will be brought in around 2:00 and continues: "It is a serious matter, thus far the prisoner has held up remarkably well. Assist him to be brave. Let all understand the situation and act accordingly."

Sheriff Scott mounts the scaffold at 1:50 to check the rope and knot one last time. He turns to the crowd, tears in his eyes and speaks with a breaking voice: "Let there be no loud word spoken. I am in a place not to be envied and I believe you all understand my position." He climbs down and, along with Deputy Hall, leaves the courtyard to retrieve the condemned.

The clock strikes the hour. At 2:03 a silent procession enters by twos through the northeast door. First, Deputy Hall and jail physician Dr. R. Bruce Gamble. Next, Kehoe, in a new and well-fitting suit of black, being led by his right arm by Sheriff Scott. Rounding out the small group are Priests James J. Dunn and Anthony Wiersbinski of Meadville's St. Brigid's Roman Catholic Church.

All spectators remove their hats when the scaffolding is reached.

Kehoe takes the stairs with a firm step and kneels while the priests offer prayers. He rises and kisses the crucifix. Scott ties his hands and feet. The condemned repeats after Dunn, "Father, into Thy hands I commit my spirit. Have mercy upon my soul."

Scott draws the black cap over Kehoe's head and adjusts the noose. After a moment's hesitation the sheriff says, "Frank, goodbye." Kehoe nods and responds. "Goodbye."

The death trap is sprung at 2:06. Kehoe drops. He's brought up short by the rope. The man never moves a muscle. It's a clean execution—to the great relief of everyone involved.

The priests continue the office for the dead. Drs. E.T. Lashelle and Gamble stand below the trap, fingers feeling for the pulse of the man hanging in front of them. Fourteen-and-a-half minutes later, at 2:20:30 in the afternoon of April 16, 1901, Daniel J. Kehoe is declared dead.

Standing on the steps of the scaffold, Sheriff Scott thanks the crowd for their "presence and good behavior." He then addresses Father Dunn, who thinks Kehoe innocent of the crime that brought his execution: "To you I give charge of this body. After a lapse of twenty minutes you may take the body and remove it from the jail."

Kehoe's last wishes are simple: He wants the few dollars in his pockets given back to the D.A.V.&P. He wants his body claimed by Father Dunn and embalmed by Striffler's Funeral Home in Meadville. He wishes for Catholic Mass be said over his body and that it be interred in Meadville's St. Brigid's Cemetery. All are granted. He is buried on April 17 with his grave unmarked.

Rumor is that Kehoe wanted to make a full accounting of himself but was dissuaded by both his sister and spiritual advisor. What might be considered an appropriate set of final words is a penciled couplet Kehoe wrote for Meadville Deputy Sheriff Bakley:

"When I am dead and in my grave, all my bone are rotten / these few lines, if you read, you'll see I'm not forgotten."

The man writing signed his ditty "D.J. Kehoe." The Commonwealth's own record of execution lists him as "Frank Major."

~~~~~

Seven months later, a short article appears in the local newspapers saying that Kehoe's accomplice, Frank Woodard, has been spotted in a "small mining town in West Virginia." Nobody pays much attention. Reports of Woodard have arrived over the months from locations far and wide. This time, however, there may be a little extra weight behind the story since the person relaying the news is from Olean, New York, one of Woodard's old stomping grounds.

Sure enough, after 2 years on the run, it's confirmed that Frank Woodard, a.k.a. Frederick Adams, has been apprehended in West Virginia, by one Mike McConnell. No less a person than Titusville Mayor J.J. McCrum has already headed out, under cover of a visit to Pittsburgh, to identify and return the criminal to justice. The now Chief of Police William Sheehy remains mum, saying if it is Woodard then the mayor, who has followed every lead in the matter, deserves full credit for the capture.

The story develops that J.W. Prentice, once a member of the Titusville city police force, and now in West Virginia, had spotted Woodard in the small town of Pine Grove, near the southwest corner of Pennsylvania. It was Prentice who alerted the good mayor. A warrant was issued, and the heavily armed wanted man was taken after a shoot-out in the small mining community of Clarksburg, West Virginia. Flush with cash, Woodard was thought to be one of a gang responsible for a series of burglaries in that part of the state.

Mayor McCrum's telegraph to Titusville is short and to the point: "Fully identified." The mayor breaks down and cries with relief while meeting with the local attorneys to arrange guards and transport for the prisoner's return to Crawford County.

Once caught, Woodard is cooperative. He's polite, bowing to people he knows. After being charged with murder and burglary, Woodard asks for the same attorneys who defended (and lost) Kehoe's case.

Extra guards are assigned to the quiet and calm Woodard but they are not needed. He is a model prisoner, spending his time reading and sleeping—at first. By the start of 1902, he's nervous, asking about letters from the outside world, anxious to hear from "the south" (West Virginia). He begins to lose sleep and is soon cussing out his jailers and complaining about his constant confinement. The corridor that holds his cell is cut off from the rest of the block so that he may take proper exercise.

His lawyers ask for a change of venue and fail even though Judge Frank J. Thomas scolds Sheriff Scott for allowing so much information about the accused to be leaked to reporters. Thomas declares that defense attorney Frank P. Ray should bring charges against local papers for the stories published about his client.

A motion by the defense to delay until the May term is refused. Woodard's trial begins on February 24, 1902. Only eight jurors are selected in the first eight hours of interviews. Like the Kehoe trial, all potential jurors from the Titusville area are rejected outright. A change of venue is tried for again, and rejected. It takes three days to seat the jury.

Police Chief Sheehy, displaying years-old scars from his ordeal, testifies. The defense struggles and then rallies. They're trying to establish murder in the second degree, based on the fact that the bullets that killed McGrath fit the gun found on Kehoe and that Kehoe has already paid the ultimate price for pulling the trigger of the murder weapon. You can't, they argue, have one gun and one shooter but two first degree murderers.

The trial takes one week. Woodard found is guilty of murder in the second. There will be plenty of prison time, but no death penalty. An obviously relieved Woodard pleads guilty to burglary.

Defense counsel is overjoyed. Some papers, especially those in Titusville, publish scorching editorials decrying the verdict. Says one: "Failures like this upon the part of juries… have a tendency to encourage rather than repress the capital crime."

March 24, 1902. Woodard smiles as he is lectured and sentenced to thirty-five years in Western Penitentiary—to that date the longest prison term ever handed down by a Crawford County judge. In interviews, Woodard calls himself "of a gentle disposition" except when under the influence of liquor. He won't discuss where he was when on the lam, denies firing the fatal shot, does not know the name of the unidentified burglar killed by McGrath.

Woodard tries to play it cool, but he shows his colors by "crying like a baby" when he arrives at the forbidding walls of Western Penitentiary.

~~~~~

The news breaks on November 4, 1913 that, thanks to the New Parole Act, Frank Woodard is to be freed after having served only eleven of his thirty-five years in prison. The relatives of Daniel McGrath retain lawyer C.W. Benedict to oppose release. It does no good and Woodard is paroled.

Titusville grows nervous. A man answering Woodard's description is said to have been in town on November 29 begging a dozen doughnuts. Another rumor is heard that he's calling on, of all people, Miss Bertha Bloom, the madam whose feet he once threatened to burn. Local papers sound a calming note, saying Woodard is unlikely to return even though he had threatened revenge on some in the city. It is insisted that the parolee's time in prison, and his instant return to his cell on any wrongdoing, will keep him to the straight and narrow.

Woodard reports to his parole officer for two years. He fails to appear on March 9 1916, vanishing, never to be heard from again.

~~~~~

Michael Moran replaces McGrath as Titusville's Chief of Police, but does not have the job for long. He dies of kidney disease in July of 1901, after Kehoe's hanging, but before Woodard is apprehended. Officer Sheehy takes over as Chief until May of 1904, when he obtains an "excellent position" with the railroad shops in Moline, Illinois (At least I think that's where. The papers aren't clear on the location.) He is replaced by Titusville Fire Chief John Laley.

McGrath, Moran, Sheehy, and Laley. Is it any wonder the stereotype of "Irish Cop" is such a strong one?

After twenty-two years of service to the community, Miss Bertha Bloom's cat-house, the Slate Roof, is shut down in 1916 by the crusading Reverend J.J. Bullen, then of Meadville, but once of the Titusville First Baptist Church. It's possible Miss

Bloom might've continued her errant ways had she not been badly crippled with rheumatism.

Edward B. Derby, the guard held at gunpoint on the rainy night of McGrath's murder, tells his story many times before dying in August of 1936, at the age of seventy-nine.

The third burglar, shot and killed by McGrath, was never identified.

Ample Reasons To Be Frightened

We've all seen hangings depicted in the movies: A hooded man, noose around his neck. Drops through a trap door. Falls a few feet. Stops with a sudden jerk. Neck broken by the hangman's knot. Instant death.

But most early hangings weren't intended to kill the victim quickly. People were "strung up" to cause slow suffocation. In the British Empire it was fairly common, even into the early 1800s, for the hung man to be cut down while still alive to be vivisected and then have his arms, legs and head removed—in that order. You've heard the phrase; "hung, drawn and quartered?" Such was part of the British penal code until 1870.

Before my fellow Americans begin feeling high and mighty about our relatively civilized executions, they should know that not all U.S. states employed the "trap-door" scaffold. New York, for instance, used a tipping scaffold and counterweight system that rarely produced the quick death of a broken neck. We should also remember that our home-grown lynch-mobs treated nearly 5,000 of our own variously-colored citizens to nearly the same extremes of British brutality and that it continued on into the 1960s.

During the mid-1800s to early-1900s real efforts were made in Pennsylvania to render court-ordered hangings more "humane." The carnival-like public spectacles were brought indoors and made solemn. Standard procedures were created to produce the quicker death of a snapped or seriously damaged spinal cord.

That didn't mean things couldn't go horribly wrong. News articles regularly described botched executions in ghoulish detail: A man dancing on the end of his rope for 20 minutes or a prisoner whose head was popped off his body. There were ample reasons to be frightened of the noose and many a condemned prisoner succeeded in avoiding their own hanging by committing suicide out of fear.

As time went on, professional executioners assisted where hangings were few and far between. Their services relieved some of the burden placed on local law enforcement like Sheriff Scott of our previous story, who reported suffering from nightmares caused by the part he played in the execution of Daniel Kehoe.

1899: Automatic coin-operated telephones begin to appear (up 'til now, an attendant sat near a pay phone, collecting coins for each use). Calls cost only five cents until 1951 when they increase to a dime.

1900: Crawford County's population is down 3% to 63,643. Zeppelins take to the air. The music styles of Country, Western, and Jazz grow in general popularity. Former President Judge S. Newton Pettis dies. Future President Judge O. Clare Kent is admitted to the bar.

1900, MAY DAY ?: Location: Cambridge Township, Cambridge Springs. Victim: Viable infant by abortion. Suspect: None. Notes: Is in September's set of Coroner's Inquests. Outcome: Unsolved.

1901: Newly-elected President William McKinley dies of infection after being shot by anarchist Leon Czolgosz. Vice President Theodore Roosevelt takes over—another year gives us his namesake bear. Thank King Gillette for the safety razor. The American Baseball League. Past President Benjamin Harrison dies of pneumonia.

1902: Lucky Lindy arrives on earth. The Rose Bowl (Michigan (49) vs. Stanford (0)—after the Stanford Captain requests the game end eight minutes early—ouch!). Automobile world speed record set at 74 miles per hour. Teddy Roosevelt is the first U.S. President to ride in a car (an electric one, by the way).

1902, SEPTEMBER 13: Location: Greenwood Township, Geneva. Victim: Martha (Neisa, Nama) Riley (Rihley). Suspect: "A well known young man, who has fled." Act: Improperly performed abortion. Outcome: No charges. (It is possible for this woman to be related to the "Elizabeth Riley" mentioned in the courthouse shootings of November 15, 1879.)

1902, SEPTEMBER 30: Location: Titusville, South Martin Street. Victim: Frank Goodwill. Suspect: Milo Peer. Act: Blow to head. Notes: After hearing coroner and witnesses, Judge Thomas declares there is no case and instructs the jury to return a verdict of not guilty.

1903: First trans-Atlantic wireless. First road trip by automobile across the United States. It takes two months and some-odd days. Wilbur Wright wins the coin toss and takes a three-second semi-controlled flight at Kitty Hawk, North Carolina. Orville shows him up a couple days later by extending the flight time by nine whole seconds. License plates for U.S. automobiles. Crayons. Windshield wipers by Mary Anderson. First World Series. The Boston Americans beat the Pittsburgh Pirates, 5 to 3 in a best of 9 series.

1903, MARCH 29: Location: Beaver Township. Victim: Herbert Rounds (son-in-law). Suspect: Frank Hogle (father-in-law). Act: Shot. Notes: Victim was drunk and beating his wife, the suspect's daughter. Victim reported dead on March 31st. *Oops. Hold on. So sorry.* "Your correspondent was misinformed by a jail official." Victim lives though the shooting and goes on to survive.

1904: Meet me in St. Louis for the World's Fair. *The song and movie* don't come along until 1944, Louis! The United States starts digging on its version of the Panama Canal.

1904, MARCH 18: Location: Meadville, French Creek near Mercer Street Bridge. Victim: Viable infant boy. Suspect: None. Act: Cord tied around the baby's neck and cut into trachea. Neck is broken. Notes: Body frozen in the ice. Found about 3:30 pm by three 12-year old boys; Willie LeCrift, Sanford Phillips and William Bierley while playing along the banks of the creek. Fully developed 7-pound boy. Lungs show it had breathed. Coroner's reports says body was tied to an iron bar. Outcome: Coroner Stockton decides a inquest is futile because there is no evidence.

1904, MAY 28: Location: East Fairfield Township, Shaw's Landing. Body found in French Creek, 4.5 miles south of Meadville. Victim: Unknown man. Suspect: None. Act: Unknown. Outcome: Unsolved.

1905: "E = mc²"—Courtesy of Albert Einstein. Teddy Roosevelt is back in office—this time elected on his own. The last U.S. veteran of the War of 1812, Hiram Cronk, dies at the age of 105. Japan invades Korea and stays there for nearly 40 years.

1906: Cornflakes by William Kellogg. Pennsylvania passes its first state-wide automobile driver license law. San

Francisco's school board orders Japanese children be taught in racially segregated schools. There is a very large earthquake. The two events are thought to be unrelated.

1907:   Oklahoma gains statehood—the first in the new century. The first financial panic of the new century, too.

1907, "PRIOR TO APRIL 21:" Location: Titusville. Victim: Viable infant boy. Suspect: None. Act: Unknown. Outcome: Unsolved.

1908 – 1928

THE HONORABLE THOMAS J. PRATHER

Frank J. Thomas does not run for re-election. Thomas Jefferson Prather is elected President Judge. His portrait shows him standing, dressed in a nice, soft gray suit, gold watch chain dangling three buttons up on a six-button vest. He wears a high-collared white shirt, a pretty tie and looks straight at you with somewhat sleepy eyes. He possesses a full head of dark hair, a large but well-proportioned nose, a wide, full mouth and a strong chin. It is the image of a man in his prime, which is what he was when first elected. Most strikingly, his hands are in his pockets.

Born a few miles west of Townville in Troy Township, November 28, 1866, Thomas Prather's log-cabin, farm-life, one room school-house upbringing make him a favorite of the common man.

He enrolls at Edinboro Normal School, graduates in 1890, teaches for a couple years and then enters Allegheny College where he is known for introducing the sport of American football. Juggling his college education and the study of law at Humes & Thomas, Prather is admitted to the bar a year before receiving his diploma from Allegheny in 1897.

Prather builds a good reputation as a lawyer in the years before he is elected. He is popular, genial, and not easily ruffled.

Prather "never gets nervous and seldom allows himself to become excited."

The new judge's calm is sorely tested from the start. He sits on a half-dozen murder cases in his first two years—more than many of his predecessors experienced in their entire careers. The Hover case (with former judge Thomas on the team for the defense) results in a retrial and change of venue based on Prather's perceived lack of control of the hundreds of courtroom spectators. But the young judge learns quickly and such mistakes are never repeated.

He is the first judge in Crawford County to be elected to two terms. Attorney Prather practices law only a few years after his time on the bench. Always active in local affairs, he is sought for advice and guidance by individuals, businesses, and educational institutions. His wife, Margaret, precedes him in death. When Thomas J. Prather dies on January 10, 1949 he leaves behind seven children and fourteen grandchildren. More than a few of his extended family follow law as a profession.

1908: Future President Lyndon B. Johnson is born. First production Model T Ford is built in Detroit, Michigan. Tunguska blasts. Oil is discovered at Masjid-al-Salaman in southwest Persia (now known as Iran). We've been fighting over that kind of thing ever since. Butch Cassidy and the Sundance Kid are, supposedly, killed by soldiers in Bolivia. Past President Grover Cleveland dies of stroke, among other things. Future President Judge Herbert. A. Mook is born.

1908, MARCH 10: Location: Meadville, just north of the Erie Railroad Roundhouse. Victim: Jose Petrole (35). Suspect: Dominick Nosti (24). Act: Shot during a gunfight after an argument. Notes: Victim shot once in the chest with the bullet entering through the right breast and passing through the body—.32 caliber six-shooter. Suspect claims it was self-defense, but witnesses say he shot at least twice before the victim returned fire. Suspect has already booked passage back to Italy and is hiding out until departure when police find him under some carpets and rags in a second-floor closet of his boarding house. Outcome: Guilty of murder in the first. Successful appeal. Guilty of manslaughter in second trial. Sentenced by Prather to twelve years in Western Penitentiary.

OPERATING WITHOUT A GOVERNOR

If you've ever watched an old steam engine run, then you've probably seen a "governor." It's that spinning gizmo, usually sitting on top, constructed of heavy metal weights hung on hinged rods. In reaction to the increasing spin of their axle, the weights swing out into the air (said to be the origin of the phrase "running balls out"). A connection between governor and throttle then reacts to slow the engine, holding everything to a safe and steady speed. The mechanism is essential. People die when an engineer is fool enough to "operate without a governor."

Guilt is the governor of many people. As such, it helps to check bad behavior. The problem with guilt is that it's reactive; its real power comes to bear only after something has happened. Just as a burst of steam can damage a governed engine, a guilt-controlled person can take a harmful action before the emotion kicks in.

Almost everyone feels guilt and that's a good thing. A healthy amount helps us to learn from our mistakes. A tiny dose is all it takes to make us understand when our behavior should be adjusted for the better.

But too much guilt can cripple. Too much guilt can kill.

Recovery is Likely

Christmas Eve, 1908. All is calm. All is bright. Until Harry Winters is shot multiple times with a .32 revolver.

Harry's shooter, childhood friend Jack Cronin, runs a block from the scene of the crime on Mead Avenue, in Kerrtown, Vernon Township, to the house of Charles Hope, who convinces Cronin to surrender to the police. He does so, saying of Winters "Yes, I shot him, and I would do it again if I got the chance. I am not sorry that I did it and I hope the ------- will die."

But Winters isn't dead by the time of Cronin's arraignment. The charge is "feloniously and maliciously wounding with intent to kill and malice aforethought." District Attorney O. Clare Kent reserves the right to change the charge if the victim dies. Pennsylvania law, borrowing a rule from the Old English, makes it murder if Winters expires within one year and a day of the attack.

Given three serious gunshot wounds and the state of medical care in 1908, you might think Harry Winters would be dead in short order. You'd be mistaken. The victim holds on in Meadville's Spencer Hospital for a week, then two, then a month and longer, all the while suffering through extensive medical treatment.

One bullet plowed through the bottom edge of his breast bone, tore his bowel, and lodged in the muscles of the back above the left kidney. Winters surrenders a nearly fatal volume of blood to that wound and subsequent surgery. A second shot entered the body under the right arm. An operation is required to remove the damaged ribs and associated infection, and to place drainage tubes. This is done under local anesthesia because Winters is too weak to take the chloroform a second time. A third surgery is later performed to remove the bullet lodged in his hip.

Winters develops pneumonia but seems to be recovering

when he dies suddenly, "his whole system thoroughly saturated with poison." It is the last week of February, 1909.

As promised, D.A. Kent changes the charge to first degree murder. Cronin admits the shooting and the crime. He wants to plead guilty and hang as soon as possible. But Judge Thomas Prather won't allow a guilty plea to murder in the first degree and its automatic sentence of death. There has to be a trial.

Waiting for justice is tough. Cronin grows erratic. He shows the jail physician, O.H. Jackson, several small, red marks on his body, one directly beneath his heart, and describes being attacked by a gang of men that held him to the jail floor and "thrusted sewing needles" into his body. He's in cell by himself and so the outrageous story is dismissed as the ravings of a man crazed by guilt. He *is* in poor condition, the doctor allows, but recovery is likely.

The prisoner is placed on suicide watch—denied knives, forks, or anything else he might use to injure himself. Not that it matters. On April 25, after a great deal of suffering and frightful pain, Cronin dies in his cell at 10:10 in the evening, four months and a day after the shooting.

His autopsy finds five large and rusty darning needles inside his body. Two traveled to the lower right and pierced his liver. Three migrated to his lower left, puncturing organs along the way. The spleen is damaged, undersized, and "dried up."

Doctors W.D. Hamaker, O.H. Jackson, and W.B. Skelton decide the needles certainly produced Cronin's suffering but could not have killed him. Opening his skull, they find meningitis. All testify that death was caused by the brain infection and not the large, corroded needles. The doctors decide the murderer died of natural causes, not suicide. But Jack Cronin is dead, all the same.

A clear motive is never established for the crime. Some claim the shooting is the whisky-bolstered result of a ten-year feud that began when the victim's father, a Kerrtown Constable, arrested the perpetrator's brother. Others are sure it is the tragic end to a love quadrangle between the two men, an Erie Railroader, and his wife. People say the woman loved Winters more than the other two. That Cronin shot him out of jealousy.

Whatever caused one man to kill a lifelong friend remains unknown. The papers, noting both men have gone to a Higher Court, say it best: The motive "will probably never be known except to the district attorney's office and to the Almighty."

The Warren State Hospital

The State Hospital for the Insane at Warren, Warren County, Pennsylvania, was the Commonwealth's third such facility. It was authorized in August 1873 and accepted its first patient in December 1880.

During the next century, Warren grew to be the home of more than 3,000 souls: from the depressed to the truly homicidal.

In 1920 the name of the institution was officially changed to the Warren State Hospital. The facility was repurposed in the last part of the 20th century to focus on handling only a few hundred criminal patients.

1908, November 13: Location: Rockdale Township, Thomastown. Victim: James Sheldon. Suspect: Eugene Hall. Act: Stabbed to death with a "jack knife" during attempted kidnapping of victim's adopted daughter (who is the suspect's step-daughter). Notes: The victim's neighbor, George Finney, subdues the drunken Hall by fracturing his skull with a white oak 2x4. It takes several months in jail for Hall to recover and he is, literally, a "changed man," going from belligerent and violent to calm and peaceful. This transformation creates consternation and confusion during the trial. Jury finds murder in the second degree, but that the suspect is now insane. Judge Prather commits Hall to the State Hospital for the Insane at Warren, "there to be kept until he recovers his mental faculties, if the same ever occurs, in such case he then to be returned to the County of Crawford for the sentence in accordance with the verdict rendered in the case." Outcome: Hall never returns to court. He is killed while under treatment in the Warren asylum after being stabbed in the abdomen with a sharpened spoon by Jacob Kosak (Cosach), a "raving maniac" and murderer from Clearfield County.

"A Nice Little Man, When He was Nice"

Many people in the small village of Atlantic, East Fallowfield Township, think there's something wrong with 23-year-old, baby-faced Alton Hover. What it is, nobody can say, but it certainly is *not* a lack of money. His father, Frame Hover, is a former dentist from Kinsman, right across the line in Ohio. He is now the postmaster of Atlantic, owner of the general store, a board member of the Bank of Conneaut Lake, and one of the wealthiest men in southwest Crawford County.

It's true that Alton has always been odd, but then, so is his family. There was his great uncle Abner Frame on his dad's side, who went bonkers after a kick in the head from a horse. After that, he'd run through his orchard, loaded shotgun in hand, looking to kill John McNoll, who had already been dead for at least 20 years. A paternal grandfather twice tried shoot himself in the mouth (good thing he was a lousy shot, people smiled). His own mother had tried to commit suicide. Alton's own attempts to take his life, once with strychnine and once by throwing himself beneath a train, had been thwarted by his family.

Things had grown worse in the two years since he married that pretty, dark-haired girl, Cora Foy, from Hadley in nearby Mercer County. It was absolutely true that his parents disapproved of her and tried to talk their child out of marrying.

As usual, Alton got his way by threatening to kill himself if they withheld consent.

At first, Alton and Cora seemed to make a nice couple, but then they started having trouble.

Plenty of folks had heard Alton verbally threaten his wife. Cora's grandmother, Maria Rhodes, swore that during one visit, Alton leveled a loaded and cocked shotgun at the girl. The old woman once heard Cora crying in her room, pleading with Alton not to throw a lamp at her. That was less than a month before their baby was born last July 13th.

When their little boy, Mason, came along, it should have been reason to celebrate, but it seemed to drive Alton further around the bend. Their neighbor lady said that Alton put Cora out of the house on more than one occasion. Another neighbor told how the girl had come with her newborn to stay at their house on the night of November 19, 1908, in a perfect terror and crying out with fear.

The next night Cora arrives in "the scantiest attire" at Cyrus Unger's across the street. The poor girl is in a state of nervous collapse after Alton tried to strike her with an axe. The next morning she catches the Bessemer train to Hadley to stay with her family awhile, until Alton calms down.

~~~~~

On November 27, while Cora is still in Hadley, her husband is hunting with Charles Minniss. Alton goes on and on, spewing wild nonsense about his wife and baby and how he wants to kill them both. Charlie figures it's all more crazy talk from Alton and doesn't think much of it. What Charlie doesn't know is that his crazy-talking friend has bought a revolver from A.C. Born, over at the hardware store.

That day, Cora returns from Hadley with her sister, Veda, in tow. They find the house locked and decide to visit with the Ungers until Alton returns. He appears a short time later, wearing a long overcoat. Cora steps out onto the porch to speak with him in private. Those in the house can hear only part of what's being said. The conversation seems normal. It's not.

Cora repeatedly asks her husband what he has behind his back.

"Nothing" is his reply.

The young woman suddenly cries out, "Oh, Alton, don't do that!"

There's a gunshot, then two more in rapid succession. Cyrus Unger leaps to his feet and rushes to the front door. Alton is gone from the porch. Cora is slumped against the screen door, bleeding from her head and body. Unger helps her into the house and onto the floor. She's talking, but is incoherent. Atlantic doctor S.L. Lewis is called.

The initial search for Alton turns up nothing. Later that night, Mrs. Jacob Kuhn answers a knock at the home of Alton's parents and is shocked to see the wanted man standing at the door. The young man says he does not know exactly how the shooting happened, that he had hopped a freight and was a distance away when he decided to return and "face the music."

Constable J.B. Laird is telephoned. He arrives to find Alton and his father sitting and talking in the dark of their stable. Once in Laird's house, Alton cooks a meal of oysters but falls asleep while waiting for the water to boil. After supper, as Laird takes Alton to the office of the Justice of the Peace, the prisoner grows afraid of the gathering crowds. Both he and Laird know that a lynching is within the realm of possibility. They cut through several empty lots to reach their destination in safety.

November 29th's early train from Atlantic brings both Alton and his wounded wife to Meadville. He is placed in jail.

She is examined by Doctors Hamaker and Skelton. They find her scalp creased by one bullet, a slug in her shoulder, and another inside her skull. There is dim hope of recovery. She is transported to Lakeside Hospital in Cleveland, Ohio where Dr. Arthur Eisenbrey performs an unsuccessful operation to remove the bullet from her head. Cora Foy Hover languishes in the hospital and dies on December 27, 1908, one month after being shot. She is buried three days later in the Hadley Cemetery. A crowd estimated in excess of seven hundred attends her funeral, more than overflowing that village's modest Methodist Church.

Alton smiles when charged with first degree murder and says the shooting was an accident. The Grand Jury indicts him. The trial is called on February 18, 1909. Alton pleads not guilty. His family's money guarantees the most powerful defense team in Meadville: former D.A.s George F. Davenport and Wesley B. Best, and the newly-ex-Judge Frank J. Thomas.

The commonwealth is represented by District Attorney O. Clare Kent and assisted by Robert Cochran of Mercer County.

More than 100 witnesses are subpoenaed for the trial. The proceedings are expected to be sensational and they do not disappoint. Right off the bat, one of the sequestered jurors talks to his wife through an open window of the courthouse and is told that Alton has killed himself in his cell. The attorneys take the jurors to the jail to see the accused alive and well and, in doing so, take a great risk of invalidating the trial.

The courthouse is jammed with people milling in the halls. Crowds estimated at more than a thousand try to find seats in a courtroom that can't hold half that many. Some bring lunch and dinner so they don't have to leave and lose their seats. During arguments, an alarm clock goes off somewhere in the throng. The owner is unable to turn it off and stuffs it under her winter coat where "its smothered wail could still be heard."

The trial is further disrupted by women spectators who overheat and faint. Judge Prather repeatedly gavels the unruly gallery to silence. He threatens groups and individuals with expulsion when they begin to mutter with disapproval and disbelief at the strategies of the defense team.

The defense wrestles with witnesses for the Commonwealth. The dead woman's somewhat frail and "sweet-faced" grandmother, Maria Rhodes becomes a crowd favorite by proving more than a match for all of Alton's attorneys. She is kept on the stand for extended periods of time as they try to break her testimony. The old lady thwarts them at every turn.

Defense attorney Thomas aggravates elderly Alvin Brockway, by asking again and again how many times he had heard of crazy Uncle Abner's armed romps through his orchard. The old farmer snaps back "How many times have you heard of Abraham Lincoln?" The crowd bursts into laughter. Thomas demands the courtroom be cleared. Prather refuses.

The defense concedes their client shot and killed his fearful wife. Their only goal is saving Alton from the hangman's noose by proving him insane. They work the M'Naughten Rules for all they're worth, trying to establish that the young man was crazy for years before the murder. Alton's parents reveal all the dark secrets they've kept hidden as they set about proving their family is riddled with mental illness.

Two well-known "alienists" (psychologists) are called as defense witnesses, Dr. Morris Gath of the Warren State Hospital for the Insane, and Dr. J.E. McCuade of Erie. They declare Alton is suffering from "'Adolescent Insanity' and utterly unable to make a selection of good or evil." They predict a near future when he will be reduced to a "helpless maniac."

The expert for the Commonwealth, Dr. Theodore Diller of the University of Pittsburgh and head of that city's St. Francis Hospital, states that Alton is not and has never been mentally deranged. He refutes statements given by the defense, maintains that dementia is not hereditary in nature, and testifies that the accused shows no signs of madness. He dismisses Alton's repeated threats of suicide as "silly tricks common to boys."

The strain of the trial shows on both the jury and defendant. One juror suffers for several days with stomach pain. Alton faints at least once and is attended by a physician for more than 30 minutes before he recovers. At first, he shows signs of nervousness and disappointment when his defense team's tactics are countered by testimony or objection. Then he grows unconcerned and begins to sleep in court. As the testimony of more than a hundred and fifty witnesses winds down, the general consensus is that the prosecution's case is strong.

The press begins to comment and complain about the cost of the trial. The amount inflates and deflates with time, but it's obvious this is the most expensive trial in county history. Stenographers have type-written 1,000 sheets, more than 250,000 words.

The last seven and a half hours of the trial are taken up by final arguments. The Commonwealth starts at 9:00 in the morning, and the defense takes over in the afternoon. Alton is apathetic throughout the final proceedings except, as the prosecution describes the murder. Then, "a cynical smile plays about his lips."

Friday, March 5, 1909, the jury is handed the case. Judge Prather reminds them Hover has already confessed to the killing. Only the sentence is in question. Does Alton pay with his life or head to the madhouse?

It takes two votes. Early the next morning, the court is summoned by the jury. Alton Hover has been found guilty of murder in the first degree.

The now-guilty man shows no concern. His father faints.

~~~~~

Alton's father states he'll spend "his last cent to save his boy from the gallows." The defense team petitions Judge Prather for a new trial based on various "light and merry" moments in the courtroom, such as the "Abraham Lincoln" comment by the old farmer. There are also the matters of pre-trial contact between a juror and his wife and the jurors' trip to the prisoner's cell to quash the suicide rumor. Most court-watchers believe a new trial will be granted.

Judge Prather denies a new trial. The defense takes the issue to the Pennsylvania Supreme Court. A hearing date is scheduled in January, 1910.

From his cell, Alton continuously expresses hope that his "wife will recover." His father says his son will grieve, once he comes to his senses.

On October 11, Judge Prather sentences Alton Hover to be hanged by the neck until dead. The condemned is calm but refuses to talk in court or answer Prather's questions.

The one-year anniversary of the shooting comes, and goes. Alton's father is failing under the strain; his once-dark hair begins turning snow white. Alton's mother is also unwell. The little boy, Mason, now 18 months, is "round, rosy and full of baby pranks and smiles to keep his grandparents from too much pain." The Hovers expect to keep him as long as they live.

Valentine's Day, 1910, the State Supreme Court grants a new trial based on the disorderly crowds that filled the courtroom and displayed hostility toward the defendant. In particular, they point out that the audible jeering at his insanity defense might have swayed the jury.

The defense team takes it one step further and makes it clear they will return to the Supreme Court if the young judge refuses to grant a change of venue for the trial.

Prather, who forever after is known for control of his courtroom, allows the trial to be taken up by Erie County's Judge Emery A. Walling. Alton is moved to that county's jail in anticipation of a new trial on the third Monday in May.

~~~~~

The defense wants more time to prepare but Judge Walling makes it clear right from the start that he will not stand for delay, inaction, or nonsense. He refuses to grant a continuance and calls the case to court on May 15. Within two days jurors are selected and testimony begins. Admission is by prior approval. There will be no disorder in the court.

At first it seems the defense is in much greater control of the case, successfully blocking damaging testimony from the first trial. But Grandma Rhodes proves, once again, to be a thorn in the side of defense. She paints Alton as a monster and his lawyers are unable to rattle her or challenge her testimony. "He was a nice little man, when he was nice but he had an ugly disposition," she says. She describes his ugliness growing with time. He was "meaner in September than he was in April," and "when he wasn't drinking he was the best man."

Thomas, for the defense, causes pandemonium in the press by revealing that Alton is being treated for syphilis and is experiencing dementia because of the disease. The lawyers begins to list their client's crazed relatives, but the prosecution rallies to shut them down, convincing the judge that the insanity of the family could not be called into light unless Alton's insanity was first established.

Defense experts counter, saying that, because of his insanity, Alton will not live more than a decade and will likely be dead in half that time. They say he claims his wife is still alive, in Cleveland, or Omaha, that he hears things, like invisible carriages clattering by.

Witnesses continue to testify to the quality of Alton's state of mind. Defense brings doctors. Prosecution brings people who have done business with the man on trial. One expert argues a person can act sane and still be crazy. Another maintains the exact opposite is also true.

Testimony ends on May 26 and is replaced with final arguments presented to an obviously impatient jury.

It takes the twelve men about ninety minutes and one ballot. After two full weeks of testimony by more than 100 witnesses, Alton Hover is, once again, found guilty of first degree murder. An immediate appeal is made for new trial, in part because testimony was not allowed to describe the supposed nuts on the Hover family tree. Judge Walling denies the motion.

Crawford County newspapers begin agitating for an end to both the legal wrangling and Alton's life. Some Erie County papers protest against the execution taking place in their jurisdiction.

Alton threatens to kill himself. Prosecuting attorney Cochran scoffs, "the best evidence of a suicide (threat) is the dead body."

The defense seems poised to take another run at the State Supreme Court. They then decide to skip the courts and go to the Board of Pardons in hopes of commuting the death sentence into life in prison. Failing that, they head to Pennsylvania's Governor Stuart to ask for clemency.

On October 9—almost exactly a year after Prather passed sentence—Judge Walling consigns Alton Hover to death. The twice-condemned man stands silent for half-a-minute after being asked if he has anything to say. The papers deem him the "coolest man in the room." Steps are taken to watch him carefully for suicide. That's a good idea.

The second anniversary of the crime passes. The Erie County jailer allows that Alton's health is failing and that he refuses to eat, but he describes the behavior "as usual in men convicted of murder."

Alton's parents meet with out-going Governor Edwin Stuart and unsuccessfully plead for their son's life. Stuart says he cannot interfere if two juries found Alton guilty. A death sentence will be carried out unless Governor-elect Tener can be prevailed upon to grant a temporary respite.

Alton's lawyers quit. A "prominent attorney for the defense" says no further effort will be made to save the murderer's life. They abandon the fight on the last day of 1910. Their client doesn't care.

Frame Hover travels to Erie to tell his son the bad news. The papers note "instead of an the active business man of 50 years that he was in Atlantic before the murder, he looks like an aged, worn-out man of 80."

Governor Stuart fixes the date of execution as February, 23 1911. It will take place in Erie County under control of their sheriff, W. Moomy. Crawford County will take no part—besides paying the bill.

In late January of 1911, Alton's death warrant is received and read. His mother spends that day with him. His father is failing so rapidly that friends say they'll be surprised if he lives to see the execution.

There are a series of protests in Erie County against the hanging of what might be an insane man. The *Titusville Morning Herald* runs a very short editorial: "Doctor said Hover was in 'no condition to be hanged.' Who is?"

A "skilled executioner" is brought from Allegheny County to prepare the gallows and rope. Alton collapses in his cell when he realizes the reason for the hammering he hears. His parents visit one last time but he doesn't seem to understand it's their final meeting. They hug and depart in silence.

On February 23, 1911, "after recovering from a fainting spell," Alton is bolstered by faith and sleeps from midnight until morning. He eats a hearty breakfast and shows no emotion during his execution. There is a prayer at the foot of the scaffold by Presbyterian Minister Dr. Bailey. Alton fairly runs up the steps to the noose, dragging his jailers behind him.

Erie County Sheriff Moomy trips the death trap at 10:25 in the morning. Alton drops. The noose breaks his neck. His last heartbeat is at 10:35. The attending physician waits four more minutes and pronounces him dead.

Alton Hover is buried in Adamsville's Rocky Glen Cemetery on the late afternoon of February, 25 1911, more than two years after shooting Clara Foy Hover. No motive for the killing, other than insanity, is ever offered.

~~~~~

The next week it's reported that Alton's previously reported pre-execution "fainting spell" was a near-successful attempt at cheating the hangman. Hover had hoarded strychnine pills prescribed to him by the jail's doctor for "extreme nervousness and bad heart action." In the early morning of his final day he took his stash of pills and ate the heads from several dozen sulfur matches he had hidden in his cell. The sheriff and doctor pumped his stomach after finding him in agony. It's something of a miracle that he lived to die. For a while, he was considered beyond human help.

~~~~~,

Six months after his son's execution, Alton's father is dead at fifty-three. Those who know him say he died of a broken heart. He's buried beside Alton. Mrs. Hover decides to send her grandson, orphan Mason, to the home of his maternal grandparents, Mr. and Mrs. James Foy. I found no trace of the boy over the following years.

Dr. Frame Hover's will, dated Dec 8, 1908, less than two weeks after the shooting, leaves all he owns to his wife who, fragile though she may be, survives another 30 years before she's laid to rest with her husband and son. Theirs are the only three graves in the Hover family plot.

1909: William Howard Taft is President of the United States. The National Association for the Advancement of Colored People (NAACP) is founded. Robert Peary gets the credit as the first to reach the North Pole— never mind the four other guys that helped haul all his stuff, and completely ignoring Fred Cook who claimed to have reached it a year earlier. The "Indian head penny" goes bye-bye when Abraham Lincoln begins to adorn the cent's head. In 1959 the back of that coin takes on the Lincoln Memorial. We are blessed with instant coffee. Edison demonstrates the first talking moving pictures.

New York Philanthropist William Ruben George founds George Junior Republic in Grove City, Mercer County, Pennsylvania. One of several such facilities in the northeast U.S., it is a "community" for unwanted, troubled, or disadvantaged children. Initial programs stress extreme discipline to modify behavior. Through the years, it modernizes its approach to rehabilitation but retains its reputation for toughness. I cannot be the only child of northwest Pennsylvania who grew up hearing the parental threat: "Behave, or I'll send you to George Junior!"

The Commonwealth gives the boards of trustees within individual prisons the ability to grant parole after a minimum sentence is served. The classic "not less, nor more than" format of sentencing comes into use. This law removes the court's ability to reach into a jail and parole prisoners once they are incarcerated—something that has been done with increasing frequency. In return, trial judges are authorized to suspend the sentence of a first-time offender "except in cases of murder, burglary of an inhabited dwelling house, and certain other heinous felonies." This helps local courts give a second chance to an individual who commits a single, stupid act and makes sure habitual or serious offenders are placed in jail where they belong. County judges across Pennsylvania begin suspending sentences almost immediately.

1910: Florence Nightingale dies in her sleep. Halley's Comet comes calling. Wright Brother's pilot Philip Parmalee makes the first air-freight delivery flight between the Ohio cities of Dayton and Columbus (about 70 miles). The first *Frankenstein* movie is released, starring (surprise!) Charles Ogle (from Steubenville, eastern Ohio) as the monster. Boris Karloff doesn't show up until 1931. Crawford County's population is down 3% to 61,565.

1910, JANUARY 6: Location: West Fallowfield Township, Hartstown. Victim: Emina Falcet. Suspect: Joe Dandren. Act: Shot in abdomen. Notes: Killed in a boxcar on railroad siding. Alcohol was involved. Outcome: Guilty of manslaughter. Fined the cost of prosecution ($5!).

Sentenced to not less than 3 nor more than 12 years in Western Penitentiary.

1910, FEBRUARY: The Grand Jury inspects the Crawford County Jail. There are rumors they will demand the construction of a new facility. They end up ordering repairs and suggesting the use of moderately-priced toilet tissue instead of newspaper.

THE LAND OF OPPORTUNITY

If you think "the problem with foreigners" in the United States is something new, then you don't know your history. Many established English families of Colonial America viewed German-speaking newcomers as hardly better than animals. At first, only a "free white" immigrant could become a United States citizen. That law changed in 1860 to include blacks, helping to propel the states into civil war. It took *another ninety years* before Asians could become naturalized citizens. A little "Yellow Peril" goes a long way.

Newspapers and politicians of the mid- to late-1800s (mostly English and the previously-hated Germans) stoked fears that the country would be overwhelmed by poor, "Shanty Mick" Irish Catholics. Looking through those years it's easy to find articles and editorials bemoaning how filthy, drunken, ignorant foreigners were destroying the moral fabric of the country, all the while stealing both genteel women and good jobs from "real American men."

The U.S. Immigration Act of 1924 controlled the flow of Slavs, Italians, and Jews. The aim was to assure the total mix of nationalities entering the country matched existing demographics.

Through the first part of the 20th century it was common for younger men to emigrate alone and married men to arrive before their families. More than 60% of immigrants were unattached males. Rootless, they moved to where there was work; canals, railroads, highways, any type of factory job. Huge numbers of men lived, worked, played, fought, and died—together.

Large companies hired certain groups for certain jobs. A sheet steel factory might have Germans rolling, Irish cutting, Swedes tinning, Italians bending, Poles stacking, and blacks hauling. Keeping like people together helped them communicate in dangerous conditions. It also "prevented trouble" and allowed astute managers to play one group against another, breed mistrust, and postpone the organization of their laborers.

It is a popular myth that immigrants swarmed to this country during the Worldwide Depression of the 1930s. Almost as many people left as arrived, aided, in part, by decades of the U.S. Federal Government forcing the repatriation of Mexicans (look up "Operation Wetback" when you have a little extra time).

The idea that the United States took in vast numbers of refugees fleeing the Nazis and Hitler's War is also wrong. We refused nearly all such huddled masses. Especially the poor ones.

For most of the period covered by this book, newspapers commonly mention the ethnicity of the people in their stories. The Germans, Poles, Irish, Jews, Italians, and others all took their turn. Sometimes with left-handed flattery: "the well-known hospitality of their race," but mostly in a lesser light: "the well-known intemperance of their race."

"Foreigner" started out as anybody who didn't speak English, especially if their name was difficult to spell. The word eventually became newspaper code for a person who was not black, but not quite as white as polite society. In Crawford County newspapers of the early 20th century a foreigner is *almost* always Italian.

The practice of noting a person's origin faded with time, at least in part because people grew more skilled at associating names with ethnicity; compare "Angelo Mastrovito" and

"Daniel McGrath." The passing of years also helped. It took, typically, three generations for a new group to be accepted as part of the crowd. It was (and still is) completely possible for the grandchild of yesterday's foreigner to become tomorrow's attorney here in the Land of Opportunity.

The only people who continued to be called out over the years were (and are) those with skin that's a color different than "white." One good reason is that you can't reliably determine the color of skin from a person's name. Honestly, what skin-tone does "George Ewing" have? Well into the 1960s, many mainstream newspapers across the country routinely regarded and described people with dark skin in what most of us would consider to be shockingly racist terms. That practice, no doubt, helped blacks find the considerable courage needed to protest the status quo.

A reporter might always include skin color because it is a physical attribute, like height or weight. But this book is not a newspaper and color is only mentioned when it is germane to the story at hand, as when it's a cause to be treated differently.

Whether it was true, or not, non-white (and not-quite-white) suspects figured the eyes of justice viewed them as horses of different color. One foreigner, accused of a 1914 Crawford County murder, was quoted as saying to his son that his sentence would be "only two years for getting an Italian (instead of) the rope for killing a white man." He received 12 to 17 at hard labor in Western Penitentiary.

Encouragingly, the shade of skin appears disconnected from the acts committed and, mostly, the results of proceedings. Even if you read carefully, it's likely you'll find it difficult to tell the color or ethnicity of a person by most of the treatment provided by the courts of Crawford County—at least in the period covered by these pages.

1910, OCTOBER, 23: Location: Meadville, Atlantic Avenue, "Italian District." Victim: Emmillio (Joe) Tartaglion,

(35). Suspect: Francesco Delcurti (Balcurti, Del Curto) (28). Act: Shot through stomach with a .32 caliber revolver. Outcome: ?

1911: Future President Ronald Reagan is born. Irving Berlin's first hit: *Alexander's Ragtime Band*. The courts declare Standard Oil a monopoly. The first transcontinental airline flight takes 82 hours—even without security checks. Eugene B. Ely is the first to successfully land an airplane on the deck of a ship (the USS Pennsylvania).

1911, JUNE 20: Location: Meadville, French Street. Victim: Lena (May, Alma, Rena) Gulick (Gullick) (14). Suspect: None. Act: Killed while sitting on parent's front porch by stray bullet fired from the West Street vicinity by a "group of drunken foreigners." Outcome: Unsolved. West Street placed under heavy police guard. Police Department censured for not enforcing laws concerning the discharge of firearms within city limits. *See 1932, November 28.*

1911, MAY 30: Location: Meadville. Victim: Alverta Orner (wife). Suspect: Sherman T. Orner (husband). Act: Struck on the back of the head, near the ear, with a glass cream pitcher. Alcohol was involved. Outcome: Murder in second degree. Fined $100 in court costs, sentenced to 20 years in Western Penitentiary unless given a pardon after serving four years and ten months.

1911, SEPTEMBER 17, 9:30pm: Location: Meadville, 1072 West Street, in front of the Thomas Boarding House. Victim: Joseph Rosso (Rosse). Suspect: Pasquall Polliquay (Dollipugnol, Pollifrone). Act: Shooting at a christening after an drunken argument over an accordion. Notes: Papers filled with vitriolic editorials:

"This Italian murder, the third one in three years with no good outcome besides teaching ignorant foreigners that the law must be obeyed." Suggesting laws forbidding selling or furnishing weapons to foreigners along with constant police surveillance. Suspect leaves Meadville, reportedly for Butler, Pennsylvania where he was offered a job. Is afraid of retribution by friends of the victim who hinted at bodily harm. Returned for trial. Outcome: Not guilty.

1911, NOVEMBER: The Grand Jury inspects the Crawford County Jail. They are expected to recommend the construction of a new building.

1912: Oreo Cookies® go on sale. The Titanic sinks. Life Saver® candy is created by Clarence Crane. New Mexico and Arizona gain statehood. More than 30,000 textile workers go on strike in Lawrence Massachusetts. Albert Berry is the first to successfully parachute from an airplane. Or was it Grant Morton in 1911? The republic of China is established. Japan gives the U.S. 3,000 cherry trees for Washington D.C.

1912: Construction begins on Rockview Penitentiary in Centre County, five miles from Bellefonte (pronounced "Bellfont," in PA-speak). It is originally intended to replace both Eastern (Philadelphia) and Western (Pittsburgh) Penitentiaries, but political and budgetary constraints prevent that from happening. Rockview is, at first, a branch prison for West Pen, housing lesser security-risk prisoners, most of whom work in the facility's extensive farm program outside the gates. By the late 1900's Rockview is a medium-security institution for men.

After 64 years, Crawford County decides to build a new

prison on the site of the old one, behind the courthouse. The new jail holds prisoners for another 66 years until it is replaced by one built in Saegertown. Let it never be said Crawford County lacks the ability to squeeze the last use from its prisons. Cells are set up in the basement of the courthouse to hold prisoners during construction.

1912, APRIL 19: Location: Bloomfield Township, Lincolnville. Victim: Sarah (Agnes) Wellmon (65, wife). Suspect: Stephen Wellmon (65, husband). Act: Shotgunned. Alcohol involved. Outcome: Suspect suicides.

1912, MAY 25: Location: Woodcock Township, Saegertown. Victim: Tony Russe (27). Suspect: Dominic Senenlillo (Sememlillo). Act: Shooting during argument over a meal. Notes: "Town has been expecting trouble. About 500 foreigners at work along the Erie Railroad line there. They sleep in bunk cars and live almost like cattle. Hardly a night passes but there is shooting and it is claimed the men spend most of the evenings in the borough saloons." Alcohol is involved. Outcome: Suspect escapes.

1912, AUGUST 7: Location: Titusville. Victim: Unknown viable infant. Suspect: None. Act: Drowned. Notes: Body is found in the mill race between Monroe and Washington Streets. Outcome: No inquest. Unsolved.

1912, MONTH ? DAY ?: Location: Titusville, Queen City Tannery. Victim: Unknown viable infant. Suspect: None. Act: Unknown. Notes: A "Polander" shoveling coal at the tannery comes across a badly decomposed body of a baby. He digs a hole and buries it. When "Americans" at the plant find out, they call police. Officials find the baby's body missing from the grave. Outcome: Unsolved.

1913: It is apparent that all but the worst inmates are being released from prison upon reaching their minimum sentences. Political fallout causes the matter of parole to be revisited. Paradoxically, things become easier for those in jail. Changes in laws allow the release of prisoners who have served just 15 years of a life sentence. To retrofit this to those already in jail, all convicts incarcerated prior to 1911 can apply for parole after they serve one-third of their sentence. The Eastern and Western Penitentiaries release a total of about 150 convicts under these new rules. The one-quarter of the total released from West Pen includes Frederick McDonnel, convicted in the 1894 first-degree murder of Johnnie McAndrew, and Frank Woodard, 1899's second-degree murderer of Titusville Police Chief Daniel McGrath.

Laws pertaining to judgeships change. Judges are now elected without regard to political party. Henry Ford gets credit for inventing the assembly line. It's a dark year for U.S. workers for another reason when the personal income tax is introduced.

Future Presidents Richard M. Nixon and Gerald R. Ford are born. Woodrow Wilson is President of the United States. He issues a 1916 executive order making the *Star Spangled Banner* the country's national anthem. Congress gets around to confirming that order fifteen years later.

Arthur Wynne invents the crossword puzzle. Mary Phelps brings us the bra. Gideon Sundback improves the zipper to the point of modern perfection.

1913, APRIL 4: Location: Woodcock Township, near Saegertown. Victims: Sam Tino and Pietro Terna. Suspect: Raphael Nuncite. Act: Gunshot. Notes: Tino shot four times and Terna twice during an argument over a meal ticket. Suspect only stops shooting when the gun is empty. "The foreigners, following their usual methods, refuse to turn informers." Outcome: Suspect escapes.

1913, MAY: The law now permits those acquitted of a death sentence by a jury, on the grounds of insanity, to be released on parole.

1913, JUNE 2: *Titusville Morning Herald* editorial: "Pennsylvania legislators have passed a law doing away with hangings in PA counties, concentrating all deaths in one location and by electrocution. This is a good thing because of the trouble and demoralization county executions cause. The *Herald* is not in favor of the death penalty, but if it is applied let it be done so humanely. Hanging is barbaric, chloroforming, like we do for dogs and cats is more humane. The law should go one further—clamp down on news to deny papers their stories of descriptions of the death, only say so-and-so was executed on such-and-such a day."

1913, JUNE 19: Governor John K. Tener signs the electrocution bill into law. Local executions are no more. Deaths will take place at the new Western Penitentiary (Rockview). The bill appropriates $50,000 for the immediate construction of the Death House, which will not be ready for use until 1915. It will be several more years after that before a Crawford County murderer sits in the Commonwealth's Electric Chair.

1913, NOVEMBER 9: Location: Cambridge Township, Cambridge Springs. Victim: Joe Wonich. Suspect: Stauko Cooklin (Stanko Cookelich, Cooklich, Cooklish). Act: Shooting. Notes: Suspect taken custody after a raid of a foreign worker's camp at Cambridge

Springs. Was found with a large cache of weapons and ammunition. Outcome: Guilty of murder in the second degree. Fine of $25. Sentenced to not less than 13 nor more than 17 years of solitary confinement and hard labor at Western Penitentiary.

1914: A nineteen year-old Bosnian, Gavrilo Princip, assassinates Archduke Franz Ferdinand of Austria during his visit to Sarajevo. This helps jump-start The Great War. More than 16 million people die. Let it never be said a teenager can't change the world. The Panama Canal opens for business. It only took the U.S. $8.6 billion (modern) and 5,600 lives.

1914, JUNE 28: Location: Meadville, West Street. Victim: Mrs. Mary Fortuna Raucci (mother-in-law). Suspect: Marggio Dimmaggio (son-in-law). Act: Stabbing. Notes: Suspect in screaming match with in-laws. The father-in-law grabs him and the mother-in-law starts beating him. Suspect yells for help. His own father arrives with a weapon fashioned from a sharpened file and hands it to the suspect. Suspect stabs mother-in-law. Knife enters slightly above the ninth rib and penetrates the diaphragm and pleura. Wound grows abscessed, turns gangrenous, victim dies. Outcome: Guilty of murder in the second degree. Prather's sentence is not less than 12 years nor more than 17 years of solitary confinement and hard labor at Western Penitentiary.

1914, SEPTEMBER 26: Location: Meadville, Baldwin Street Extension. Victim: Joe Suraci. Suspect: Joe Constatino. Act: ? Outcome: ?

1915: The Rockview Prison Death House opens for business. On February 23, wife-murderer John Talap, sentenced in Montgomery County, is the first to be electrocuted. On April 2, 1962, rapist/murderer Elmo Smith, also sentenced in Montgomery County, is the last of 350, including two women to die sitting in "Old Smokey." The Chair remains in place at Rockview until December, 1990 when Governor Robert Casey signs legislation making lethal injection the Commonwealth's method of execution. Old Smokey now resides with the Pennsylvania Historical Museum Commission in Harrisburg, the state capital.

1915, SEPTEMBER 13: Location: Meadville. Victims: Sarah A. Smith (mother-in-law, 90) and Isabella (Isabel) Henry (wife 48). Suspect: DeLoss W. Henry (45). Act: Shooting after a quarrel. Alcohol was involved. Outcome: Suspect commits suicide by gunshot.

"WHAT AN ODD PLACE FOR A SCARECROW"

It's mid-November, 1915. Gryn Proper of New Castle, Beaver County, is tromping through the trees with his hunting buddies on the William Woods farm in Troy Township. They're about a mile and a half north of Prather's Corners and traveling towards Clappville, maybe a third of a mile back and away from the road.

The men are moving along within sight of each other, trying to stir some game. It hasn't been a particularly productive morning, as far as hunting goes, but the weather has been fine.

Up ahead, through a break in the forest, there's a large object hanging from a tree. Proper's first thought: "What an odd place for a scarecrow." The air is soon filled with the stench of rotting meat. It's not a scarecrow, but a well-dressed man that's tied by the neck to a tree limb eight feet in the air with twine combined from nearby shocks of corn.

The group alerts nearby resident J.C. Ghering. He contacts

Deputy Coroner Robert A. Kerr who gathers undertaker E.L. Cummings, of Titusville and proceeds to the scene. They determine the man has been dead at least six weeks, basing the decision on both the state of decomposition and the fact that his bedroll has fallen leaves on, but not beneath it. The autumn leaves, they figure, started falling about six weeks back.

Is it a simple suicide by hanging? No, it's not. Examination of the body indicates the man, in addition to being strung to the tree, has been shot once, from the front, through the abdomen, slightly below the floating ribs and into his right lung.

Is it a not-so-simple suicide by gunshot and hanging? No, it's not. As would be expected, there is an entrance hole made by the bullet in the man's shirt. But there is no hole in either his buttoned vest or fastened overcoat. If he did it on his own, he would've shot himself from the front and at an awkward angle. Then, while suffering from the effects of his wound (that included a collapsed lung), put on and buttoned his vest, donned his overcoat, and then hung himself. Or did he hang himself, shoot himself, and then put on the rest of his clothing?

Neither scenario seems likely. Add the fact that there's no firearm to be found at the scene and things look mighty suspicious.

On the other hand, there's no indication the man was robbed, and nobody noticed any strangers in the area. Then again, they didn't notice the hanging man, either. There are no witnesses and no other evidence except the dead man's hat-band being stamped either "Burcher" or "Vircher."

The Coroner's Jury determines suicide by hanging, or suicide by gunshot, or suicide by some combination of hanging and gunshot, or murder by someone unknown to the jury.

The hanged and shot man is never identified. His body is buried in Titusville. The crime, if there ever was one, is never solved.

1916, April: Philadelphian wife-murderer James Reilly

is Pennsylvania's last official hanging. Reilly shot his spouse before the electrocution law was enacted and so gets the noose and not the Chair.

1916, APRIL 11: Location: Spring Township, Conneautville. Victim: Francis M. Covell. Suspect: P.A. McHugh. Act: Shooting over control of a business location. Outcome: Suspect commits suicide.

1916, OCTOBER 6: Location: Meadville, Cottage No. 5 on Erie Railroad's "Company Island." Victim: Clarence Haymer. Suspect: William Burgess. Act: Shooting. Notes: A .45 caliber revolver is used in a robbery after an argument following a game of chance; some say craps, some say cards. Outcome: Judge Prather delivers a "fatherly lecture" on the sins of gambling and the consequences of same. Sentence is costs, including $10 to cover the prosecution along with not less than 11 nor more than 16 years at Western Penitentiary. *This is the first killing I found where the race of either the victim or suspect (in this case, both) was noted as "colored," "black," or "Negro."*

1917: Future President John F. Kennedy is born.

AT THE OPERA HOUSE

From the *Titusville Herald*, September 1, 1913:

It is more than likely that "The Common Law," to be offered at the opera house on Wednesday of this week, will prove a sort of dramatic revelation as a broadside against the logic which has made so many people blindly confident in love that, they are eager enough to break all conventions. Robert W. Chambers' book from which this play was adapted, tells the story of a misguided girl thrown upon her own resources, in a skillful manner and with flawless delicacy....

"The Common Law" is a tale of amazing frankness and one of unflagging interest. It is the story of love and passions told with terseness and accumulative vigor while dealing with the vital subject of marriage.

"Respect and Honor in the Community"

Harry E. Gerson, manager of the Titusville Opera House, is a man on the move. Schooled as a stenographer, possessing a head for business, and able to keep secrets, the 35-year-old traveled widely, spending time working with Colorado's Barstow Mining Company and running restaurants and hotels. He was secretary to the Titusville Iron Company, the Olmsted Art and Decorative Company, and now, besides managing the Opera House and working as a notary, he's secretary to J.C. McKinney, former oil man, present banker, and one of the richest and most powerful men in the region.

Gerson is a popular man. He is a member of many fraternal organizations and founder of the one of the best, city-wide baseball teams in the country. He is, also, a Jew.

Not that it matters much in 1917 Titusville. The city has two synagogues with one right across the street from the Gerson home. Jews counted among the early settlers of the city and are respected members of the social and business communities. Harry's father, Abraham, was a pioneering resident who for years operated a thriving cigar business at 31 South Franklin, despite near blindness and an invalid wife.

Harry Gerson's sweetheart is the 25-year-old Miss Laura Wood. Her considerable physical beauty and obvious charm hide a somewhat tragic past. Her father, Charles Wood, committed suicide several years ago. Her mother remarried John Daugherty and moved to Buffalo, New York.

Laura has lived in Titusville since 1912 when she came to stay with her aunt, Mrs. E.E. Ricketts, after attending Villa

Maria School in Erie, Pennsylvania. As the name may suggest, it is a Catholic, faith-based institution.

A Jew and a Catholic make a somewhat unusual couple. Still, the handsome, young, and lively pair has been seen together often of late and give the strong impression of being betrothed.

But something is going haywire in their relationship. Wednesday, June 13, 1917, in the mid-evening, after a visit with her mother in Buffalo, Laura returns to Titusville. She goes to the Gerson family home in the 100-block of West Spruce Street, where she has been staying. The door is locked against her. Harry tells her she's no longer welcome.

Laura walks around the corner to the home of her cousins and stays there "quite into the night." She then returns to the Gerson's and angrily demands admittance. Again denied and now furious, Laura breaks the glass in the door. Police are summoned. She agrees to stay away from the house to avoid arrest. But Laura also makes her own charges against Harry. She threatens proceedings for a breach of a promise to marry.

The matter is taken up by lawyers C.W. Benedict (for Laura) and James R. Gahan (for Harry) and all is settled by Saturday, June 16. Or so it seems. Later that same day, Miss Wood arrives at the Bue Brothers Store on Diamond Street to buy a .32 caliber bulldog revolver.

~~~~~

Two days later she stands before District Justice Kerr and the Crawford County Grand Jury on charges of the murder of her sweetheart, Harry Gerson. District Attorney Albert Thomas is present. C.W. Benedict is counsel for the defense. The beautiful Laura Wood, dressed in a dark blue suit, is extremely nervous and trembling in the witness chair.

Her testimony:

On June 16, three days after the incident outside the Gerson family home, Harry convinced her to travel to Oil City, Venango County, for dinner. After some initial car trouble, the two enjoyed a meal at the Arlington Hotel. Harry wanted to stay for the movie. But Laura wore only a light coat against the cool night. She wanted to return home to "spend the evening with him."

During the return trip, Harry promised all would be fine, that they'd take the "moonlight train to Buffalo," and spend a few days. "Everything would be the same as before."

Upon retuning to Titusville, he told her he would visit where she was staying, with the William Morans (the dead Chief of Police Michael Moran had a son, William) in the 300-block of North Drake. A few minutes before 10:00, Harry called to confirm that Laura was alone and said he'd be over.

Harry appeared. The two sat in the dining room. Laura asked if he was going to keep his promises. He said he was. Harry asked Laura to come sit in his lap. She did. They talked for a few minutes.

The Grand Jury hears how she had bought the .32 to commit suicide after being rejected by Harry, but now "he seemed so kind that I decided to tell him what I had contemplated doing and show him the trouble he had saved."

She went to the coat she was wearing earlier in the evening, now hanging on the back of a chair. She pulled her revolver from the pocket. Harry leapt from his chair and grabbed her. The two struggled. The weapon fired. Harry staggered and fell. Laura ran from the house, screaming for help.

Miss Wood breaks down. Sobbing, she is unable to continue.

Witness and neighbor William F. Cron tells how he was returning home from a fishing trip when he heard a woman screaming outside. It was Laura, running about the lawn and shouting, "My God, I did not mean to do it! I did not mean to do it!"

Cron ran into the house and found Harry, in the corner of the dining room, on his side, partly doubled up but not yet dead. Cron could feel a pulse and see breathing. He telephoned for a doctor, couldn't get the one he wanted, and so told the operator to send anybody. Cron said the condition of the room indicated a struggle.

C.B. Eller, the first doctor on the scene, corroborates Cron's testimony about the condition of the room and placement of the body. Harry was on his right side. He still had a pulse and was almost rolling forward, his face in a pool of his own blood. Eller was about to begin treatment when Dr. W.G. Johnston arrived and told him it was pointless since the victim was practically dead.

Dr. Johnston testifies that he was called to the Moran home a little past 10:00 in the evening. He heard a woman shouting "For God's sake, doctor, save him! Don't let him die!" Johnston later found out it was Laura Wood. The doctor says Harry would've remained conscious for no more than thirty seconds after such a wound.

Deputy Coroner Robert A. Kerr says he found powder burns on the victim's clothes, indicating the extreme closeness of the weapon on discharge.

Dr. H.H. Hildred testifies that the bullet entered Gerson's left chest about two inches from the breast bone and between the second and third ribs. The slug took a path down and into the body, cut the superior vena cava, pierced the right lung and lodged in the thoracic cavity. The victim might've lived for, maybe, ten minutes but would've lost consciousness in a short time.

A decision from the Grand Jury is not forthcoming, and Laura Wood is received as a guest in the county jail at Meadville.

Harry Gerson's Orthodox ceremony and burial takes place on June 19. He's interred in the Jewish Cemetery on the south side of town. Titusville Iron, where he had worked as a secretary, shuts down during the funeral out of respect for the dead.

Gerson had registered a will a month before his death. The estate is estimated to be worth between $50,000 and $100,000

($850,000 and $1.7 million modern). Minor sums go to his synagogue, its cemetery, and to various societies. The remainder, Harry stipulates, is for his parents to "share and share alike." The will also includes a last clause: "In the event of my marriage the provisions heretofore mentioned will stand and the residue of my estate shall be divided according to law." The Oil City Trust Company is the executor.

Meanwhile, Laura Wood is doing poorly in jail. She is the only female prisoner and is uneasy and nervous. She spends most of her time crying. Father Thomas W. Cavanaugh of Titusville visits, but she continues her hysterical weeping. The jailer invites nuns from Meadville Spencer Hospital to visit and provide comfort.

Judge Thomas Prather holds a bail hearing on June 26. Laura's testimony matches that of her Grand Jury appearance. Dr. Johnston states the shot that killed Harry was made at such a peculiar angle and location that it could not have been fired deliberately. A petition is presented, urging for Laura's bail. It's signed by many citizens of Titusville.

Prather sets the amount at $5,000, and she is out of jail. Better news comes on September 11 when the Grand Jury fails to return a true bill and all charges against her are dropped.

The next day an advertisement by Maxwell Chick's Real Estate in Titusville features the Gerson family home. Harry's parents announce plans to move to Canton, Ohio, to be with the family of Mrs. Gerson's sister. Their West Spruce home is eventually purchased by Mrs. Sidney Curry.

~~~~~

In late November, the Benevolent and Protective Order of Elks holds a ceremony to honor members lost in the previous year. Jacob Goldstein says of Harry Gerson:

This lodge has lost an ideal brother; a self-made man, burdened from childhood with the responsibility of creating a place for himself, as well as caring for a blind father and an invalid mother. He brought himself in early manhood to a position of respect and honor in the community. In the death of Brother Gerson we lost a member who was ready to identify himself with any project for the good of the order, one who, had he lived, would have done much for the principles for which our order stands.

~~~~~

Two weeks later, Laura sues the estate of the principled Harry Gerson for $5,300. The young woman claims that she and her now-dead sweetheart were, in fact, husband and wife—and had been so for the last several years. She files the action using the name "Laura Gerson."

The estate immediately experiences trouble collecting thousands of dollars of insurance because Harry never claimed to be married. The insurers deem all contracts invalid due to "misrepresentations at the time he (Gerson) took out the policies."

Laura is, once again, in front of Judge Prather at the end of April 1918. This time she's asking for a Widow's Appraisement of Gerson's estate. She repeats her claim of legal marriage to Harry and that she lived with him as his wife until his accidental death. She seeks $5,300 of the $137,200 estate Gerson left behind.

Laura has R.P. Marshall and Albert Thomas representing her. Harry's old lawyer, James R. Gahan of Titusville, along with William Parker of Oil City defend the estate.

Laura's star witness is her cousin, Anna R. Edwards of Cleveland, Ohio. She testifies that, in her presence on August 15, 1912, Laura Wood and Harry Gerson clasped hands and declared they were married and, what's more, had spent several days on a "honeymoon" at Bemus Point on Chautauqua Lake in western New York.

Laura relates how she always feared their "contract marriage" was not legal and repeatedly appealed to Harry to wed her before a minister or court official, which he steadfastly refused to do. She came to believe they were legally married, even though Harry would not allow her to declare herself his wife because he was a Jew and she a Gentile.

Prather defers judgment, saying the matter should be decided by jury. That trial begins in December of 1918.

The testimony remains the same. Laura's cousin and friends corroborate the young woman's story of her contract marriage. C.W. Benedict, Laura's attorney at the time of the shooting, claims he and his client called on attorney Gahan to institute a $10,000 action against Harry for breach of promise. Benedict tells how Laura had appealed to Harry to save her honor and marry her in a formal ceremony and how the man had refused.

To prove Gerson's intent, attorney Marshall produces several hotel registries, including the Virginia at Conneaut Lake, Pennsylvania and the Pickard at Bemus Point, Lake Chautauqua, New York. In them, and in his own hand, Harry had registered himself and Laura as "Mr. Gerson and wife."

On December 5, and by a vote of 11 to 1, the all-male jury finds Laura to be the wife of the late Harry Gerson. She is due not only her $5,300, but a full half of anything that remains after the estate is settled. There is an appeal to Judge Prather for a new trial. He refuses. The verdict stands.

After the trial, Laura Wood Gerson picks up and moves to the city of Franklin, in Venango County.

~~~~~

Let's close this story with a line from *The Common Law,* a play that Laura and Harry no doubt attended together at the Titusville Opera House: "The girl who gives herself without benefit of clergy walks the earth with her lover in heavier chains than were ever forged at any earthly altar."

By the way, the book, which you should read, has a happier ending.

A Woman in Need

A crippling social stigma used to go hand-in-hand with "bearing a child without benefit of marriage." The single mother and fatherless offspring were ostracized. Such a birth stained the entire immediate family and could count against several subsequent generations. There was an overwhelming drive to avoid illegitimacy. Many unwed mothers took extreme measures to bring their pregnancies to premature ends: drinking near-fatal potions, subjecting themselves to physical violence, seeking the assistance of someone who might attempt an abortion.

In the period covered by this book, the legal standing of abortion was very much decided by individual states. As early as 1812, lawsuits were brought against both the women who sought to end pregnancies *and* the people providing such services. Connecticut outlawed abortion in 1821. New York followed in 1828, still allowing the procedure when necessary to preserve the life of the mother. Such laws were rarely applied. There was always someone willing to help a woman in need.

During the 1850s and 1860s, it's estimated that 20% of all U.S. pregnancies ended in abortion—a number amazingly close to modern statistics. Pennsylvania responded in 1870 by making it a felony to seek *or* provide an unnatural end to a pregnancy.

All this ignored the most severe penalty that could be paid. Terminations performed before modern medicine were notoriously unsafe. Up through the 1930s, it's estimated that abortions killed one in four of the desperate women who took the chance. Russian Roulette kills only one in six.

"The Diseases of Women"

As a teenager, Miss Nellie Denison moves from Georgetown, north-central West Virginia, to East Titusville and grows to be a well-liked and respected member of the community. A few years later, she opens a small grocery on the Pleasantville Road, across from the Mack Brothers Mill.

She dies at her home the morning of August 23, 1917 a few weeks after celebrating her 25th birthday, leaving behind three sisters. One of them, Mrs. James McDonald, lives a few miles away in nearby Titusville.

Miss Denison was taken ill with intestinal troubles just one day before her death. Dr. M.J. Haley, a specialist in "women's diseases" was called. Her good friend Herbert Clark, also from East Titusville, was visiting when she was, again, taken with extreme pain. Clark summoned the doctor once more, but the young lady passed before Haley arrived.

Everyone is shocked by her rapid demise from "acute indigestion." Her death is so sudden that Deputy Coroner R.A. Kelly orders an investigation with the autopsy performed by Doctors H.H. Hilderd and J.C. Wilson. The results are in and the inquest organized as Nellie Denison's funeral is held at the small Enterprise M.E. Church. Her body is buried in the windswept Cheney Cemetery at the crest of Goodwill Hill, off Route 27, a few miles into Warren County. The grave is marked with a severely elegant stone.

Much to everyone's surprise, the coroner's jury finds death was caused by peritonitis as the result of a perforated uterus. In other words, Nellie Denison died from an improperly performed abortion.

Herbert Clark, who was with her at the time of her death, is arrested and charged with having knowledge of the facts leading up to the abortion. Dr. Haley, who was out of town for a few days, is arrested upon his return to his home at the corner of East Walnut and Martin Streets. He is charged with having knowledge of the causes that led to Nellie's death.

Lawyer C.W. Benedict arranges a $1,000 bond for the release of Clark. Attorney J.R. Gahan manages bail for Haley at twice that amount.

Both Clark and Haley stand before the September 1917

Grand Jury on charges of complicity in the death of Denison. Clark is not held. Dr. Haley is indicted.

Haley's subsequent criminal trial is a fiasco. A key witness fails to testify as expected, and Judge Thomas J. Prather instructs the jury to find the doctor "not guilty." No other charges are pressed. No other trial takes place. The papers hold no details.

By November 1917, Nellie Denison's estate is closed. Her small grocery and its contents are sold at public auction.

Nellie's friend, Herbert Clark, fades into the past.

Nellie's doctor, M.J. Haley does not.

~~~~~

Haley is a native of Wilkes-Barre in east-central Pennsylvania. A bright young man who studies medicine in Philadelphia, he brings his wife Anna to Titusville in January of 1916 and opens an office on the corner of Main and Martin Streets. He also purchases a twenty-acre "farm" and house on the outskirts of town. His first advertisement in the local papers: "M.J. HALEY, Physician and Surgeon, special attention to diseases of women."

He seems off to a good start—until Miss Denison's death and the subsequent trial.

1918 — MAY: Haley is arrested on complaint of his wife Anna for drunk and disorderly and threatening to kill her. Anna takes off "for the east" to avoid appearing in court against her husband.

September: He is arrested and fined $25 for driving his automobile in a reckless manner. Found guilty of intoxication for another $5. Also arrested and charged with driving while intoxicated. Pleads not guilty. Held for the January 1919 Grand Jury on the same charge but is released on $200 bail.

October: He is fined $5 for public drunkenness. House on West Main goes up for sale and is bought four months later by John J. Harvey.

1919 — JANUARY: Haley skips bail and is a no-show at his Grand Jury trial for drunk driving.

February: He surrenders to police. Changes his plea to guilty. Receives a $100 fine and 60 days.

April: Haley opens a new office for the general practice of medicine in the 200-block of West Central.

October: He's arrested and fined $10 for intoxication and creating a disturbance in his home. Neighbors note he's awake until all hours of the night playing the same phonograph record over and over again. They can hear him through his home's open windows. There is, unfortunately, no mention of the song's title.

October: Haley's arrested for drunk and disorderly and threatening the lives of wife and others: Tries to choke his wife who is visiting a neighbor's house. Threatens the 84-year-old lady of the house with bodily harm when she interferes. Leaves when another elderly neighbor lady appears with a stove poker and threatens to strike him over the head. Fined only $25 because witnesses will not testify against him.

October: Say the papers: "It is a matter of much comment on the street that in the past months Dr. M.J. Haley was almost continually in a state of intoxication."

December: Haley purchases a home and office in the 100-block of East Main.

1920 — **FEBRUARY:** The doctor leaves for Philadelphia to attend three months of medical classes on "stomach diseases."

1921 — **JULY:** Haley and Anna leave on a motor trip to points east. His patients are told he will be absent from his office until further notice.

1924 — **MAY:** The Haley residence on East Main goes up for sale and is purchased by Mrs. Mary E. Fleury. The doctor and wife leave for their new home and practice in Jermyn, Pennsylvania, a few dozen miles away from his hometown of Wilkes-Barre.

October: The "M.J. Haley Farm," twenty acres of land and six-room bungalow near Titusville, goes up for sale for $1,400. That's the last we hear of the good doctor.

1918: Judge Prather's back on the bench, becoming the county's first President Judge to be re-elected. Gavrilo Princip, assassin of Archduke Franz Ferdinand, dies in prison. The War to End All Wars officially ends for the U.S. in 1921, but the world-wide pandemic of the "Spanish Influenza," helped to spread by the war Princip started, begins killing 50- to 100-million more people. Czar Nicholas and his family are killed by other means. Charles Jung peeks into our future with his fortune cookies. Past President Theodore Roosevelt dies of a coronary embolism and infection.

1918, MAY 6: Location: East Fairfield Township, Shaw's Landing. Victim: J.M. Schnepp (an old man). Suspect: Raymond Waters (21). Act: Blow to the head with some sort of blunt instrument. Outcome: One of the witnesses changes his testimony. Acquitted of murder.

1918, MAY 26, EARLY MORNING: Location: Meadville, Athletic Park, "just off of Water Street." Victims: Ray Oxley (22) and George Mickle. Suspect: William G. Smith. Act: Shooting. Outcome: Arrested, charged, acquitted by Grand Jury and released.

1919, JANUARY 8: Location: Vernon Township. Victim: Mrs. Peter Dernfanger (wife). Suspect: Peter Dernfanger (husband). Act: Hacked and slashed to death with hatchet and razor. Outcome: Suspect commits suicide with razor.

1919, APRIL 28: Location: Meadville, 200-block of Linden Street (victim's home). Victim: Pasquale Munno. Suspects: Angelo Mastrovito (using a shotgun) and Thomas Vardarno (using a revolver). Act: Shooting. Outcome: ?

1919, OCTOBER 28: President Woodrow Wilson vetoes the National Prohibition Act. Within two days his objections are overridden by both houses of Congress, paving the way for the Volstead Act.

1920: Crawford County's population is down 2% to 60,667. The Band-Aid® begins covering wounds. League of Women Voters is formed in Chicago, Illinois. Detroit Michigan is home to the first commercial radio station in the U.S., 8MK (now WWJ). Or was that 8YK (now KDKA) in Pittsburgh? At any rate, Westinghouse starts selling household radio sets for ten bucks ($100 modern). The U.S. Census adopts the "one-drop rule." People with *any* "black blood" in them are now considered "colored," no matter their appearance. This definition was or became legal in many southern U.S. states until 1967, when the

U.S. Supreme Court ruled it unconstitutional. That doesn't mean that folks still don't try to apply it.

1920, JANUARY 17: The 18th Amendment to the United States Constitution, ratified by the states and approved by Congress, takes hold, criminalizing the manufacture, sale, transport, import, or export of intoxicating liquors. The duty to sponsor the bill before Congress falls to the chair of the Judiciary Committee, Republican Andrew J. Volstead of Minnesota's 7th Congressional District. Despite serving in congress for several previous terms, he is not re-elected to his seat after the passage of what is known as "the Volstead Act." Many backers of Prohibition expect alcohol-related crimes to vanish. That does not happen. With simple intoxication now a crime, drinkers inform on sellers who inform on suppliers who inform on distillers. The air is filled with revenge. Liquor-related crimes take a serious turn for the worse as organized gangs begin establishing control over the supply, distribution, and sale of booze.

1920, APRIL 6, ABOUT 10:00pm: Location: Meadville near the Page Boiler Plant, 1127 Main Street. Victim: John E. Morneweck (35). Suspects: None. Act: Attacked, robbed and shot by two assailants. Outcome: Unsolved.

1920, APRIL 24, ABOUT 5PM: Location: Meadville, Gable House Livery Barn, 900 block of Water Street. Victim: Oswald Schultz. Suspect: Clyde Smock. Act: Shultz is dating Smock's ex-wife. The violently jealous ex-husband shoots Schultz in the head. Outcome: Smock suicides.

1920, JUNE DAY ?: Location: Meadville railroad yards. Victim: John Kulich (Kulick, Gulick). Suspect: Charles M. Cullen (Erie Railroad Detective). Act: Shot during theft. Notes: Suspect claims self-defense. Coroner's Jury decides the victim was resisting arrest. Outcome: ?

1920, AUGUST 18: The 19th amendment to the Constitution of the United States is ratified by the states and approved by Congress. Woman now have the right to vote. Lists of prospective jurors are created from the voting roles and so women are now also eligible for jury duty. Many states accept this change, but not all Pennsylvania men are convinced their delicate females can withstand the rigors of politics or crime. The battle to keep women's votes out of the ballot boxes and butts off juries is fought all the way to the Commonwealth's Supreme Court.

1921: Warren G. Harding is President of the United States. It's a landslide in both popular and electoral votes. The first birth-control clinic is opened in London, England by Marie Stopes. The province of Northern Ireland is created. The U.S. formally ends World War One. Adolf Hitler becomes leader of the Nazi Party. Sweetest Day starts in Cleveland, Ohio. More Jews begin immigrating to Palestine when the U.S. drastically limits immigration from Eastern Europe. Non-partisan judicial elections prove unpopular. Judges for Pennsylvania courts of record are again aligned with specific political parties.

1921, JUNE 9: Location: Titusville, private drive leading from South Monroe Street to the east at the rear of the Howard & Beaver Wholesale Grocery Store. Victim: John Sieczka. Suspect: Charles Pendolino (Cologero Lauricello). Act: Blunt force about head and neck during a robbery. Notes: Victim had been flashing large rolls of bills earlier in the week. Arguing with wife over the same. Alcohol is involved. Outcome: Suspect arrested, produces an alibi, is set free. Case is unsolved.

A Good Place To Stop

Hartstown, the scene of our next story, was incorporated in 1850. The tiny village is located in the northern part of West Fallowfield Township, toward the southwest corner of the county. It's named after James and William Hart, early settlers and land owners, and came into existence with the digging of the Erie-Beaver canal just to the east. A huge basin for canal-boats guaranteed customers for local businesses.

Heading north, Hartstown was the last village on the canal before the Pymatuning Swamp and several miles of marshy and lonely desolation. It was, literally, a good place to stop.

Hartstown never grew much bigger than it was back in its heyday. By the time of our story, a railroad had replaced the canal.

It's a good bet that the route taken by our main characters was the western Pennsylvania portion of present-day U.S. RT 322. An early Federal Highway, it was one of the first in the county "improved" from rutted dirt, choking dust, and sucking mire to a hard surface.

The "Mud Lake" mentioned below, just across the border in East Fallowfield, is the largest of three closely-spaced kettle ponds formed in northwest Pennsylvania's last encounter with continental glaciation. Locals have named the body of water a more picturesque "Crystal Lake."

"Three of The Hardest Boiled Safe-Crackers"

June 27, 1921. Pretty and young, Miss Lillian Bogart, of Poland, Ohio, is out for an automobile party. She and a few friends take advantage of a splendid day to drive a few hours to picnic in Hartstown, Pennsylvania.

They stop to eat lunch at "Mud Lake," a large, almost circular pond a half-mile east of the village. Miss Bogart, first to finish her meal, strolls along the shore. She comes to a fork in the path and wanders to the left. Had she gone the other way, she never would've found the dead body, half-covered by bushes, a few feet from the water's edge.

The unfortunate young man, about 25 years of age, is just over five feet tall and "darkly foreign." He is nattily dressed in dark trousers, a white and blue striped shirt, and tan oxfords. Cause of Death? Being shot three times; in the top of the head, at the base of the brain, and the left side of the neck. What remains of his head has a cut and severe bruise over the left eye. A club matching the last two wounds is found a short distance away. The index finger of the left hand is nearly severed.

County Detective John Laley and Coroner Byham figure the murder took place elsewhere and the body was dumped in Hartstown. This is based on the fact that, despite the great violence, there is little to no gore where the man is found.

The victim carries no identification. His pockets hold 40 cents, a ring with several numbered keys, and some cartridges for a .32 revolver.

The story hits the papers. Detectives are contacted by the proprietor of the Iroquois Hotel in nearby Conneaut Lake. It seems the midnight before the body was discovered, foreigners, "three of the hardest boiled safe-crackers" the man had ever seen, had stopped for directions to Youngstown, Ohio. They had specifically asked for a route that would take them on the road past Mud Lake.

Crawford County lawmen contact police in Youngstown. Officials share phone calls and follow leads. Within days it's apparent the cause is hopeless. The case is never solved.

The well-dressed body of the small man with the ruined head is held for a few days before burial in the potter's field of Rocky Glen Cemetery near Adamsville. His gravesite overlooks the valley that holds the little lake along the shores of which he was found.

THE COUNTY DETECTIVE

Crawford County created the job of County Detective in 1903. A civil position, the detective was appointed by the President Judge upon recommendation of the District Attorney. The job was one of liaison between the courts, the general public, regular law enforcement, and other county offices. Typical duties included serving warrants and subpoenas, along with the investigation of matters brought before the grand jury. "Real police work" was added as years passed, but at first, the job was more of organizing after the fact than actively fighting crime.

Frank J. Lowe was Crawford's first County Detective. An extremely well-educated man, Lowe was raised on his family's Richmond Township farm, attended public schools, and graduated from Yale University. He was admitted to the bar to practice law in 1884 and worked as a lawyer as well as a teacher and principal in a number of the county's borough schools. Lowe was serving as the warden of the Meadville Jail immediately before his appointment to detective.

Lowe had the job for three years before resigning because of problems with his health. He suffered from tuberculosis which, despite the best available treatment, killed him at the age of 52 in November of 1907.

All total, about a dozen men served as County Detective throughout the time covered by this book. The man in the job longest was recommended by then District Attorney O. Clare Kent to replace Frank Lowe.

John L. Laley, a Titusville native, was born in 1868. He was in his early teens when his mother died. Abandoned by his alcoholic father, young John was raised, almost as an indentured servant, in the less desirable part of Titusville: his home was the daughter-filled house of South Washington Street blacksmith John Haehn.

Laley's childhood built the person he became; he spent his life in temperance—the result of a promise to his mother never to touch alcohol. He did not use tobacco, rarely lost his temper, and hardly ever cursed. Haehn pulled the youngster from school to gain more help at the smithy, so Laley lacked formal education. He compensated with a life of voracious reading.

Laley grew to be well-liked in his community. Pictures show him as a blonde, curly-headed, obviously strong and handsome man with broad, open features. He had a reputation as a good cook and excellent baker and was known as an organizer. Almost 6 feet tall and weighing in at 200 pounds, blacksmith Laley was a competitive man with a real knack for getting along and getting things done. Quietly supporting the County's Republicans, Laley was a fixture at meetings, serving coffee to the party faithful throughout much of his life.

It was with these skills and connections that he was appointed Titusville's Fire Chief, a job at which he excelled. Said the *Titusville Herald* of his actions during the city's 1892 flood and fire: "Chief Laley was everywhere present directing the [fire fighting] force with his accustomed skill and energy." Laley and his crew helped save many lives in that catastrophe. Unfortunately, the mother and several daughters of the family that raised him were lost.

In 1904, though he had little in the way of relevant training, Laley was named Titusville's Chief of Police to replace the departing William Sheehy. It was from that position that Laley was brought on as County Detective. He served for more than six years, then was off for about a decade.

He made an unsuccessful 1915 run at County Sheriff (no shame there, it was an office many detectives failed to win). Laley was reappointed as County Detective in 1917, after O. Clare Kent, his old crime-fighting partner, was elected President Judge.

That same year, Laley (a "confirmed bachelor" of 49) married the 25-year-old Gertrude Mosbacher, a distant cousin of the Meadville jewelers. The couple raised their eventual family of three boys and a girl on the uphill end of Meadville's Randolph Street.

A dozen years later, and after working together for several months, District Attorney Stuart Culbertson suddenly replaced the 61-year-old Laley with Raymond McIntosh, a man who was not from Crawford County.

Laley's dismissal remains something of a mystery. A likely cause was the clashing of methods or personalities; Culbertson was aggressive in his work of trying (and failing) to clear booze out the county. He didn't care whose toes he stepped on. Using State Police and Laley, Culbertson staged a successful 1929 New Year's liquor raid on three of Meadville's biggest lodges: the Eagles, the Elks, and the Moose. The D.A. was happy to claim all the credit—well past the point of grandstanding. These traits may have rubbed the amiable and consensus-building Laley the wrong way. The detective was replaced a few months later.

Whatever the cause, Laley was not out of a job for long. Judge Kent appointed his long-time friend to the position of Health Officer and later to Probation Officer, work that Laley, and his wife, performed for years.

A silver-haired John Laley died of prostate cancer in 1943. He was 75. His wife went on to live for more than another half-century, passing on in 1996, at 104 years from, one supposes, old age. Both are buried in St. Agatha Cemetery, not far from their Meadville home.

1921, JULY: The Pennsylvania Supreme Court upholds the law that makes women eligible for both voting and jury duty.

1921, DECEMBER 8: Location: Vernon Township, Kerrtown on Lake Road. Victim: Philip Tropksi. Suspect: Albert Toms (20). Act: Blunt-force trauma to the skull. Notes: Both men work in a road construction gang. Toms confesses to beating Tropksi during a robbery for $6.00. Outcome: Pleads guilty to murder. Found guilty of murder in the first and is sentenced to death. Papers surmise he'll be the first from Crawford County to be electrocuted at Rockview Prison in Bellfonte, Pennsylvania. Sentence is appealed to the State Parole Board and is commuted to life in prison.

1922: Washington D.C.'s Lincoln Memorial is dedicated. Insulin begins treating diabetes. James Joyce's *Ulysses* begins confusing readers. The movie *Nosferatu* is released. He's a blood-sucking vampire. She's a gorgeous victim. The plot hasn't changed much, has it? This is not the first movie about such a fiend, but it's the earliest one still around. In case you're wondering, Béla Lugosi doesn't show up for another decade. The Union of Soviet Socialist Republics (USSR) is created after much trampling of various neighboring sovereignties. It's a passing thing.

1922, FEBRUARY 5, SHORTLY AFTER NOON: Location: Meadville, 1000-block of West Street. Victim: Harry Breed (25). Suspect: Frank Larosa. Act: Shot during drunken argument. Outcome: Larosa is found guilty of murder in the first degree. Judge Prather sentences Larosa to die in the electric chair. Papers surmise he'll be the first from Crawford County to be electrocuted at Rockview Prison in Bellfonte, Pennsylvania. Defense attorney O. Clare Kent thinks Larosa may be "mentally deficient" and takes the case to the State Pardon Board. Before the pardon board acts, Prather recommends clemency on the basis of Kent's opinion. Death sentence commuted to life in prison.

Figure It an Open and Shut Case

It's hot and muggy in the late night hours of August 22, 1922. Meadville Police are called to West Street. The surrounding neighborhood is home to many of the city's prostitutes and bootleggers and they draw a mean crowd.

There's an Armenian boarding house in the 1000-block. Inside the door is an appalling scene: Thirty-five-year-old William Roberts is dead on the floor, nearly decapitated, his throat cut ear to ear. An occupant of the place, middle-aged Dokoran Kudrian, is sprawled in a nearby chair bleeding from a bad gash on his right forearm. Kudrian, along with the dead man and the walls and carpet are spattered and soaked in blood. It's not pretty, even by West Street standards.

The straight razor used to slice Roberts is on the ground next to the outside stoop. Kudrian readily confesses to the killing. To prevent their flight, police hold as witnesses Sresansh Papazian, proprietor of the house, along with his wife and a few of the boarders.

The victim, a married man from Bellvue, New York, was living in the city and working as a guard at the Meadville Machinery Company. According to his drinking buddy, a man known as "Turzay," the two spent most of that day's afternoon enjoying the questionable wares of the boarding house ladies and drinking a considerable quantity of bootleg liquor. They left after a stay of several hours but decided to return when Roberts was outraged to discover the proprietor had short-changed him a dollar.

Their liquor-laced logic convinced them that it would be best to break in, find the money owed, and sneak out. This would avoid any chance of confrontation with the front doorman whose main attributes were his considerable size and strength.

They broke a rear window, entered, and snuck upstairs to the bedroom where the transactions had been made. Angered by their inability to find their money, the two trashed the room.

The ruckus woke Kudrian who followed the men downstairs. It was Roberts who started the fight, viciously attacking the man who eventually killed him. Turzay fought alongside his friend until the battle became too hot to handle—then he ran.

Officials, including District Attorney August Delp, figure it an open and shut case. The papers publish stories trumpeting the perpetrator's guilt, surmising he'll be the first from Crawford County to be electrocuted at Rockview Prison in Bellfonte, Pennsylvania.

The police trace Turzay's story. There is the back window, smashed, where the drunken duo gained access. They find an upstairs bedroom in disarray. But there is no booze to be found anywhere on the property. The owner and occupants of the building heatedly insist theirs is an honest boarding house and not one of ill-repute. Interviews with neighbors support their claims of innocence.

Further investigation leads to a similar-looking building a few doors down where four women identify the victim and his friend as visitors on the day of the murder. There, police easily find an abundance of evidence pointing both to the sale of illegal liquor and to other various and sundry unsavory activities.

It seems Roberts and Turzay were so gloriously drunk that they returned to the wrong house, broke in, and kicked off a chain of events that brought one of them to their death at the hands of Dokoran Kudrian.

Roberts died for nothing. Well, almost nothing. He died for nothing more than a dollar.

Kudrian is brought in front of the September Grand Jury. The good and honest citizens of Crawford County find no evidence of a crime. The confessed killer of William Roberts is set free.

1923, JANUARY: Drawing of prospective jurors from the voting rolls takes place. For the first time in the history of Crawford County, the list contains the names of women.

1923: Adolf Hitler begins writing "Mein Kampf" (My Struggle) after being jailed for trying to overthrow the German government. The National Flag Conference alters the *Pledge of Allegiance* to: "I pledge allegiance to the Flag *of the United States* and the Republic for which it stands, one nation indivisible, with liberty and justice for all." Birdseye frozen food? Thank the Clarence with the same name. Past President Warren G. Harding, dies of congestive heart failure, probably.

1923, JANUARY 5: Location: Meadville, West Street. Victim: Frank Petrolia. Suspect: None. Act: Shooting. Notes: May be related to the sale of illegal liquor. Outcome: Unsolved.

1923, JANUARY 6, EVENING: Location: Meadville, Arch Street, across from the Byham Funeral Home. Victim: Respected Meadville businessman Ford W. Weber. Suspect: None, Act: Random shooting. Outcome: Unsolved.

1923, JUNE: In Uniontown, Pennsylvania (Fayette County, to the southeast of Pittsburgh), a jury with four women finds Charles Ingram guilty of murder in the first degree for the shooting death of William Joy.

THE FAIRER SEX

As noted above, all eligible women in the United States were granted the right to vote in August of 1920. Some states (including Pennsylvania) took the battle for voting rights to the courts. It was another eighteen months before that process ended in the Commonwealth, and then an additional half-year before a new jury pool was drawn from the voting records of Crawford County.

Many doubted a woman's ability to condemn another human being to death—one would think personal experience might have suggested otherwise. It was soon apparent from trials around the country that women were capable of both forgiving a single mistake *and* sending a killer to execution. Within a short period of time, both the defense and prosecution in cases of murder actively sought female jurors.

Crawford County's first women jurors in a murder trial were: Mrs. Sadie Arthur (Rome Township), Mrs. Maude Rickerson (Saegertown in Woodcock Township), Mrs. Augusta Mosier (Cussewago in Cussewago Township) and Mrs. C.H. Kuler (West Shenango).

What follows is the case they helped decide.

"Unusually Clever With the Dice"

Major highways in Crawford County are improved to macadam "Pinchot Roads" through the 1920s and 30s. Almost all of the work is done by regional companies that bring gangs drawn from across the country by the relatively good wages paid for the hard, semi-skilled labor. The ethnically- and racially-mixed workers are boarded in large camps that follow the leading edge of the construction. Like canal and railway camps, the roadway sites tend to be hotbeds of crime, most of it minor—some of it deadly.

The J.C. Devine Company is improving the highway between Spartansburg and Sutton Corners. In the early morning of July 16, 1923, Georgia-state native Prince Crawford, (black, in his 20s) and George Ewing of Beaver Falls, Pennsylvania (black, in his 20s) are walking to work from their camp on the Charles Weidner farm. The two men are considered peaceable with Crawford "quite a favorite with the white men in the (work) gang."

Others in the work party, ahead of the duo, hear a gunshot. They turn back to see Crawford on the ground and Ewing running in the opposite direction. He's last seen headed south out of Spartansburg on the tracks of the Pennsylvania Railroad.

The area's Acting Coroner, John I. Thompson quickly convenes a jury. It's murder with robbery as a probable motive.

Both Crawford and Ewing are gamblers, "unusually clever with the dice." Witnesses testify the two had shot craps the previous Sunday and then quarreled over their gains and losses. Ewing had lost heavily to the victim who, before the crime, was supposedly carrying more than $500 in winnings. When Crawford's body is searched, a little more than a dollar is found.

The alleged perpetrator was last seen in dark trousers, a blue shirt, and a blue overblouse with blood on it. Surrounding counties are alerted. All area police, along with a good number of armed citizens begin the search. Papers describe George Ewing as "a full-blooded Negro" with a "swarthy growth of beard on his face" and a "peculiar smile which causes his lips to turn upward and out."

Given the fact that nearly 100% of the area's residents are white, and those who aren't are well known to everyone, it seems impossible for Ewing to stay hidden long. Sure enough, after fleeing to the north (the eyewitnesses were incorrect) he grows hungry and stops at a farmhouse to ask for food. The occupants call authorities.

The next afternoon, Ewing is found in a swamp several miles to the north near Corry in Erie County, Pennsylvania. The large number of police, not to mention the mob of citizens armed with all manner of weapons, convince the man to drop the revolver and surrender.

Ewing has only $60. He claims the argument was over $40,

not the $500 witnesses described. He says the murder weapon belonged to the victim and he had taken it and shot the other man when attacked on the way to work. The arrested man states he killed in self-defense and then shuts up.

Nonetheless, George Ewing pleads guilty to murder and is bound over to the September 1923 term of Judge Prather's court with Frank J. Thomas of Meadville and Blaine Kinkaid of Corry for the defense and D.A. August Delp representing the Commonwealth.

Dr. E.E. Maitland of Spartansburg testifies that the bullet entered Crawford's left side between the third and fourth ribs, was deflected upwards and to the right, puncturing the ascending aorta, just above the heart. The victim died almost instantly.

Marvin Miller, area resident and one of the first to reach the slain man, says he did not hear the shot but happened to turn and see the victim topple into the ditch and the shooter take off towards Spartansburg.

George Dunkle, Corry Police Chief, tells of the arrest and testifies that Ewing maintained that the gun belonged to the victim who had made threats with it. The accused stated he had taken the weapon from Crawford and shot him in self-defense.

George Ewing withstands heavy questioning from the prosecution and tells his story in a convincing and compelling enough manner for the four women and eight men to find him innocent by reason of self-defense. It takes only two ballots, the first being 11 for and 1 against acquittal.

This surprising decision is reached despite the fact the District Attorney presented fair poof that it was Ewing who had purchased the murder weapon. It also ignored the accused own previously-entered plea of guilty.

It takes Ewing a few minutes to understand what has transpired. The *Meadville Tribune Republican* notes the "defendant was happy when he realized he was free of his charge."

No doubt.

~~~~~

Letters in the victim's belongings suggest he and his family—mother and sisters—are well educated. The last note he receives expresses hope that he would soon return.

The dead man's home town ("Cave," Georgia) is too small to have its own telegraph office. A courier is sent to ask family members to telephone as soon as possible, because the body of their son is being held for burial at the funeral home of Spartansburg undertaker J.E. Winans.

Comes a sorrowful reply: The victim's family cannot afford the return of the body. The J.C. Devine Company refuses to pay for transport. The county prepares to bury the body locally.

This will not do for Reverend G.W. Corey of Spartansburg. He, and the kindhearted citizens of the area, donate more than enough money to return Prince Crawford to his mother.

~~~~~

The Klu Klux Klan was actively recruiting in Crawford County at the time of this shooting. It's interesting to imagine what might've happened had either the victim or suspect been white.

1923, July 18: Location: Summit Township, Conneaut Lake Park, Conneaut Hotel Annex. Victim: Unknown baby girl. Suspect: None. Act: Drowning. Notes: Child found dead in a bath crib. Outcome: Unsolved.

"Two or Three Times Every Week"

Forty-year-old Charles L. Weatherbee has been a cop in Titusville for a half-dozen years and has seen his share of action, even survived being shot while arresting a madman.

He's trusted enough to serve as "Acting Chief" when his boss is on vacation.

Despite his success, Weatherbee has three big problems: his young, pretty, blonde, and hot-tempered wife Sadie; Titusville postman, Ed Sterling; and the fact that it takes Postman Sterling an hour or more to deliver the mail to Weatherbee's home in the 700-block of West Elm.

It's not as if the policeman is surprised. He knows Ed and Sadie have been lovers for the past three years because she throws it in Weatherbee's face whenever they argue—and just before she steps out on him again. He starts divorce proceedings against her twice. Both times she promises that she'll do everything on God's earth to be taken back so she can have a hand in raising their only child, Charles J.

Then she's good, for a while. But she cannot resist her postman. Sterling showers her with gifts—money, jewelry, clothing, even underwear. They spend nights in distant hotels registered as "E.S. White and wife."

When Weatherbee confronts the postman and demands he stop, his wife's lover laughs in his face and says "Weatherbee, you're not in it; go and get a chicken for yourself."

Sterling's busted for transporting liquor, a fairly serious crime in 1923, but the charges don't stick. Weatherbee later roughly arrests Ed and his brother for disorderly conduct, an act that brings a charge of unnecessary brutality upon the officer. These confrontations only serve to bring Sadie closer to Sterling who promises he's "willing to die for her."

In the early morning hours of October 2, 1923, Weatherbee's working the night shift. He's home late for a meal. Sadie and her friend, Mrs. Isabella Mitchell, are running the player piano and having a good time. Weatherbee drives Mrs. Mitchell the twelve blocks to where she lives. He then circles back to his own home, thinking he'll leave the car in case his wife needs it the next morning. The house is dark when he arrives. He parks the vehicle in the garage behind his home and starts east along West Linden for his walk downtown.

He has not gone far when an unfamiliar automobile slows in front of his house, blows the horn in a peculiar fashion, and travels on. Curiosity piqued, the policeman cuts back down the alley to where he can stand in the narrow, dark space between his own house and the next. The unknown car pulls to the curb, facing the wrong direction on West Elm. The horn blows again. One long, one short toot. The porch lights go on, then off. Out comes his wife, wearing his bathrobe. The driver's side door opens. Sadie puts one stocking-clad foot on the running board and leans in to talk to the driver.

Weatherbee steps into the light, recognizes the man in the car, and moves closer. Sterling shouts "There he comes!" Sadie turns, yells "Charley, what are you doing?" She runs at her husband as he draws his service revolver, points it at the vehicle, and fires three times.

The first shot parts his wife's hair but does no harm. The second embeds itself in the frame of the car. The third hits Sterling in the shoulder as he's stooping to exit the vehicle. The man staggers, turns, and runs across the street. With Weatherbee in pursuit, the postman travels 200 feet in the direction of 3rd Street before collapsing in the side yard of Sam Smith. Smith exits his house.

Weatherbee tells him to call an ambulance.

Sadie arrives. She holds her postman in her arms and kisses him.

"Sadie," he says, "I am gone. I died for you."

The wound doesn't look all that serious, but the bullet has traveled through Sterling's body and pierced a lung. He lives for ten minutes after arriving at the hospital.

After witnessing Sterling's death, Officer Weatherbee draws his revolver, aims for his own heart and pulls the trigger. The weapon doesn't fire. The attending physician, Dr. Hugh Jameson rushes to take away the gun. Emptying it, the doctor finds three spent cartridges and three unfired. The dud has a dent where it was struck by the firing pin.

Weatherbee is arrested by his boss, Chief of Police Edwards.

At the Coroner's Jury, Sadie's attempt to commit suicide by jumping from a second floor window is thwarted. She fights her arrest the whole way to the station. Once in her cell at the Titusville jail, she climbs to the top of the bunks and threatens to throw herself, headfirst, to the concrete floor. She calms with the promise of seeing her husband. They visit in the corridor, retiring to sleep in separate cells.

Husband and wife are put on suicide watch that first night. When Sadie is released the day before Weatherbee is moved to the county lockup in Meadville, she begs and pleads until she's allowed to stay with her husband one more day.

Charles Weatherbee is visited regularly in the county jail by his wife and his sisters, with whom she is staying. Sadie brings him home-cooked meals. They sit, eat, and converse with apparent ease.

The policeman's trial, held in a packed courtroom under the tight control of Judge Prather, is remarkable. The unfaithful wife is completely unrepentant for her improper relations with the postman. When asked if the victim had bought her jewelry she shows off the watch she's wearing during her testimony. When asked if her lover carried a revolver, she says she took it from his pocket whenever she was with him, "and I was with him two or three times every week."

For her own part, the postman's wife, Lucy Sterling, mother of three, testifies her wandering husband "was not coward enough to carry a gun. He had a good pair of fists and could use them."

District Attorney August Delp refers to Sadie as "that blonde" and "Mrs. Macbeth," causing her to half recline in her chair and cover her forehead with one hand. Her statement of the bullet parting her hair is dismissed likewise "as if we know that's really her own hair."

Questioned by his lawyers C.W. Benedict and Frank J. Thomas, Weatherbee makes an excellent witness for himself, telling of multiple humiliations and overpowering helplessness, how he tried all he knew to get Sterling to stop, even asking County Detective John Laley for advice.

Weatherbee describes how he provided for his seven-year-old son and wife of fourteen years, cared for them, doing everything he could to make his wife faithful. How everyone knew what was going on. How he could do nothing about it.

The defense is one of momentary insanity. The night of the shooting, according to his attorneys, Weatherbee had no idea what he was doing. Immediately after the unfortunate act, the policeman showed great tenderness towards the man who had caused him so much trouble. Not the action of a premeditated murderer. If he had murder in his heart, he would've emptied the gun into Sterling and not stopped shooting when injury occurred. If Weatherbee wanted to kill, he would have never, upon realization of what he had done, tried to kill himself.

The prosecution maintains that the trial is not to judge Sterling or the unfaithful wife, but to decide the guilt of Weatherbee. Sympathy is not a cause for finding for the defense. The loss of control is no excuse for murder. The laws of the land do not allow us to seek revenge—no matter the reason. The suicide attempt was not born of regret, or insanity, but because of the guilt of a capital crime.

Prather's forty minutes of instructions to the jury boil down to deciding if Weatherbee was of sound mind when he shot the postman. It takes the twelve men four hours and one vote to declare Weatherbee "not guilty." The spectators break into applause despite warnings against demonstrations when the verdict is read. Local newspapers fill with editorials for and against the decision. Letters are written, using the case as evidence of what can happen when a marriage is lacking sanctity, "something tragically common in these United States."

Weatherbee announces that he's taking his boy on a two-week vacation to visit family and friends, to calm his shattered nerves. He hugs and kisses his wife and departs. The community wonders if the two will stay together. They do, for a while, and then divorce.

~~~~~

In 1941, the son, Charles J., has marital problems of his own. He marries a wealthy woman who then runs away to Florida. He sues her for $15,000, claiming she promised to support him. He loses the suit.

In 1947, "Mrs. Sadie Lefford Weatherbee, aged 54, formerly of Titusville, died on April 4 at her home in Celeron, New York. Mrs. Weatherbee is survived by a son, Charles Weatherbee of Celeron, and a sister." There is no mention of a husband.

In 1971, old man Weatherbee takes a bad fall at his home in Bristol Springs, NY. He is hospitalized and dies shortly thereafter.

~~~~~

Four months after the shooting, the victim's wife and family, Lucy Sterling and her three small children, Clinton, Beatrice, and Leola are all ill with Scarlet Fever. They survive.

Lucy marries Daniel R. Goodwill in 1923. They remain together until his death in 1956. Lucy Sterling Goodwill dies three years later at the age of 72 and is buried in Titusville's Greenwood Cemetery. She is survived by her children, step-children, 16 grandchildren, and 4 great grandchildren.

Instead of the Gallows

William Kemmler was the first person in the world to die in an electric chair. The execution took place on August 6, 1890 in New York's Auburn Prison. It did not go well. The first 17-second shock with 1,000 volts struck the condemned unconscious.

A second shock with twice the voltage burst blood vessels beneath the skin. Witnesses mistook the smoke and stench from electrically-scorched skin and hair as signs that the body had caught afire. Said George Westinghouse, whose Tesla-designed generators were used to provide the juice, "they would have done better using an axe," a somewhat ironic statement, considering Kemmler had axe-murdered Tillie Ziegler, his common-law wife.

It wasn't until 1913 that Aaron B. Hess, a State Representative from Lancaster County, in southeast Pennsylvania, proposed the Commonwealth adopt the electric chair as its form of execution. The bill was spurred, in part, by a widespread desire to centralize, standardize, and render Pennsylvania's executions "more humane" than hangings. It was enthusiastically endorsed by lawmakers, passing the house by a vote of 159 to 2. With senate approval, it was signed into law by Governor John K. Tener.

Along with changing the Commonwealth's method of execution, the Hess Bill also specified the then-being built Rockview Prison as the site of the "Death House" and appropriated $50,000 for the construction of a building to hold the condemned, the Chair, and all necessary equipment.

In contrast to the semi-public hangings held in county lockups, electrocutions were private. The prisoner was kept in solitary, except for visits from family, spiritual advisers, and officials of the penitentiary. Witnesses were restricted to a physician, a spiritual adviser, six "reputable citizens" selected by the warden, and no more than six reporters and/or prison officials: a total of fourteen.

The condemned waited in their local jail until the governor set a date of execution, whereupon the prisoner was transported to central Pennsylvania. Sentence was carried out within days of arrival. Those headed for the Chair never lived long once they reached Rockview, even though they might remain for an eternity.

The Death House, which still stands, is a low, horizontal, stone-faced building that contained a small number of cells and separate rooms for both the generator and chair. Executions usually took place in the early morning, right after the prisoners heard the spin-up of the generator. Brought into a near-empty room, the condemned was belted into "Old Smokey," an extremely sturdy, square, wooden chair. A leather mask was placed over the face. Electrodes were strapped to the head and left ankle. Last words were requested.

The current was then applied. Two bolts were almost always fatal. A third was used "to be sure." A practiced crew took a cooperative prisoner from life to death in very few minutes. Burns to the skin where the electrodes sat were the only signs of violence.

Once the attending physician declared death, the body was removed for autopsy. If unclaimed, it might have been sent to the State Anatomical Board. More often than not, the executed was buried on the prison grounds.

Wife-killer John Talap was the first in Pennsylvania to be executed—7:14 on the morning of February 23, 1915. Aaron B. Hess, author of the bill creating the Commonwealth's power to electrocute the condemned, was on hand to witness the proceedings. From then, and until April 2, 1962, three hundred and fifty Pennsylvania murderers were killed in this uniquely American form of execution.

"Now We're Gonna Get You"

Albert Platt is a small man. He is a little over 5 feet tall and weighs not even 150 pounds. He grew up on a family farm in Ashtabula County, northeast Ohio. Farm work has always been dangerous and Albert is living proof. He wears a wooden peg to replace the right leg his 17-year-old self ground off to the knee with a fall into a steam-powered threshing machine. The peg, and 40 additional years of wear and tear, makes it difficult to get along. At times, he's barely mobile.

Under different circumstances, Albert might be able to pass for a well-to-do businessman. He has a full head of thick, wavy, steel-gray hair that, combined with a prominent, hooked nose and strong chin, gives him a look of character. As long as he doesn't smile. His teeth are stained, rotted, and ruined, the result of his constant habit of chewing tobacco.

Nothing about Albert's life is easy. His lack of education makes him suitable only for the physical labor that his disability makes almost impossible. He drifts from state to state, farm to farm, and relative to relative. There has been some trouble with the law, but nothing serious.

There is something else that makes life difficult for the small man: his mercurial moods. He is gregarious then silent, agreeable then unpleasant, happy then inconsolable. His own relatives "don't think him just right." He sits silently for hours, then bursts with anger. Once riled, he'll take actions he sometimes regrets. A farmer once fired him for striking a cow with a pitchfork despite Albert explaining it was the animal's fault for stepping on his good foot.

Nothing bothers the man when he's happy. Contrariwise, his downs are so miserable that he has tried at least twice to kill himself. His last attempt left him an ugly scar across the base of his throat.

On New Year's Day, 1924, Albert starts work at the McGowan farm at Dennison's Corners about halfway between Linesville and Harmonsburg in Summit Township. The family needs an extra hand since 18-year-old Ellis began teaching at the nearby school on Gherton Road. The young man's new job and Mr. McGowan's regular work leaves only the wife and 14-year-old daughter, Mary Etta, to tend to the farm's unending chores.

The pay isn't much, but that doesn't matter to Albert. He's good to go as long as he has enough cash to buy tobacco, the occasional bootlegged pint, and necessary clothing, like his new, sheepskin-lined khaki overcoat. The work's light, the food's tasty, and there's a clean, safe place to sleep.

Albert's not bothered by Mr. McGowan. He departs early each morning to travel 40 miles south by train to his work as a manager at Westinghouse in Sharon, down in Mercer County. Between his job and long commute, he's hardly ever around and is exhausted when he is.

The boy's another story. About the age Albert was when he lost his leg, the young McGowan is everything the small man never was: tall, handsome, athletic, educated, and well-liked. Ellis spends his time teaching, singing in the church choir, attending socials, and cheering the local basketball teams. The two share sleeping quarters when Albert first arrives. Then the boy asks his mother to move the hired hand to a separate room.

Mrs. McGowan explains it's to allow the older man to sleep undisturbed by Ellis and his night-owl habits. Albert doesn't believe it for a second. The boy doesn't like him. Refuses to do even simple favors, like buying tobacco when he's in town. Albert thinks the youngster rude, lazy, and smart-mouthed. He's also a sloppy worker, leaving tools scattered about when the job is done. The boy's mother admits her son doesn't care for chores, but defends him, saying it doesn't matter because his real job is at the school, not on the farm.

Despite her standing up for Ellis, the one-legged man takes an almost immediate shine to the "bright-looking" and smart Mrs. McGowan. It doesn't seem right to him that such a pleasant, kind, and handsome woman is left on her own so much of the time. Before long, he can hardly keep his eyes off her. He has to be careful when the kids are around, especially the girl, Mary Etta. She has noticed Albert's infatuation and is watching him like a hawk.

After being at the farm a little more than a month, when the two are alone, Albert asks Mrs. McGowan if maybe she'd like to spend some time with him. Even offers her a little of her own money back. He says it off-handedly, as if it could be a joke, but he can tell she hasn't taken it that way. He spends the next two days in fearful agitation because he knows he'll be fired if the Mister finds out.

Friday morning, February 8, starts out like many others. Mr. McGowan leaves home a little after 5:00 to catch the early train at Linesville. Mrs. McGowan, still cold from Albert's proposition, calls him to breakfast in the kitchen and then goes to the dining room to prepare her son's lunch. She knows the hired hand is worked up over something, but thinks little of it.

Ellis joins Albert at the table and starts in about the improper advances towards his mother. "Now we've got you where we want you," the boy hisses. "Now we're gonna get you."

The upset hired hand leaves the table and takes the back door to the barn. Worry is replaced by anger as he works. "Get me?" He rages to himself. "Get ME?"

Abandoning his chores, the now-furious, peg-legged man limps back through the snow to the house. He stops at the woodshed to pick up a double-bitted axe. He reenters the kitchen the way he left.

Ellis is facing the opposite direction, sitting and eating while reading a newspaper propped up on the sugar bowl. He ignores Albert who stands behind him, raising his weapon.

Albert drives the axe into the base of the boy's skull, leaving a deep, four-inch wide, horseshoe-shaped gash. Ellis is thrown forward by the blow then slides off, backwards and to the left, onto his right side, pulling along the tablecloth and sending everything on it crashing to the floor. The older man stands over the boy as if he were felled timber, spins the axe in his hands to gain the fresh edge, and swings again. The blade cuts the boy's skull in an arc above his left ear. Twisting the axe and pulling it free, Albert peels back skin and bone, exposing the brain inside.

Mrs. McGowan rushes from the other room to find her

fallen son and Albert, axe raised for yet another chop. Screaming, she attacks the small man, striking him on the face and arms. Mary Etta, hearing the commotion from her bedroom, rushes downstairs. Grabbing the iron poker from the kitchen stove, she joins her mother to disarm her brother's attacker and drive him from the house.

Mother and daughter pull Ellis to his feet. With their help he stumble-walks to and is placed on the living-room couch. The last words of the once-eloquent young man are a mumbled "oh boy, oh boy, oh boy." He loses consciousness and dies several hours later after being transported by trolley to Meadville's Spencer Hospital.

By coincidence, that same day, the Crawford County Grand Jury is meeting on their usual quarterly schedule. They immediately consider Albert's case and return a true bill.

The criminal trial starts before the week is out. The judge is Thomas Prather. District Attorney Augustus Delp prosecutes. O. Clare Kent, past-D.A. and future-judge, is assigned to defend the destitute man.

The now emotionless Albert pleads guilty. The Commonwealth is rabid for execution. They reject any potential juror "with scruples against the death penalty." The all-male jury is drawn in less than two hours, which probably still stands as a county record for a murder trial.

A stream of morbidly curious citizens file through the sheriff's office where they see the bloody and brain-spattered axe being held as evidence. There are mutterings of short-circuiting the legal process and hanging the killer from one of the elms out in Diamond Park.

The trial is a potential powder-keg. Judge Prather holds his packed court under tight control. The McGowan family provides excellent testimony. The mother, especially, wins the admiration of men and women alike as she clearly and fearlessly testifies to the horrors visited by a man she brought into her house out of pity and in the spirit Christian charity.

From the start, it's obvious that the only goal of defense attorney Kent is to keep his client out of the electric chair. The lawyer tries repeatedly to bring to light his client's past: his bouts of uncontrollable fury, depressions, and attempted suicides. D.A. Delp successfully objects each time. Albert's past, Judge Prather decides, has no legal bearing on present actions.

Kent argues that Albert's inhuman fury lead him to murder. He's portrayed as possessing some intelligence but losing all judgment when angered. The defense contends the small man did not comprehend what he was doing at the time he attacked Ellis.

For his part, Albert claims no memory of the act until the mother told him what he'd done. The problem is that cross-examination proves he recalls details of the crime.

It takes the jury ninety minutes of deliberation and one vote to reach their unanimous decision. The newspapers wonder how it took twelve reasonable men even that long to reach a verdict. Albert is found guilty of murder in the first degree. Judge Prather gavels for silence as the packed courtroom breaks into applause. Several women cry with relief. The murderer is unmoved. Within an hour of hearing the jury's decision, he's back in his cell, laughing and playing checkers with fellow prisoners.

Another week passes before sentencing. Judge Prather asks the murderer if he wishes to make a statement. Albert tells the judge what he has mentioned to several others, that he didn't tell the whole story when he was on the stand. That he's holding his tongue to spare the family more pain. But nobody's interested in what secrets the murderer might possess.

Judge Prather condemns the prisoner to death by electrocution, "and may God have mercy on your soul."

Albert displays no emotion. He turns, hands his watch and chain to his cousin, Wilbur Brooks, of Steamburg, Conneaut Township, and says "Here, take this. I guess I'll have no further use for it."

Platt's lawyer makes no motion for a retrial. Nor does he appeal to the state for commutation of sentence to life in prison.

At first, waiting for the end is an easy task. There is no "death guard" assigned to Albert because he appears unfazed by the sentence and remains a model prisoner. The press reports, in amazed prose, that the killer shows neither guilt for the past nor concern for the future. He sleeps well, eats enough for two, and spends his time dozing and joking with other prisoners. He does ask his jailers for some warning before the trip to the Death House, so he can give away what little he owns.

By the first week of April, Albert has grown nervous and lost his air of indifference. He's heard arguing with himself and has begun to talk with a minister who visits the jail every week. The prisoner shows his temper. He grows angry at small problems and minor frustrations. He steadfastly refuses to take any responsibility for his actions. He blames the McGowans in general, and Ellis in particular, for his plight.

Governor Pinchot sets the execution for April 28. Albert can't be told because Sheriff Cutshall doesn't receive official word, but the condemned already knows from the other prisoners who read the papers. He is now calm, worried only about the date he'll be taken away. Through a bureaucratic snafu, the sheriff never receives any written orders to transport his prisoner to Rockview. It's handled by a simple telephone call.

Albert is jovial when he is stirred for his early morning automobile ride to Titusville. He says it's pretty short notice, but he thinks he can make it. Waiting at the station for the train that will take him to his death, he eats a hearty meal of pork chops and potatoes, joking, "I may not get any more."

The sheriff and his condemned prisoner travel to Rockview via Pittsburgh. It's a 12-hour trip through the coal fields of western Pennsylvania and on to the state's central province of valley and ridge.

The men arrive in the early afternoon. As he's transferred to the Death House guard, Albert hands his almost new overcoat to the sheriff and asks it be given to his sister.

At 7:15, Monday morning, April 28 1924, after a good night's sleep and a big breakfast, the small, one-legged man is strapped into the Chair. With Edward E. Moss, uncle of the victim as one of the witnesses, electrodes are set on the prisoner's head and around his only ankle. He has no last words.

The executioner pulls the switch at 7:19. Eight minutes later, less than three months after murdering young Ellis McGowan, Albert Platt becomes the first man electrocuted on a sentence from Crawford County.

~~~~~

Newspapers reported that Ellis was buried in Pittsburgh, Pennsylvania. But there is a headstone for him in the McGowan family plot in the Evergreen Cemetery at Harmonsburg.

A few years later the McGowans adopted Jack Moss, an orphaned member of Mrs. McGowan's extended family. Tragedy struck in February 1936 when then 11-year-old, sled-riding Jack was accidentally killed by a passing car. It was twelve years, almost to the day of the murder. Jack's grave lies next to that of his murdered cousin.

Mr. Robert McGowan persisted in his long commute to Westinghouse Electric in Sharon, eventually trading train for automobile, until retiring in 1943. Three years later, at the age of 70, he died suddenly at his farm.

Mrs. McGowan was well-respected in her community, with leadership roles in many of Linesville's civic and religious organizations. She suffered a decline in health over several years and died in December of 1956. She is buried beside her husband.

June of 1928, Mary Etta married Dale Henderson, of Pittsburgh, eventually bearing two daughters, Maryette and Lois Adele. Dale Henderson died in 1974; Mary Etta, in 1992. Both were buried with the McGowans.

Albert E. Moss, Jr., Ellis' cousin and son of the Albert Moss who witnessed Platt's execution, was a Staff Sergeant in the Army Air Corp during the Second World War and spent three years as a prisoner of the Japanese. He moved to Linesville after his return. Like his Aunt Henrietta, Albert Moss gained respect in his adopted hometown. He died in March of 1997 and was buried in the Linesville Cemetery.

Linesville's Veterans of Foreign Wars Post #7842 bears his name.

1924: The National Flag Conference alters the *Pledge of Allegiance* to: "I pledge allegiance to the Flag of the United States *of America* and to the Republic for which it stands, one nation indivisible, with liberty and justice for all." Lenin dies. Stalin grows even meaner. Newly elected U.S. President Calvin Coolidge grants citizenship to all U.S. Native Americans. Future Presidents Jimmy Carter and George H.W. Bush are born. IBM is founded. Past President Woodrow Wilson dies of stroke.

1924, MAY 25: Location: Meadville, Erie Railroad yards. Victim: Emmett Plummer (black). Suspect: Duff Shorts (white, detective for the railroad). Act: Shot while trespassing. Notes: Despite exoneration by the Coroner's Jury, Shorts is arrested and charged with murder. Page 3 of the September 11, 1925 *Titusville Herald* reports this as the first murder case with women jurors, but that's not true. It's the first murder trial of a *white man* where women are jurors. Outcome: Jury deliberates five days before finding Shorts not guilty.

1924, JULY 12: Location: Conneaut Township, near Steamburg, ditch on side of the road. Victim: Harry Tedesco. Suspect: None. Act: Shot and hurled from moving

automobile, perhaps as part of "bootlegger wars."
Outcome: Unsolved.

1924, August 5: Location: Sadsbury Township, Conneaut
Lake. Victim: Mrs. A.H. Terril. Suspect: J.H. Hotchkiss.
Act: Deliberately killed by automobile (first case of
its kind in Crawford County). Notes: Well-known
animosity between victim and suspect over property in
the Conneaut Lake area leads some to suggest murderous
intent. Outcome: Charged with willful murder, then
accidental homicide. Grand Jury reduces to "aggravated
assault and neglect to stop a motor vehicle."

Now You See It...

Clarksville, Mercer County, Pennsylvania—hometown of the
subject of our next story, no longer exists. Laid out along the
Shenango River in 1829, the little town grew and then thrived
after the construction of the Erie-Beaver Canal along the
Shenango's bottom land.

The river that provided so much life undid the village. The
Shenango Dam was built to the south, below the confluence of
the Shenango with Pymatuning Creek. The reservoir behind the
dam drowned the site of the original town which was moved to
higher ground in 1968 and renamed "Clark, Pennsylvania."

"Ridding Themselves of the Obligation"

William M. Locke is a 42-year-old cattle buyer from Clarksville,
midway between Greenville and Sharon, in Mercer County just
to the south of Crawford. He is a businessman who loves to
make money, is "thrifty" and will "go almost any place at almost
any hour to put through a legitimate transaction promising a
profit." Well known for driving a hard bargain, he is said to have
the grudging respect of all those who deal with him.

On Wednesday morning, April 15, 1925, Locke and his brother, David take a load of dressed beef to Farrell, Mercer County, Pennsylvania. They part ways at noon. Locke tells his brother he plans to stop by the local A&P for groceries before visiting their sister, Mrs. Lawrence Giewitz, in the nearby city of Sharon. He never arrives.

It's a shock to everyone when William Locke is found dead in his car, bright and early at 7:00 the next morning by Walter Bierman and his son.

The vehicle sits in the middle of the road, stalled in high gear, A&P groceries in the back and the driver dead behind the wheel. Locke's head is terribly mangled. Police think an initial revolver wound to the chest caused him to stop the car, after which he suffered two shotgun blasts, one to the back of the neck and the other behind the left ear. There's a shotgun-barrel-sized hole in the isinglass behind the driver's seat.

More puzzling is that Locke's car sits on Dickey Road, a mile north of Hartstown in West Fallowfield Township, more than an hour's drive from his home. Crawford County authorities are pessimistic from the start. County Detective John Laley: "We are completely baffled by the case." Coroner W.E. Byham: "My personal opinion is that the mystery will never be solved."

A large part of the problem is the lack of motive. It isn't robbery. The dead man's pockets still hold the $42 he had made with the previous day's sale of beef. Locke was not a drinker and was not thought to traffic in liquor. He lived with his brother and was not a lady's man. With no romantic entanglements, a jealous husband seems unlikely.

Since the murder victim was known to lend money and "had the reputation of being rather hard and relentless with those who were in his debt," police advance the theory that the killing was one of a rough collection gone bad. Brother David shoots down the idea, saying the dead man knew nobody so far from home and had no business there. Nevertheless, authorities interview all of his debtors to be sure none were "ridding themselves of the obligation."

Locke's three other brothers and two sisters are estranged, and none have much good to say about the other. Still, they allow that Locke was an honest man, though he could be disagreeable in business. To a person they maintain he had to have been decoyed or forced to the murder spot since he was neither given to whim nor the type to have traveled so far on a lark.

The day before his murder, the victim stopped to buy three gallons of gas at 1:30 in the afternoon from F.L. Sweet along the Mercer-Sharon road. Sweet reports the presence of two men in the rear seat, taking particular notice because there was no cushion there, it being removed by Locke and his brother to haul beef.

The gas-station owner describes one of these men as young, about 25, with the other larger, around 50. He couldn't get a good look because of the curtains in the car, but both are deemed "foreign in appearance."

Locke *had* stopped at an A&P for groceries, but it was in Greenville, fifteen miles north of the Sharon store he said he was going to use. He was there between 2:00 and 3:00 in the afternoon, accompanied by a smooth-faced man in his late 40s who was short and heavily built. The clerk said he didn't know the man but could identify him, if need be.

Investigators are convinced the men riding with Locke are his slayers. The meager descriptions don't give much hope of finding them. Two men are arrested, then released.

The mystery deepens when it's found that Locke took a $5,000 short-term loan from McDowell Bank in Sharon three weeks before his murder, He said it was for his brother, David. But he gave David only $500. When the note expired two weeks later the victim was granted an extension on collateral of mortgages valued at $6,000.

Brother David was contacted for payment a week after the murder. He went in thinking the loan was for half-a-grand and was confused and then horrified to discover he owed ten times that much. What's more, the now-dead William had forged David's signature on the contract.

Perhaps Locke used the extra money "for a booze deal," or some other shady venture. Perhaps the transaction somehow went wrong. Perhaps the victim became so desperate for money to pay the $5,000 loan that he leaned too heavily on the people who owed him, causing violence and death.

Speculation is rampant, but in the end there is no way to tell. The case is never solved.

1925: The Grand Ol' Opry starts radio broadcasts and begins fusing what has been two styles of music: Country and Western. The Scopes "Monkey Trial" confirms the illegality of teaching evolution in Tennessee. In 1967 Tennessee repeals that state's Butler Act which prohibited the teaching of evolution in public schools. Malcolm Little is born—you might recognize him as El-Hajj Malik El-Shabazz. No? Then how about Malcolm X?

1925, MAY: Up 'til now, those found guilty of murder in the first degree had to be sentenced to death. The Guerin Bill now gives Pennsylvania courts another option. First degree murderers can now be punished with either death *or* life in prison. The jury fixes sentence in the case of a trial. The judge decides when the defendant pleads guilty. These changes hold throughout this book.

1925, JUNE 11: Location: Vernon Township. Victim: John W. Hill (61, father-in-law). Suspect: Clarence Kuhn a.k.a. Connie Drayer (25, son-in-law). Act: Strikes head on floor in a fall during a fight. Outcome: Charged with murder. Pleads not guilty. Found guilty of manslaughter.

But Later, He Grew "Real Vile."

Glenn and Marie Ogram moved to Custards, in Greenwood Township several years back. They've not had the best of luck, suffering crop failures and a run of cattle deaths. They've lost some property to the sheriff for non-payment for goods received. To add insult to injury, their home burned to the ground a few months ago. Since then, they've been living in a set of small farm sheds.

They'd have lost everything if not for Glenn's milk delivery business. He leaves early each morning to make his rounds and then travels the several miles to Meadville and back. He's gone most of the time, every day of the week. It's hard work, but it pays the bills.

For the past couple of years, they've had forty year-old Burton Williams, from nearby Geneva, as a hand on the farm. He and Glenn had worked together at the Ogram family sawmill near Conneaut Lake. Burt is a good, kind, and hard working man—as long as he stays on the wagon. There is no doubt to anyone who knows him that he's one mean drunk.

~~~~~

Marie Ogram's trial for the murder of Burton Williams begins on September 28, 1925. She has retained attorneys Walter J. McClintock and O. Clare Kent for her defense. The accused does not deny the shooting, but maintains it was self-defense against a drunken assault.

Representing the Commonwealth is District Attorney August Delp, assisted by Albert L. Thomas who is, presumably, being paid by the victim's relatives (it's no secret that Burt's extended family harbors "decidedly bitter" feelings against the Ograms). The prosecution admits Burton Williams was drunk but plans to prove he was shot and killed while walking away from the victim.

With a female defendant, the trial is expected to be

particularly newsworthy. Judge Thomas Prather warns the unusually large numbers of spectators to behave. He insists on order. "The court is not a curiosity shop."

It takes but two hours for the lawyers to seat the six women and six men of the jury. This is the first case in Crawford County tried under the Guerin Bill. If Marie Ogram is convicted of murder in the first degree, the jurors will set the sentence: life in prison, or death by electrocution.

Ogram's neighbor, George Alexander, is first on the stand. He tells how Burt had been laid off from time to time due either to the Ogram's lack of money or Burt's drinking and that Burt showed up tipsy at his farm on August 18 between 6:00 and 7:00 in the morning and left not quite two hours later. During the visit, the man took several good pulls from a jug containing hard cider.

Burt reappeared in another forty minutes, drunker than before. He told how he'd been at the Ograms' and how he'd slapped Marie on the side of the head and knocked her down. The woman had fired a rifle at his feet. The bullet had ricocheted and almost hit him on the neck.

After more hard cider, Burt said he was going back to the farm to get his clothes and then head to Meadville to get a lawyer to get the money the Ograms owed him for his work. Alexander testifies he warned the victim not to go back. "I told him to go straight home, that if he went back to Ograms' she would shoot him again."

Sure enough, a short time later, Alexander's mother came to him saying Burt had been shot. Alexander describes how he'd gone for the doctor after he found the drunken man on the roadside, weak from the loss of blood.

Thelson Williams, the victim's third cousin, testifies that he and his brother Marshall were riding a horse-drawn hay wagon on the road near the Ogram farm. They were only a few hundred feet away when they spied Burton, walking in their direction on the road. They heard a report of a gun and saw their cousin fall to the ground. It was Thelson and Marshall who raised the alarm at the Alexander farm a short distance away.

Soon after the shooting, Thelson says, he saw Marie Ogram pick up her small child and run toward Custards.

Frank Crist, of Custards, testifies that Marie came to his place saying she had shot Burt. Crist was at the Ogram farm when the ambulance came to take the wounded man to Meadville.

Dr. William Marshall, of Geneva, attended the victim and describes how the bullet struck Burton in the thigh. The injury wasn't thought to be serious until they discovered the victim must have been in a stooping position when shot. The bullet took a course into and through the intestines.

The doctor says when he arrived, Burton was in shock and already suffering from loss of blood. His opinion that the victim was drunk was based on his slurred speech, that the victim was confused enough to accuse the doctor of shooting him, and that he had vomited liquid that smelled like hard cider.

On cross, Dr. Marshall is willing to allow that shock and loss of blood could have also produced some of the delirium and maybe even magnified the effect of the cider.

Small and dark-haired twenty-nine year-old Marie Ogram takes the stand. Her lawyers advised her not to testify at either the Coroner's Jury or her arraignment. This is the first time the public hears her story.

Burton, she says, worked until noon the day before but became too drunk to continue. He retired to the small building he slept in, making a "good deal of commotion about his shed until midnight."

The farmhand was still drunk the next morning, but able to walk. "His tongue was all right" at first, but later, Ogram says, he grew "real vile."

The accused woman ordered him from the farm. Burton replied that he'd get his clothes and leave. He did get his clothes, but didn't leave. He came to her and struck her down with his fist, threatening to kill her.

Ogram retrieved a .22 rifle. She fired into the ground, first at her feet, then at his. Burton said that if he had a gun he would kill "any old woman" and stormed from the property.

A half hour later he burst into her shed where she was trying to sleep and moved a step or two in her direction. She jumped from the bed and grabbed the rifle. When he turned to pick up a piece of wood from the floor, she shot him.

She claims to have had no choice. She is small, her health is bad, and she has no strength. There was no way to escape through the closed windows of the shed. Burton was large and strong and had once told her how "he had shot his brother and beaten up his father." She was sure the drunken farmhand was capable of killing her.

According to Marie Ogram, she scooped up her child and headed for Frank Crist's place in Custard as Burton stumbled his way to the road. When she passed the wounded Burton on the way he said "You needn't get any doctor for me. I'll take my medicine here."

Four men were at her farm when she returned. She brought water to help bathe the blood from the man she had shot. Burton asked "Marie, aren't you ashamed?" She replied, "I can't say that I am ashamed, but you will never know how sorry I am that you forced me to do this."

The ambulance arrived and took Burton away. That was the last time she saw him alive.

The prosecution rebuts her testimony, saying she'd supplied her victim with the hard cider that got him drunk, that she'd shot him at a distance when he was leaving the farm or standing on the road.

She denies their accusations, repeating she had shot only when defending herself, only when threatened with death.

Attorney Thomas begins to question her character. She is unable to give any account of her origin. She is accused of living with her husband before marrying. Thomas states she is prone to violence and makes a habit of carrying firearms. The defense manages to shut down the personal attacks with objections to Judge Prather.

Glenn Ogram takes the stand and says of Marie "she is supposed to be my wife." He says many in Greenwood Township think he and the accused are not married but a look in the county records would prove they were, in the clerk's office, on April 19, 1920.

The husband says his milk-delivery business keeps him away a good part of the day. He was ready to leave early on the day of the shooting, when he saw Burton, who was already giving good evidence of drinking. Glenn testifies he told the farm-hand to go home until he sobered up. Then, he got his milk ready and started for Meadville.

Ogram describes how he had known Burt for six years, having first worked with him at the family saw mill. He says the victim did not behave himself when imbibing.

He describes the area around Custards as "a drinking country down there if you want to know it" and that he would have never had moved to the area had he known what it was like.

When asked why he kept Burt around, Glenn replies that if he had laid him off for drunkenness once, he'd done it fifty times.

Glenn Ogram's testimony is followed by fifteen prosecution witnesses claiming the reputation of the Ograms for the truth was bad and they weren't to be trusted—even when under oath. Then seven defense witnesses swore just the opposite.

On September 30, after five hours of deliberation, the jury finds Marie Ogram not guilty in the shooting death of Burton Williams.

Judge Prather warns against outbursts. There are none.

~~~~~

I took Glenn Ogram's challenge, traipsed to the courthouse, and checked for a marriage license for him and his wife, Marie.

There it was: Docket 18, page 280. Took a little figuring, though, since they weren't listed as expected. Instead, they were "Alva G. Ogram" and "Leah M. Geer." It's odd that both of them used their middle names.

Alva and Leah's luck never improved, as far as their property was concerned. Their farm was seized and sold in a sheriff sale in February 1928.

1925, OCTOBER 12: Location: Meadville, South Main. Victim: Frank Malek, Suspects: Alexander Lavinsky (Alec Levinsky) (37), wife Julia Lavinsky (Levinsky) (38), and George Patterson (Persns [*sic*], Pershin) (44). All arrested and charge with murder. Act: Hole in skull caused by blunt force. Alcohol is involved. Outcome: Alec Levinsky sentenced to pay $250 and sent to Allegheny County workhouse for a period of two years for violations of the liquor laws. Julia Levinsky placed on parole (because of her "serious medical conditions") for violations of the liquor laws. George Patterson found not guilty of murder by jurors after 24 hours of deliberation and fourteen ballots. He is immediately re-arrested on charges of failure to pay for earlier violations of liquor laws. He's placed in jail until he pays $27.50 in fines or sweats it out with hard labor. No one else is ever charged with the crime. The case goes "unsolved."

1925, NOVEMBER 3, 5:00am: Location: Titusville, Dairy Street near the Pennsylvania Railroad underpass. Victim: Bert (Bruno) A. Krenz. Suspects: Frank H. Flanders (Titusville undertaker) and Miss Jane Moran (the dead Chief of Police Michael Moran had a daughter Jane, who was a school nurse). Act: Krenz struck by automobile. Notes: According to three witnesses, victim dies of a heart attack, falls into the street, and then is hit by a car. Alcohol is involved, perhaps philandery on the part of Krenz. Coroner's Jury returns the cause of death as accidental. Victim's wife will not let matter drop and keeps at the case until warrants are issued for Flanders and Moran. Outcome: District Attorney Stuart A. Culbertson takes no action because there is no criminal act.

1926: *Winnie-the-Pooh,* by A.A. Milne. The NBC radio network begins its broadcast days, beating CBS by one year. Robert Goddard launches a liquid-fueled rocket at Auburn, Massachusetts. Harry Houdini escapes this life with help from a ruptured appendix. Charles Edward Anderson "Chuck" Berry is born. So is Miles Davis.

MAKE MINE PALE DRY

Brothers Arthur and Patrick McGill arrived in 1795 to be among the first white settlers in what is now Woodcock Township, Crawford County. About five years later, Roger Alden built a sawmill near their property.

The settlement was generally known as "Alden's Mill" until 1824 when forty-four year-old Daniel Saeger from Egypt, Jefferson County, north-central Pennsylvania bought the mill and surrounding land. He named his village after himself, "Saegertown."

The town gained some fame during the mania for curative spring water in the late 19th and early 20th centuries. The Saegertown Mineral Springs Company won international awards for the best soft drink of the day. Many still remember "The Aristocrat of Ginger Ales."

Saegertown shows up several times in this book. It was a frequent site of railroad work camps, never a calming influence. It was also home to the "Saegertown Inn" which, as it fell from premiere tourist attraction to a state of neglect, attracted more and more questionable clientele.

But there was always good with the bad. Saegertown was also the home of Mrs. Maude Rickerson, one of the first of four women to serve on the jury of a Crawford County murder trial. It also helped raise Herbert Mook, a President Judge who executed his duties so well that he ran unopposed for his second term on the bench.

"He'd Have One as Nice When He Died "

Polish immigrants John and Josephine Muztuck fight constantly through their fourteen year marriage. You can't hide that kind of thing in a place as small as Saegertown. Everyone knows it: neighbors, friends, co-workers. It's impossible to ignore their threats and public acts of violence, the pitched screaming, the scratches on his face and bruises on hers.

Most of their battles are over real and imagined middle-aged jealousies. Josephine, at 47, is no angel. It's true she instigates some of the arguments, but as tiny as she is, five-feet tall and 90 pounds, there's no way she can stand toe-to-toe against her larger, stronger, and younger husband, a brutish man with a full head of dark hair standing straight up from his head. As years pass, she ignores him when he argues. It infuriates her violent husband, especially when he's drunk, and he's drunk a lot.

Josephine separates from the 34-year-old John while he's serving six months in the Allegheny County Workhouse on a conviction for bootlegging. He has threatened to kill her several times since his release but has, so far, left her in peace.

The evening of November 16, 1926, John is in Erie where he holds a job as a laborer. Drunk, he calls Josephine at the Saegertown Inn, where she has worked hard and well as a domestic for the last dozen years. John begs his wife to take him back. She refuses. He grows abusive. Josephine holds the phone so that 17-year-old Miss May Sobeski can plainly hear the drunken man shout his intent to return home and commit murder.

Josephine throws on a shawl and runs home shortly thereafter. Those living nearby hear her calling to the large German shepherd dog owned by neighbor and co-worker Jack Wright. The dog does not show.

The inter-urban streetcar arrives from Erie at 10:11pm. Later, the neighbors hear Josephine screaming. They don't pay much attention. It happens all the time when the Muztucks quarrel and fight.

Josephine fails to show up the next day at work. Her friends figure it must've been a pretty bad beating.

Within the week, John appears at the Meadville police station. He says that he had awakened a couple days ago to find his wife gone and that she hasn't returned. He explains how he'd asked several people if they had seen his Josephine. They had not. The worried husband brought along a picture of his wife because he wishes to report her as missing.

John says he's afraid Josie has drowned herself in French Creek that runs fifty feet from their home. County Detective Laley arranges to drag the water. He also investigates the Muztuck's relationship.

John is arrested.

A few days later, neighbor Jack Wright contacts police after noticing his dog behaving oddly around the Muztuck's hen-house. Josephine's tiny, battered, kimono-wrapped body is found, buried three feet under the floor of the coop.

Muztuck is hauled to the scene and forced to clear the last of the loose, manure-ridden dirt from his wife's grave. He shows no emotion and continues to deny any involvement. He tells police that "one of her enemies did it" and that he would tell them who it was, if he could think of anybody with enough of a grudge.

The husband offers no plausible explanation for the death of his wife and denies guilt to the Coroner's Jury. He testifies that the door to his house was locked when he arrived from Erie and that he left and returned to find it unlocked. He looked around the house and the yard for his wife but couldn't find her. John contradicts himself several times during testimony. When it's pointed out, he shrugs his shoulders and says "Well, all right."

Mike McDonnough, manager of the Saegertown Inn, testifies he'd seen husband and wife quarrelling and knew John had attacked Josephine on numerous occasions. McDonnough had, at least twice, stopped him from choking her in the hallways of the Inn and ordered him out of the building.

Miss Sobeski says she'd lived with the couple for two months and there was "seldom a day that they did not quarrel." She saw Muztuck knock his wife to the ground and kick her and heard him threaten to shoot and kill her, same as he had over the phone the night of November 16.

Doctors H.C. McFate and John Hazen's autopsy describes a brutal death. The tiny woman had no broken bones but the body was badly bruised on the legs, thighs, arms, and torso—from the second ribs up to the top of her shoulders. She had been pulled, wounded, from her bed and struck several blows to her head with a pick handle found in the bedroom. Her head was damaged, but death was caused by a violent choking that crushed and hemorrhaged the tissues of her throat. Josephine died of slow suffocation.

The community that did nothing to rescue Josephine from repeated beatings by her abusive husband is outraged by her murder. As Detective Laley and John leave the Coroner's Jury, they are attacked outside the back of the courthouse by "an unorganized but ugly mob of several hundred citizens with a ten-foot length of stout rope tied to the rear of an auto."

A half-dozen unidentified strongmen, hats pulled low over their eyes, make a grab for the prisoner but miss their chance when Laley manages to shove Muztuck back inside the building. The entire Meadville City Police Department and reserves are called. It takes a half-hour to calm and disperse the crowd before the accused can be escorted back to his cell. Officials say the mob might have been successful had they been well-led. It's about as close to a lynching as Crawford ever gets (the courthouse and jail are later connected by a tunnel to facilitate the movement of prisoners).

The Coroner's Jury finds Josie was killed by her husband. When arraigned for the murder, Muztuck enters a plea of "not guilty."

But... following the arraignment, John is taken to the back office of Alderman J.D. Roberts. Coroner Byham tells John they have "buried Josie in a nice Polish ceremony" and, if John is lucky, "he'd have one as nice when he died." Byham implores the prisoner to tell the truth. Meadville Chief of Police Himebaugh takes it from there, telling John things will be better if he tells the truth, that he might have a chance to live. Detective Laley reminds John how they had taken care of him during the attempted lynching.

Muztuck starts talking and makes the following confession as recorded by Court Stenographer Ivan Culbertson:

The devil did it. But the blood is on my hands.

When I start, from Erie, when I get my pay from Erie, from the office. I start uptown and I buy me a quart of whiskey, and before I got that quart I got about five shots in me, before they gave it to me. I go down to the depot to wait for the car and I take some more shots out of the bottle. That don't satisfy me. I wait a little longer and take some more; about half a pint is gone out of quart bottle.

After I get my street car I go in the back end. In the smoking room and sit down there. There was nobody there. I was still drunk. Every little bit I take a shot. Well, before I get home, well, I might as well say over half the bottle is gone. I come home, and I have some left.

Well, I come home and say "hello." She was sitting in the chair alone. I said "hello," and she answered me "hello," and that is all. I started to talk to her and she wouldn't talk and I take some more drink and I finish that bottle. She wouldn't say one thing or another.

I just grabbed her and slammed her down one time and

another, and picked her up and slam her again. I guess maybe I kick her, I can't remember. But I remember I hit her with a piece of wood over her right thigh. She don't want to talk to me, not talk to me at all and I pick her up and I twist her and that is all. That is all I was doing and drop her down again and then I guess I fell asleep.

After I wake up and see her lay on the floor, so I pick her up and put her on the bed and laid there with her. I talked with her and she wouldn't talk. She can't talk then. She wasn't dead then. She was breathing.

I talk with her and she don't know what to do, or one thing or another, so I had her sit on the couch in the sitting room, and the stove burning, so I have her on my knees to talk with her. She wouldn't talk. She is pretty near half gone, and she died right on my knees.

I put her in the front room and lit the candles and lay a cross on her chest. I got down on my knees to pray for peace for her, and then I don't know what to do. I just go down and dig that piece of hole for her and drag her down. That was Thursday. I put her in the hole 6 o'clock Thursday night.

I was crazy drunk. I didn't do it; the devil do it. I am guilty in this case, and that is all. The devil do it, that is all. By my hand do it. There is a blot on my hand right now, there.

~~~~~

Shortly after, stories appearing in the Erie papers describe John as going insane. He is a "cringing, writhing man, suffering untold agonies." He constantly cries, "Look at my hands. There is blood all over them!" It is claimed that he sits on his hands so he can't see them.

Not so, reply officials at the Crawford County Jail. Muztuck hasn't gone around the bend. In fact, he's eating well and sleeping soundly. He isn't even in a separate cell. John spends his time playing his harmonica and beating other prisoners at cards. It is observed that he seems better for the confession, though he may not realize he could be executed.

Lawyers examine 101 potential jurors before filling the box. Mrs. Otto Calrin of Vernon Township is the only woman chosen. She faints before the proceedings begin and is replaced by an alternate. Muztuck ends up with an all-male jury.

At his trial, John sticks to "not guilty" despite his previous full confession. It is an apparent effort to escape the electric chair. His defense attorneys, Wesley B. Best and Walter J. McClintock seek to convince the jury that John was so intoxicated at the time that he should escape with something less than death.

The Commonwealth, represented by District Attorney August Delp and C. Victor Johnson build their case against John "thread by thread." They start with the fact he has a past of threatening and abusing Josephine and do not dwell on drunkenness being a factor.

The prosecution never enters the "alleged" confession into evidence. Instead, they ask detailed questions of Byham and Laley as to their understanding of what John described.

Miss May Sobeski testifies that John repeatedly threatened his wife with death. "He said he was going to get another girl: Josie was too old." It seems John usually started the quarrels, and Josephine would call him bad names. For her part, Josephine was jealous of John and would get angry when he talked to women in the street or at the Saegertown Inn.

Josephine's sister, Mrs. Valentine Posestieski of Erie, tells the court that she saw John kick Josie in the back, and that he often threatened to kill his wife, and was always drunk when he did so. On cross-examination, she says the death threats were the result of what John considered to be the failure of his wife to keep their house in order. Brother-in-law Valentine Posestieski testifies he once took a butcher knife away from John as he chased Josephine with it.

John makes a poor witness in his own defense. He begins by

claiming he was pressured into his confession. He asserts he was "just joking" when he said he wanted to kill his wife.

The accused denies remembering taking any action against his wife. Every time he's asked a pointed question by the prosecution, he replies, "I don't know." He says he thinks somebody else broke into the house and killed Josephine. He buried her and kept it quiet because he wanted to discover for himself what happened.

When asked why he hadn't gone for a doctor when he discovered the severely injured Josephine, John answers it was because she was pretty much gone anyhow and he didn't think a doctor could help. The defendant grows angry and loudly denies accusations. His testimony rambles and contradicts itself. He repudiates his confession then backtracks, saying Josephine disappeared as he slept. He tried to find her but couldn't, then called relatives and friends for help.

Commonwealth lawyer Johnson suggests John quit the stand and go back to his attorneys for more coaching. Defense attorney Best strenuously objects to the statement, saying such an accusation is unprofessional, uncalled for, and ungentlemanly.

When the jury is charged, Judge Thomas Prather tells them they have three choices—guilty in the first degree, with death or life imprisonment, guilty in the second degree, or not guilty.

It takes six ballots before John is found guilty of murder in the first. For the first time in Crawford County history it is the members of the jury who order the execution of a condemned man.

After sentencing, on his way back to jail, Muztuck slips and nearly falls on the icy sidewalk. He quips, "I may fall down and kill myself before I get my death."

It is reported that John cries for a few minutes in his cell, then stands, plays his harmonica, and begins to dance around the corridor. "Oh well," he says. "We all got to die sometimes." He remains a popular inmate and the leader of the socially inclined prisoners, making plain his desire to be merry during the remainder of his numbered days.

But John is not all fun and games. He and fellow prisoner Cecil Kennedy (breaking, entering, and robbery) are caught by Sheriff Charles H. Jones passing notes that detail a jail break and escape. Placed in segregation, the murderer grows violent, throwing all the loose items in his cell through the bars, scattering the corridor with splintered glass and chinaware. He stages a short-lived hunger strike in protest. John angrily tells the sheriff he'll never die in the Chair, that the killing was justified because Josephine wouldn't speak to him.

Sheriff Jones later catches John trying to saw his way to freedom. A search finds a dozen-and-a-half hacksaw blades, three bottles of acid used to soften the metal, and several partially severed bars. The prisoner has been playing the harmonica to cover the sounds of the blade against iron. The source of the contraband is John's many visitors. Access to the murderer is curtailed.

John fakes insanity after seeing fellow prisoners taken to the Warren State Hospital instead of the penitentiary. He constantly mumbles to himself and sets fire to his bed-sheets, claiming unheard voices told him to burn down the jail.

He becomes a "model prisoner" after his failed escape attempts and feigned insanity, but his jailers take no chances. He is placed in solitary confinement and watched, twenty-four hours a day.

Pennsylvania Governor Pinchot sets the execution for July 12, 1926. John already knows the date when he is officially informed, being told by fellow prisoners who read the daily news. Defense attorneys fail to gain a new trial. All legal action ceases. John, like axe-murderer Albert Platt, is one of the few executed in the Commonwealth without seeking pardon, clemency, or reduction of sentence.

~~~~~

The electrocution at Rockview takes place right on schedule. With Catholic Priest O'Hanlon by his side, John enters the death chamber at 7:00 in the morning, eyes closed and in obvious terror. He is strapped to the Chair and connections are applied to his forehead and ankle. The killer offers no last words. The first 45-second contact is at 7:02; the second at 7:03; the last at 7:04. The prison physician pronounces John dead at 7:06.

After the required autopsy, Muztuck is buried in the penitentiary's graveyard. He does not receive the "nice Polish ceremony" afforded by the church to the wife he murdered.

1926, APRIL 26: Location: Titusville hospital. Victim: Baby Dow. Suspect: Miss Dow. Act: Death due to lack of proper attention. Notes: Mother is a nurse at Titusville City Hospital. Gives birth, puts baby in the locked closet of her room. Nobody at the hospital has been aware of Miss Dow's "condition." Outcome: Not Found.

1926, AUGUST 15: Location: Union Township. Victim: Fern D. Dawley (male, 43). Suspect: George Stitt (70), Act: Shot during an argument. Notes: Suspect admits shooting but claims self-defense. Is uncooperative and contrary on the stand. Outcome: Found guilty of murder in the second. Sentenced to not less than 7-and-a-half nor more than 15 years in solitary at Western Penitentiary.

1926, NOVEMBER 8: Location: Meadville. Victim: Frank Mariarz. Suspect: Mike DeMaio. Act: Death due to being struck on head with a water glass during an argument over a poker game. Notes: The victim does not regard his injuries as serious until weeks pass and he is found to have severe meningitis caused by hemorrhaging of the brain together with an internal fracture of the skull. The suspect is arrested on complaint of the victim's wife, Sophie. DeMaio is originally charged with assault and battery but that's changed to murder in light of the victim's death. After six hour deliberation the jury finds him guilty of manslaughter with a recommendation for mercy. State admits DeMaio has reputation of a peaceful, law-abiding citizen. Outcome: Judge Prather sentences him to 2 to 4 years in Western Penitentiary, a fine of $5, and the costs of prosecution. Parole may be applied for at the end of the first year provided good conduct in prison.

1927: Werner Heisenberg's uncertain. Pez® candies by Haas. The guy with the best inventor's name ever, Philo Farnsworth, builds a complete electronic TV. Technicolor comes to life, as does the iron lung. Lucky Lindy lands at Le Bourget Field in Paris, France. *The Jazz Singer.* The Academy Awards. On May 26, the last Model-T Ford rolls off the assembly line. It's the 15,000,000th!

1927, July: Of 71 sentences in Crawford County Court so far this year, 33 have been for liquor convictions of one sort or another. That about matches the average for the rest of the United States.

Let's Take a Trip to the 'Burg!

Sadsbury Township, in the west-central portion of the county, is a cornucopia of glacial landforms, the most striking of which is the largest natural body of water in the Commonwealth: the two-and-a-half mile long and mile wide Conneaut Lake.

The area was settled fairly early in the county's history. Though he was not the area's first white settler, Abner Evans established a gristmill and a town, Evansburg, in 1796 at Conneaut Lake's single, southern outlet. A litigious individual, Abner appears as plaintiff many times in Crawford County's earliest civil court records. He stuck around for several years, then vanished by 1813. Some think he became the first white settler (1816) of Bean Blossom Township, Monroe County, west-central Indiana.

In the 1830s, Conneaut Lake was raised ten feet to provide water for the Erie-Beaver canal that was dug a few miles to the west to connect the Ohio River and the Great Lakes. The extra-large lake possessed huge marshlands that bred great swarms of insects. The fear of disease they might carry nearly de-populated both Evansburg and the surrounding area.

The canal years ended in 1871 with the collapse of the Elk Creek Aqueduct, near Erie, Pennsylvania. The dam holding the lake was cut in 1873 and the modern shoreline was established.

Rail passenger service arrived along the old canal rights-of-way in 1881. Eleven years later, the city fathers officially changed the name of their tourist-oriented town from Evansburg to "Conneaut Lake."

"I Never Saw a Sweeter Smile"

Seventeen-year-old Clinton Schroedel's family hails from Pittsburgh, Pennsylvania where his father, Philip, has retired from People's Natural Gas. Seeking to improve Clinton's health, impaired by the influenza epidemic of the previous decade, the family leaves the famously-smoke-filled city and moves to a farm in Sheakleyville, Mercer County. When it proves too large, the family buys a smaller plot of land near Conneaut Lake in Sadsbury Township.

Clinton is a bright young man, standing near the top of his junior class at the local high school. Popular, he has good manners, good looks, and drives his own car. He's happy to taxi his many friends to and from school, church, picnics, and other activities.

Among his acquaintances are the two Mellon girls who

live about a mile and a half west of the Lake on the paved road to Linesville. Clinton often drives Lorraine, 15, and Bonita, 13, to school and home again. He sometimes ferries them to social outings, but has never paid romantic attention to either girl. They are all just friends and nothing more.

Such is the case following a football game at Conneaut Lake High School on October 8, 1927.

Lorraine happens to be the last of several kids Clinton drives home. As any proper young lady would, she asks her mother's permission for her friend to sit on their front porch. Beside planning for a bonfire, the girl wants to show Clinton her new guitar.

A short time later, Edward Peterman, the girl's 37-year-old stepfather, arrives at the house with his farm-cart and team of horses. He and Lorraine's mother had married in May of 1926. It took only a few months to become obvious that Peterman was seriously, perhaps pathologically infatuated with his 15-year-old stepdaughter.

He doesn't like Lorraine having contact with anyone outside the family and does his best to deny her visitors, girls or boys. If his stepdaughter is visited when he is around, Peterman sulks, silent and angry. Last winter he saw her at a dance with a boy and refused to speak to her for the next half-year. Young Schroedel is not aware that Lorraine's step-father harbors such obsessive feelings.

Peterman recognizes the car. He urges his team forward, pulls close, and uses his farm cart to scrape the fenders of the vehicle. The man mounts the steps of the front porch.

"How long is this going to continue?" Peterman asks the girl.

"My mother said it was all right for me to have this young man call."

Peterman walks into the house and immediately returns with a .28 Colt automatic pistol. He fires at the girl who slumps forward in her chair. Clinton vaults the porch-rail and makes a dash for his car.

Peterman jumps to the ground and takes careful aim. Clinton is shot once through the neck and spine. The man places the revolver against the right side of his own head and pulls the trigger. He does not immediately fall from his self-inflicted wound but runs towards the boy before collapsing. The automatic slips from his grip and lands a short distance from his right hand.

Mrs. Peterman does not see, but hears the shooting. Once outside, she checks Lorraine. The girl is unconscious, but unharmed. She had fainted at the sight of the gun and fell forward as her stepfather tried to shoot her. Peterman missed the girl, but probably thought he'd shot her dead.

Bonita, the younger sister, is sent to the Schroedel home about a mile away. County Detective John Laley, Deputy Sheriff Lyle Jones and his younger brother, Martin Jones, arrive at the scene to find Dr. H.L. Brush of Conneaut Lake giving aid to Clinton.

It is obvious the boy is mortally wounded. Laley tries to get a dying statement. Says Laley: "I asked him if he knew me and I never saw a sweeter smile when he indicated by the nod of his head he did. I then asked if he knew what I was there for and he nodded again."

"'Did this man shoot you?' I asked him, and he said 'yes' loud enough for those about him to hear. By that time his father was there, and when Mr. Schroedel told those in charge he 'wanted the best of care taken of his boy,' the lad heard and understood, for again his countenance lighted up with his wonderful smile."

The victim and perpetrator are taken in same ambulance to Spencer Hospital in Meadville. There, Drs. Snodgrass and Gamble agree with Brush that there is no hope for either.

Clinton is paralyzed from the shoulders down but remains conscious and able to talk. Nurses and family members speak encouragingly about his condition, but when an older brother tells him he'll still be around in a week or two, Clinton replies. "That's a lotta baloney. I know what's going to happen to me and it's not going to be very long, either."

Shortly after, he sends for his mother and asks her to kiss him. Then he asks for his father. When he appears the boy says he is sleepy and thinks he might take a nap. Clinton dozes off and never awakens, passing on at 1:50, the morning of Sunday, October 9th. Edward Peterman never regains consciousness, dying of his self-inflicted wound three and a half hours later.

Funerals for both were held from their respective homes on the afternoon of October 11, 1927. The shooter was buried in Cochranton, the dead boy in Conneaut Lake's Lakeview Cemetery. I was unable to find his grave.

1927, NOVEMBER 29: Location: Vernon Township, two miles west of Meadville on Conneaut Lake Road. Victim: William Michael Waitschis a.k.a. Michael W. Waite a.k.a. Michael W. Stain a.k.a. Michael W. Stein. Suspects: None. Act: Shot in lower stomach. Notes: Been in the area for three weeks having arrived from Syracuse, New York where local police say he is a bootlegger. Staying at the Midland Hotel. Has lots of money. Is invited by friends "for a good meal." Found alongside the road by a motorbus driver. Gives a disconnected and evasive story of shooting. Cops think he knows who his attackers are, but will not say. Outcome: Unsolved.

1928 – 1948

The Honorable O. Clare Kent

Thomas J. Prather loses re-election to a third term. O. Clare Kent becomes President Judge. His portrait has us disturbing his reading of what looks like a book of laws. He glances up at us, a stray forelock mischievously falling away from the rest of his brown-shot-with gray hair. He has a full, oval face with dark eyes behind round, wire-rim glasses perched on a somewhat thin nose and a neat, brown moustache over a thin-lipped mouth graced by the slightest hint of a curious smile.

Born June 15, 1876 in North Shenango Township at Espyville, Kent attends school there until the age of nine when his parents move to Linesville where he finishes his public education. He starts Allegheny College in 1892, graduating four years later. Law student Kent reads at the office of Josiah Douglas in Meadville and is admitted to the bar on May 30, 1900.

In 1906 Kent begins the first of two, three-year terms as Crawford County District Attorney where he builds a reputation for aggressive eloquence. He then serves as the County Solicitor from 1912 to 1916. He is a "stalwart Republican" and chairman of that party's county committee for two successive terms. Attorney Kent is in demand for both defense and prosecution as he sharpens his practice of law in the ten years before his 1927 election to President Judge.

Kent is the first person born in the western part of the county to win the job. He successfully runs again in 1937. Judge Kent begins wearing a judicial robe while on the bench at the start of his second term and is the first county judge to do so on a regular basis.

He is in charge and organized from the start. He is seen as dignified, honest, and fair. He never misses a day in court. No matter the case, he remains faithful to his principles. Well known as a stickler for detail, he insists the preparation of papers submitted by attorneys in his court be entirely correct. The judge loves to keep the lawyers "on their toes."

An avid family man, his courthouse chambers are filled pictures of his children and grandchildren. He also has a knack for growing flowers.

He is nearly seventy when his second term comes to an end. Citizen Kent retires and stays busy, spending his time with family and friends, community work, and gardening. His health begins to fail, and 81-year-old O. Clare Kent dies in Meadville's Spencer Hospital on June 23, 1957.

1928: Amelia flies the Atlantic. Bubble gum invented. Penicillin discovered. Mickey Mouse® created. Shick® electric razors are the cutting edge. What could be better? How about sliced bread and Velveeta®? Both go on sale. Former President Judge John J. Henderson dies.

COLT'S NEW STATION

Linesville, in Pine Township, western Crawford County, had what could be considered a stuttering start. In the early days of the county, the Pennsylvania Population Company, charged with selling tracts of frontier, was trying to establish villages to draw buyers. In 1800, company agent Jabez Colt built a mill on a small run in what would become Pine Township. He called it "Colt's New Station" to distinguish it from "Colt's Station," a venture that had failed a few miles to the north.

Alas, the serious lack of neighbors meant a serious lack of grist for Jabez Colt's new mill. It, and a nearby tannery, failed. Mr. Colt and associates went on their way.

Enter one Amos Line. A surveyor for the Pennsylvania Population Company, he bought a few tracts of land in the same area Jabez Colt had pioneered and, in 1818, started to work. He established something like a general store in his first house, a log structure.

Five years later, his frontier home burned to the ground. Relocating a few miles to the south, Line came upon the remains of Colt's New Station. After living in what was an abandoned log cabin, he moved his family to the west of the run, up the hill and, in 1825, built what was the first wood-frame home in Pine Township. Line laid out his "ville" around that same time. The plat was recorded in 1838.

First known as "Line's Mill," the town's first attempt at incorporation, in the spring of 1862, failed because an enrollment tax was not paid and elections for officials could not be held. It was another two years before the village was able to fulfill all of its obligations and come to life as "Linesville Station." It dropped the last half of its name in 1883.

Amos Line did not live to see the elections. He had died nine years earlier at the age of seventy-seven. He left behind a family of four sons, two daughters, and a village that was built because he was fortunate enough to have his first home burn down.

A Figure Steps From the Shadows

It's the early morning hours of November 4, 1928. Frank Garthman, from Greenville, Mercer County, and thirty-four year old Mary Wallace of Linesville, are at the end of an enjoyable evening spent together at the nearby Maple Corners Dance Hall. The two have been keeping company for several weeks. Frank knows his lady-friend separated four months back from her husband and has started divorce proceedings against him.

They arrive at the Linesville home of Mary's mother, Mrs. Hilda (Nettie) Jack, at about 1:30 in the morning. Frank walks Mary to the door and gives her a goodnight kiss. The woman bids him farewell. He turns from the porch and starts back to his car.

A figure steps from the shadows, aims a .38 caliber revolver, and fires three times. The first shot goes high, burying itself in the ceiling of the porch. The second strikes Garthman, shattering his left arm and collarbone. The final shot hits Mary in the abdomen. The bullet perforates her intestines several times as it goes in one side and out the other.

Hilda Jack calls the cops. The first to arrive is Conneaut Lake Police Chief Joe Cannon. Mary tells him "Ray shot me." Ray being her not-quite-ex-husband and father of their fourteen-year-old daughter, Irene.

Upon questioning, Mary's mother reveals that Ray had telephoned several hours before the shooting. She describes him as sounding "quite badly intoxicated." Another person volunteers he saw Ray at the Maple Corners Dance Hall, armed with not one, but two loaded revolvers.

More damning is his overcoat, found on the ground 150 feet from the shooting. In one pocket, the sliced bacon he'd bought at a Lineville butcher earlier in the day. It's obvious Ray was laying in wait. When Mary dies on November 6, the charge is murder in the first degree, if Ray can be found. With as many clues as he left the night of the shooting you'd think that'd be easy. But Wallace proves himself invisible in the days after the crime.

There are rumors of gunshots in the nearby woods of

Pymatuning Swamp. Many locals figure Ray killed himself out of remorse. The police aren't so sure. Sheriff Charles H. Jones and Detective John Laley arrange for Pymatuning to be searched as well as it can be for the murderer's body, but both are of the opinion their suspect planned his escape; Ray Wallace had secured a large sum of money before the shooting, disposing of anything that might be turned into cash.

They begin their search for the fugitive by checking several Ohio cities where the suspect has relatives. No luck. They expand their search, sending out bulletins, first to regional authorities and then to police across the nation. All fruitless.

~~~~~

Five years later, almost to the day of the shooting, police in St. Louis, Missouri encounter a wild-looking, mostly incoherent man. He talks of wandering the country on the run from the law. He raves about going blind, how he needs to surrender because of the crimes he's committed.

It's Ray Wallace. He's extradited to Crawford County to stand trial for the premeditated murder of his wife.

From the moment Wallace arrives, it's obvious he's not right in the head. Judge Kent orders a psychiatric examination that finds the accused insane. He is sent to Warren State Hospital until cured, at which time he will be returned to court for trial. I found no record of a release.

1929: Herbert Hoover is President of the United States. The car radio is invented. The N.Y. Stock Market crashes, starting the Great Depression. The Yo-Yo® becomes an American fad that has its ups-and-downs. Martin Luther King is born a year after his assassin, James Earl Ray.

1929, July 12: Location: Meadville, 1000-block Bessemer Street. Victim: Philip Toppo (65). Suspect: Andro Trotto. Act: Stabbed during a drunken fight over a game of "Briscoloa." Notes: Six men held and released in connection with the death of victim, a retired railroader. Trotto flees the area, convincing cops he's guilty. Every clue is followed but the suspect vanishes. *Trotto is arrested in Newark, New Jersey, fourteen years later* and returned for trial. He feared vengeance, particularly from the victim's two sons. In all the years he was gone, he never once wrote his wife or thirteen kids in Meadville. Outcome: Jury finds for involuntary manslaughter after four hours deliberation. Judge Kent's sentence, not less than 3 nor more than 12 years at the Allegheny Workhouse.

1929, AUGUST 31: Location: Woodcock Township, Saegertown. Victim: Edward Brown (40). Suspects: Mrs. Cora Stainbrook and Mrs. Sue Dewey in complicity, and Mr. Clark (Claude) Boulton for murder. Act: Several blows to head with an automobile crank. Notes: Victim is a "yard boy" at the Saegertown Inn. Came from Canada several months ago. Is beat over head because "he would not shut up" while returning from a "booze joint" in Paigeville, Erie County. Found the next day, dumped at the rear door of the Inn. Boulton admits striking victim on head with the crank during a drunken argument. Did not intend death. Didn't know the victim's skull was fractured when they dumped him. Outcome: Charge reduced to involuntary manslaughter.

1929, SEPTEMBER 18: For the first time in Crawford County, all 12 jurors in a criminal trial are women. Mrs. Anna Geyeuski (40), South Street, Titusville, is found guilty of shooting, with intent to kill, her neighbor, John Sagan (45), a man she claims is responsible for both her yet unborn child and snitching her husband out to police for violation of the liquor laws. Accusations that Sagan, widower and father of eight, denies.

1929, November 9:00: Location: Meadville. Victim: Rodney Jones. Suspect: Dathon (Dathan) Gilbert. Act: Shot during argument. Notes: Victim is well know as a car washer at various garages in Titusville. Is killed instantly when shot through his body twice with one bullet piercing the heart. Gilbert admits shooting. Crime committed after both men had done some heavy drinking. Gilbert says he shot when he thought the victim was going to pull a gun from his own hip pocket. Victim's wife had to be threatened with jail to gain cooperation on the witness stand. Outcome: Murder in the second after three hours of deliberation. Sentenced to pay costs, and not less than 8 nor more than 16 years of solitary confinement and hard labor in Western Penitentiary.

1930: A new planet, Pluto, is discovered. It's later decided the poor thing isn't a planet after all, or maybe it is. Our own planet grows much neater thanks to Scotch Tape®, and traveling about it will be much faster due to the jet engine. The "differential analyzer" is invented at MIT by Vannevar Bush. Crawford County's population rebounds 4% to 62,980. Past President William Howard Taft dies of heart disease.

1930, month ? day ?: Location: Randolph Township, H.M. Cutshall's farm. Victim: Viable infant boy. Suspect: None. Outcome: Unsolved.

1931, April 15: Location: Meadville. Victim: John W. Holt (white, 43). Suspect: George Wade (black, 60). Act: Gunshot. Notes: Victim is Captain of Detectives for Erie Railroad. Shot April 7 (his birthday) attempting to "arrest a gang of Negroes trespassing on railroad property." Suspect says he shot after Holt had already shot twice. Witnesses tell the same story. Trial is fairly stormy. Judge Kent allows no more than 100 spectators, then locks the door. Outcome: Jury decides murder in the second degree. Wade receives no less than 8 nor more than 16 years in Western Penitentiary.

1932: A practical method of mechanical air conditioning is invented. Zippo® lighters are introduced from Bradford, McKean County, Pennsylvania. Duke Ellington's *It Don't Mean a Thing if It Ain't Got That Swing.* The "Bonus Army" marches on Washington D.C. and is, eventually, repelled with troops and tanks. The Lindbergh's baby is nowhere to be found. Future President Judge Herbert A. Mook is admitted to the bar.

1932, FEBRUARY 8: Location: Meadville. Victim: Albert Boush (husband, 65). Suspect: Mrs. Blanche Boush (wife, 55). Act: Shot through left eye and head with a rusty .32 caliber revolver. Notes: Husband had repeatedly threatened the suspect. Suspect admits shooting. Claims self-defense and pleads not guilty. Husband was drunk and threatened to shoot her after she refused to comply with his demands of "unnatural acts." She was prompted to fire first by "a strange look in his eye." Outcome: Acquitted by the jury after 5 hours of deliberation. Judge Kent gavels the court to silence when the spectators burst into applause.

1932, MARCH 30: Location: East Mead Township between Frenchtown and Meadville. Victim: George Slingluff (71). Suspect: Clinton Hamilton (brother-in-law). Act: Gunshot during argument over personal property on a farm. Notes: Also shot two other men, one in the groin and leg and the other (his brother) in both calves. Suspect surrenders immediately after shooting and claims it was in self-defense. This is denied by his own brother. Hamilton speaks freely with police though warned it could be used against him. In jail suspect tries to slash his wrists with a safety razor and then goes on a hunger strike. Outcome: Court finds him to be of unsound mind and mentally unbalanced. Sent to Warren State Hospital.

SPELL IT RIGHT — "PYMATUNING"

Much of Pymatuning Swamp, in the southwest corner of Crawford County, was ill-suited for use by anybody except Mother Nature. Early settlers found its spongy and water-saturated surface too wet to farm except in the driest of conditions. Plans to transform the swamp into something more useful date to the 1860s, except, back then, the idea was to channel the water and drain it from the marsh.

People living on the edge of Pymatuning found the place alive with all kinds of animals, some of them big enough to bring down livestock that might wander into the swamp. It could be a treacherous place, with hidden pools, quicksand, briars and brambles, not to mention blood-sucking insects, dangerously big snapping turtles, and biting snakes.

Building a flood-control dam on the troublesome Shenango River below Pymatuning had already been discussed when a disastrous flood in 1913 spurred the Commonwealth to action. The Pennsylvania General Assembly approved a control dam for the river and budgeted a little over a million dollars. Governor John Tener did his part by slashing that amount to a paltry $100,000. It took nearly two decades to raise the four million in funds it took to build the dam at the foot of the swamp, just upstream from Jamestown, Mercer County.

Pymatuning Reservoir is estimated to hold about 64 billion gallons of water, cover around 17,000 acres, and possess somewhere near 70 miles of shoreline. Its original purpose of flood-control is usually forgotten by the people who use the area for recreation in their visits to the Pymatuning State Parks located in both Pennsylvania and Ohio.

The name of the swamp and lake is said to be a corruption of "Pihmtomink," a Native American reference to a Lenape chief whose group lived in the area. The chief must have had quite the reputation. The original word is typically translated into something like "The Liar Lives There."

"Not so Badly Decomposed"

Late April 1932. Norman E. Hartweg of Warren, Pennsylvania, doctoral candidate of Herpetology at the University of Michigan, is tromping along through the cold muck of the north end of Pymatuning Swamp. He's looking for turtles and snakes. Head on a swivel, he works to cover as much territory as possible. Construction is underway on the Jamestown dam. Once it's completed, Hartweg knows, the land he's walking will be under a heck of a lot of water.

The young man is almost a caricature of a scientist: skinny, glasses, smokes a pipe. Little interests him besides his work, but he's about to have a field experience that has nothing to do with reptiles.

Hartweg is near Linesville, a good distance from the unimproved road that runs through the area. He's bushwhacking through the tangle when he stumbles upon a woman's body, wrapped in a torn overcoat and half-buried in the soft earth. She is wearing galoshes.

Norman hurries to the road and his car. He drives to Linesville and reports what he's found to police. He marks a map with his discovery. Then, seemingly unruffled, returns to his field work.

The brush is so thick that, even with Hartweg's map, officials can't find the body. They must wait until the scientist returns to town so he can lead them to the spot.

The police think the woman was killed elsewhere and brought to the swamp to be hidden. They base this on a piece of heavy rope they find near the body, surmising it was used to drag her from the road to her resting place. They note no effort was made to hide the body after it was placed in the brush.

Deputy Coroner Arthur E. Byham examines the corpse. He thinks the woman was a foreigner and around forty-years old. He finds the skull broken as if with a hammer and the throat cut from ear to ear. It's Byham's opinion that the body has been in the swamp for about six months. He thinks someone who knew the woman might be able to identify her, because her face is "not so badly decomposed."

There have been no local reports of missing women. That leads State Police to think that she may be from Ohio, but all leads fail. The unfortunate woman's body is buried in Linesville the week after she's found.

She's exhumed a month later so that Mr. Anthony Parado and his mother, from Venango Township in the north-central tier of Crawford County, can view the body.

It seems Parado's wife, thirty-seven year old Caroline, had grown weary of farm life. He had given her money to return to her native Poland but had not heard from her since December 22, 1931. Officials find no record of a passport issued to her. The clothing on the body matches what she owned. The height and hair are similar. But neither Mr. Parado nor his mother will confirm or deny it is Caroline. The body is reburied. The case is unsolved.

~~~~~

Student Norman Edouard Hartweg went on to become a Professor of Zoology at the University of Michigan, picking up the odd nickname "Kibe" along the way. He worked thirty years as the Curator of the Division of Reptiles and Amphibians at his university's Museum of Zoology.

Dr. Hartweg described several new species of animal and

was honored by being the species namesake of at least a soft-shelled turtle, Apalone spinifera hartwegi (Hartweg's Spine-bearing Soft-shell), and a salamander, Bolitoglossa hartwegi (Hartweg's Climbing Salamander). He died suddenly, February 16, 1964, a few days shy of his sixty-fourth birthday.

P.S. A "kibe," is typically defined as "a chapped or inflamed area on the skin, especially on the heel, resulting from exposure to cold." There are worse nicknames, I guess.

1932, NOVEMBER 28: Location: Meadville, Mead Avenue. Victim: Elma (Gulick) Kinley (wife, 37). Suspect: Walter Kinley (husband, 39). Act: Multiple gunshots to the abdomen. Notes: Estranged husband arrives from Corry, Erie County, in the late evening to talk. Son, Walter Jr. (8) is put to bed. Husband wants to reconcile. Wife refuses. He pulls out .22 revolver and shoots her three time in the gut. Then, places the revolver in his mouth and pulls the trigger. Boy runs to nearby home of his uncle, Harold Gulick, who returns to find the bodies. Murdered woman is daughter of Mr. and Mrs. Eugene Gulick of Mead Avenue. Their other daughter, this victim's sister, was stuck and killed by a stray bullet on June 20, 1911. Walter Jr. (who possess a touch of the trouble-maker in him) is raised by his grandparents, graduates from Meadville High School in 1941, joins the marines, and survives the Pacific during the Second World War. He marries the pretty and exotic-looking Miss Doris May Meyers of Southampton, England in a hometown ceremony on May 18, 1950 and vanishes from the local papers.

1933: Franklin Roosevelt is President of the Unites States. The Dust Bowl. The U.S. says "Cheers!" when the Twenty-First Amendment to the United States Constitution is ratified by the states and approved by Congress. Citizens are happy to toast the end of Prohibition. Past President Calvin Coolidge dies of a heart attack.

1934: The cheeseburger is "invented." Really? It took that long? The board game, Monopoly® is invented (so they say), so is the tape recorder, for the, uh, record. Japan says it doesn't have to follow international treaties, if it doesn't want to. Sounds like trouble. Former President Judge Frank J. Thomas dies.

1934, FEBRUARY 5: Location: Bloomfield Township, Lincolnville. Victim: Mary Richards (mother, 50). Suspect: John Richards (son, 28), Act: Beating. Death caused by fractured skull and blood clots on brain. Notes: Pleads not guilty due to lack of legal representation. Death occurs during a drinking party. Son tells mother to return with him to their home. Mother refuses. Son knocks mother to the floor, stands astride her, "and rained blow after blow upon her head." Victim portrayed by defense as being an overweight alcoholic with a bad heart. Some question about the skill of the doctor performing the autopsy. Outcome: Jury finds, on second ballot after 90 minutes, guilty of murder in the second degree. Judge Kent sentences the guilty man to not less than 8 nor more than 16 years in Western Penitentiary. Richards goes crazy a short time into his jail term. Kent orders treatment for his criminal insanity at Fairview Hospital in northeastern Pennsylvania. During the transfer, the prisoner attacks the deputies in the car and must be subdued and tied down with ropes for the remainder of the ride.

1934, MARCH 2: Location: Meadville. Victim: LeRoy Sugar (28). Suspect: None. Act: Multiple gunshot wounds. Notes: Victim was a fruit dealer. Killed upon opening an outside door of his brother-in-law's home. Two shots enter his body, a third grazes his cheek, a fourth is found in the door's jamb. Sugar had been implicated in bootlegging cases. Said to have made enemies by turning "stool pigeon" for the cops, a charge police emphatically deny. Outcome: Unsolved.

1934, June 11: Location: Meadville. Victim: Joseph Cardinale (56). Suspect: Thomas Belifore (65). Act: Gunshot to the head. Notes: Suspect surrenders to cops right after shooting saying the victim had threatened him and his family unless he paid $10,000 in protection money. Pleads not guilty. Had complained to police since the first of April that he was receiving threatening letters from "*La Mano Nera*" ("The Black Hand") of Warren, Pennsylvania. Questions about the authenticity of the letters. Outcome: Found guilty of manslaughter after less than four hours of deliberation. Judge Kent's sentence is not less than 3 nor more than 6 years at Allegheny Workhouse. Belifore's age and illness prompts Kent to direct parole after about a year into his sentence. An editorial in the *Titusville Herald* states: "We had no feeling whatever about the recent murder trial in Meadville, but it is rather reassuring that a man who deliberately shoots down another on the public street does not go scot-free."

1935: Nylon for stockings. Canned beer. Radar. Benny Goodman, Tommy Dorsey, Glenn Miller, and the rest of those "Big Band" guys. Social Security starts collecting, to begin paying two years later. The Hoover Dam. Alcoholic Anonymous. Elvis Presley is born.

"I Had a Scary Feeling"

May 9, 1935. Nineteen year old Anna Shellenberger runs, crying and exhausted, into Kerrtown's Maltbie & Morrisy Garage and shouts for somebody, anybody, to call the cops. Mr. Maltbie does just that. Highway Patrolman Corporal C.H. Blocker, County Detective R.O. McIntosh and Deputy Coroner A.E. Byham respond.

They arrive to find the nearly hysterical woman sitting alongside the road. She instructs them to take her the mile to her home that sits across the street from her in-laws, the Harry Colemans. There, they find her twenty-six-year-old husband, Joseph Shellenberger, in bed. He's barely breathing and that's something of a surprise considering most of the top of his head is missing. The 16-gauge shotgun Anna used to remove his crown is still in the room.

Anna says they quarreled when her husband returned from his third-shift work at Hookless Fastener (a forerunner of Meadville's famous "Talon Zipper"). They had gone to bed where the argument continued. As she put it, she decided, "I might as well end it." She got up, went across the street, and snuck into the house of her in-laws. There, she stole the weapon she used to blast her sleeping husband's head.

When asked why, she replies, "Joe liked his mother better than he liked me, so I shot him."

The wounded man soon dies. Shellenberger appears remorseful for her crime. She asks to view the body and does so in the company of police. She violently weeps and cries, over and over, "I wish it was me!"

The Coroner's Jury finds her actions to be the cause of her husband's death. At her arraignment she's told she has to enter a plea of "not guilty" because she has no counsel. "What's the use," she asks, "of me pleading 'not guilty'?"

At her preliminary hearing, a court-assigned physician judges her mentally imbalanced and sends her to Warren State Hospital for examination, evaluation, and treatment. Dr. Ira A. Darling declares her mentally fit at the end of the summer. Judge Kent orders Shellenberger returned to the Crawford County courts. It's time for her to face the consequences of her actions.

The Grand Jury returns a true bill against what the press describes as the "attractive, modishly dressed Polish girl." Her criminal trial starts on September 12, 1935, eight days before her twentieth birthday. Judge O. Clare Kent is on the bench. District Attorney Stuart A. Culbertson seeks murder in the first degree. Arden D. Mook, her court-appointed defense attorney, sticks with the plea of not guilty.

With the victim's sister alongside the accused, jury selection begins. The lawyers reject many potential jurors, either because of opinions already formed or opposition to the death penalty. They settle on nine men and five women for the panel of twelve jurors and two alternates.

The first witness against the "comely young woman" is her mother-in-law, Mrs. Mary Coleman. She testifies that she saw her son arrive home the morning of the shooting. She later left her own house to visit friends. Upon returning, she found the shotgun missing. It's easy to see Mrs. Coleman doesn't think much of her daughter-in-law. She admits to once calling the girl a "cock-eyed Pollack."

Shellenberger's neighbor, fifteen-year-old Kelly SanFelice describes how the accused appeared at her parent's home the morning of the killing and asked to borrow a shotgun and some shells. SanFelice did not lend them because Shellenberger "looked so queer."

Dr. Paul Rastatter, Shellenberger's personal physician takes the stand. He testifies the accused has been mentally ill for the past two years, particularly since last February when she had to quit her job at Hookless Fastener. The doctor says she once told him, "I'm going to kill Joe. Something tells me to." Rastatter admits on cross-examination that he supposes the young woman could probably "realize the consequences of shooting Joe," despite her illness.

The dead man's sister, Mrs. Mary Dilley says she noticed "a change" in her sister-in-law after she left her job. She grew melancholy and was always crying. She said she had no friends and everyone was down on her.

When Anna Shellenberger takes the stand, she is nervous and emotional with an unstable disposition. She never lived with her biological family, now in New Jersey. She has no childhood memories of her parents other than the name "Urbanwaicz." Shellenberger was raised by and used the name of the "Reezolski" family who lives on Mill Street in Kerrtown.

She was sixteen years old when she married the victim. They moved in across the street from her in-laws. Trouble soon developed between her, her husband, and his mother. The three of them fought constantly about Joe's drinking and relationships with other women. Joe's mom always sided with her son.

After searching for and finding her biological mother in a New Jersey sanitarium, Shellenberger says she was obsessed with the fear of being "sick, just like my mother." When she confided in her husband, he responded that, if it happened, he would leave her.

Her attorney asks the young woman to describe her February breakdown that forced her to quit her job. She replies, "I hollered and I screamed and cried, and I felt like nobody cared. I had a scary feeling."

After three hours of questioning by prosecution lawyers, Shellenberger bursts into hysterics, shouting, "I've admitted I killed him and that's all I know about it and hope you're satisfied!"

In closing arguments, defense attorney Mook describes the preponderance of the evidence as clearly showing the young woman to be "generally insane." She is, he says, a clear victim of "homicidal mania."

D.A. Culbertson refutes that characterization, pushing strongly for murder in the first degree. Not for the death penalty, he says, but so Shellenberger can be put away for life, where she can have care and treatment.

When Judge Kent charges the jurors he explains their task, and options, and sends them into deliberation.

The jurors are experiencing their own set of problems. Clifford McKay is taken ill earlier in the day and rendered unable to hear testimony. He is replaced by alternate Virginia McDaniel. As required, the other alternate is excused once the jury is charged by Judge Kent. Then, several hours into deliberation, juror Minnie Langworthy becomes "terribly nervous" and is removed from the room. It's hoped a good night's rest will solve the problem. A mistrial will result if she's unable to continue.

Langworthy rallies to complete the deliberation. Shellenberger is found not guilty, acquitted "for the reason of insanity." The vote is 10 to 2 for acquittal. The two jurors who think her guilty are women.

Judge Kent explains the verdict: The young lady was incompetent at the time of the crime. She may or may not be that way now.

Anna Shellenberger weeps when the decision is announced. She is kept in the Crawford County Jail for a few more days and then sent to her birth-family in New Jersey. Her father is there. She has a sister who is a nun. They will care for her.

1935, AUGUST 13, 6:00am: Location: Meadville railroad yards. Victim: Harry Johnston. Suspect: None. Act: Gunshot to left chest. Notes: A "youthful transient" finds the victim drunk, partially clothed, and shot. Is cut on his right hand. Victim lives for 2 days and, during that time, is of no help to authorities other than insisting he does not want the cops involved. Outcome: Unsolved.

1936: Guitars are "electrified." Hoover Dam is completed. Polaroid sunglasses. Sunblock. *Gone with the Wind*, the book, that is. Helicopters begin flying. The last public execution in the U.S. takes place in Owensboro,

Kentucky, when the confessed rapist/murderer Rainey Bethea is hanged (for rape).

1937: "Oh! The humanity" in the Hindenburg. On happier notes, the Golden Gate Bridge and the Appalachian Trail. The science fiction convention gets its start in Leeds, England. Pennsylvania makes Flag Day an official state holiday. Amelia Earhart loses her way—for good. Japan attacks China—not good. Steinbeck's *Of Mice and Men*.

1937, NOVEMBER 3: Location: Meadville, Mercer Street Poolroom, near "West Street District." Victim: Fain Strickland (black). Suspect: James Walls (Wals) (black) of Niles, OH. Act: Shot after a fight over eight cents in a poker game. Notes: Walls enters the pool room, drunk, shortly after 8:00 in the evening and gets into an argument with a local. Suspect leaves the bar for about 15 minutes, returns with a concealed weapon, renews the trouble, pulls out the revolver, and fires six times. One bullet strikes the victim who runs into the street and dies. Suspect has previous record. Outcome: After six hours of deliberation, jury finds Walls guilty of murder in the second degree. Sentence is a fine of $25 and costs and not less than 6 nor more that 12 years at Western Penitentiary. Judge Kent also comments: "Trouble springs from the poolroom at Mercer and West. It is an unwholesome atmosphere operated exclusively for Negroes. It encourages gambling and there's a connection with an adjoining West Street 'house.' It would be a good thing for the officials to take care of the place and it should be either 'washed out' or 'washed down' French Creek." Both businesses remain open.

1937, NOVEMBER 9, 8:10am: Location: Meadville, Garden Street. Victim: Margaret Catalino (divorced, 32). Suspect: Charles Dellario (Meadville liquor dealer, 36). Act. Gunshot 4 times to the chest and abdomen. Notes: Victim and suspect are carrying on an "illicit love affair." Meadville Police Chief Hays says victim had reported physical abuse and death threats by the suspect on "numerous occasions" and knew her life was in danger. Suspect leaves a signed note on a chair in the victim's kitchen: "I hope that the whole world forgives us, for we both have done wrong and both will suffer for we are both to blame." After the shooting both stumble into the street where they lay, wounded. The victim dies December 5 leaving behind three children. Outcome: Suspect dies the day of the shooting from self-inflicted gunshot.

1938: Judge Kent is back on the bench after re-election. Roy Acuff becomes popular, along with ball-point pens. LSD shows up. So do strobe lights, Teflon®, and freeze-dried coffee. National Minimum Wage Act (25 cents an hour). Orson Welles' *War of the World* scares the pants off a whole heck of a lot of people on the night before Halloween.

1939: Baseball Hall of Fame. The Second World War begins when Germany invades Poland. The U.S. remains neutral, for the time being. Einstein briefs President Roosevelt on the possibility of building an atomic bomb. The United States Supreme Court sets aside the conviction against a Louisiana Negro because Negroes were excluded from the Grand Jury that indicted him. *Gone with the Wind,* the movie, that is. Lee Harvey Oswald is born.

1939, MARCH: District Attorney Herbert Mook assails the Parole system because of "the politics" involved.

1939, MAY: A bill to abolish the State Pardon Board, relieve county courts of much of their power to parole, and create a new, five-member board to deal with long-term convicts begins working its way through the Commonwealth's legislature. The bill is vetoed by Governor James, not because of its content, but because the legislators fail to provide funding. Prisoners continue to be released after serving their minimum sentence, even though that's clearly not the best thing to do.

1940: The United States Supreme Court rules for the first time that public school students can not be compelled to recite *The Pledge of Allegiance*. Similar rulings follow throughout the years. They are, at first, based on violations of student religious beliefs. Later rulings declare forcing people to recite or even stand for the pledge violates First Amendment rights to free speech. John Lennon is born. So is Richard Starkey (you may know him as Ringo Starr). Crawford County's population grows more than it has in the past 70 years. It's up 14% to 71,644.

1941, JANUARY 18: Location: Richmond Township, Teepleville, a mile southeast on Little Cooley Road. Victim: Mrs. Hazel Reuchart (42). Suspect: Sylvester Ikenburg (Ickenberg) (72). Act: Point-blank shotgun blast to the chest. Notes: Both work on the Robert Dunlap farm. Dunlap describes Ikenburg as "deeply religious" and showing no mental stress prior to the shooting. Victim has been employed for past eight or nine weeks as housekeeper. Suspect is a farmhand. At 8:30am, as the victim is ascending to the second floor, Ikenburg appears at the top of the flight and blows her down the stairs with the shotgun. Outcome: Immediately after the shooting, Ikenburg walks downstairs, around victim's body, and into the kitchen. There, he tells Dunlap's granddaughter, 16-year-old, Dorothy Morse of Buffalo, New York, what he has done and that he is ending his own life. He walks to the barnyard behind the house, places the muzzle of the gun against his chest and pulls the trigger. He dies almost instantly. Victim and suspect have no real relationship. No motive is discovered except for "a mental quirk."

1941: Governor James signs a bill into law setting up a new parole system for Pennsylvania. Cases involving sentences of death or life are handled by the State Pardon Board. County courts can suspend sentences less than two years. The Governor-appointed, five-member Parole Board has jurisdiction over everyone else. A prisoner is reviewed for released when minimum sentence is reached, but parole is not guaranteed.

1941, OCTOBER 10: Location: Meadville, Waelde Alley. Victims: Josephine DePascale (wife, 33) and Mrs. Merle Miller (neighbor, 33). Suspect: Jerome DePascale (husband, 43). Act: Both victims shot through the chest. Notes: Husband and wife have quarreled with considerable violence over a period of years. Suspect mortally wounds his wife and chases her from their home to Vauda Johnson's, next door. Mrs. Miller, living in another part of the Johnson home, runs to see what is happening and is killed for her curiosity. Outcome: Suspect commits suicide with a gunshot to the head. Left behind are eight kids, ages 3 to 19 years. Coroner Luther J. King decides an inquest is not needed. He attributes the crime to temporary insanity complicated by domestic trouble.

1941, December 7: Japan attacks Pearl Harbor. The U.S. enters the Second World War. Within two months Japanese-Americans are relocated to camps away from the U.S. west coast, there to stay for three years. Within two years the U.S. and Britain begin joint development of an atomic weapon.

1942: The Japanese drive General MacArthur from the Philippines. He vows to return. The Nazis start in on concentration camp killings in a serious way. Gasoline is rationed in the U.S. The first self-sustaining nuclear reaction is established under the bleachers at Stagg Field at the University of Chicago. The Grand Coulee Dam is finished on the Columbia River. DDT gets it's first use. Carol Lombard is killed in a plane crash. Paul McCartney is born. So is Cassius Clay who changes his name, in 1964, to Muhammad Ali.

1942, January 16, 8:45pm: Location: ? Victim: Geraldine Johnson (wife). Suspect: Emil Johnson (husband). Act: "Misuse." Notes: Cause of death is peritonitis. Outcome: ?

1942, July 22: The United States Congress officially recognizes the *Pledge of Allegiance:* "I pledge allegiance to the Flag of the United States of America and to the Republic for which it stands, one nation indivisible, with liberty and justice for all."

1943: Silly Putty® and the aqualung. George Harrison is born. The State Parole Act is amended to require consideration of the recommendations of the District Attorney and the jail's warden or superintendent who has been in charge of the prisoner in question.

1943, JUNE 28: Location: Summerhill Township, Dicksonburg. Victim: Miss Jeanne Phelps (37). Suspect: Andrew Kinch (brother-in-law, 37). Act: Shot in car after accident. Notes: Both of Conneaut Lake. Kinch has been married to victim's sister for about ten years. The morning of the crime, he drives the victim and her uncle, Fred Hanselman, to their work in Meadville. Drive in is normal. Getting out at Walnut is the last Fred sees of them. Forty minutes and 20 miles later, Dicksonburg residents see the Kinch vehicle careen from State Route 18 into their small town and crash over an embankment into a stream. They hear a woman shout, notice the passenger door open, and see the flash of two shots fired. There is no other sign of physical harm to the victim. Outcome: Suspect commits suicide by gunshot to head. Weapon was a 32-20 Colt revolver used by suspect for target practice with the Meadville State Guard unit. Deputy Coroner Samuel Gottlieb finds no motive, other than a man suddenly gone insane.

1943, JULY 9: Location: Cambridge Township, two miles south of Cambridge Springs, in a boxcar. Victim: Julius Allen (43). Suspect: John Russell (49). Act: Punctured lung due to stabbing during a fight over a dice game. Notes: Victim from Bellefontaine, Ohio. Suspect from Cincinnati, Ohio. Both worked in Erie Railroad construction crew. Suspect said he did not intend to murder the victim but bought a knife in a Springs hardware to "settle a dispute" with the victim. Outcome: Prosecution expecting a conviction for murder in the second. After deliberating twenty-two hours, the jury finds voluntary manslaughter but makes a request for "no mercy" as a compromise for those wanting a more severe judgment. Judge Kent comments that, through the years, he's received many requests for mercy but this was the first for none. The extreme penalty is 12 years. Kent's sentence is not less than 6 nor more than 12 years at Western Penitentiary.

1943, JULY 17: Location: Titusville, 300-block East Central Avenue. Victim: Harold R. (Red) Muir. Suspect: Mrs. Caroline Hogan Marvin. Act: Gunshot. Notes: Suspect denies intent to kill. Says there was considerable trouble between her and Muir, some of it leading to prior violence. She has not been "sleeping" with the man. Each has separate rooms. In the course of a booze-fueled argument Muir strikes her on the chin and knocks her down. Then he picks up an end table and swings it at her. At this point she gets his rifle to bluff him. He takes the weapon from her. Seconds later, he hands it back and tells her "to use it." She raises the gun to his head. The weapon fires but she claims she never intended to shoot him, that she does not remember pulling the trigger. While examining the weapon as evidence, one of the jurors discovers it has a "trick safety" that only the dead man could have readily known. This leads everyone to conclude the victim had slipped it off before handing the rifle back to the suspect. Outcome: Four hours of deliberation. Acquittal on first ballot.

1944: Kidney dialysis. D-Day. More than 200,000 American troops help MacArthur keep his promise to return to the Philippines. The U.S. Supreme Court validates the Japanese-American relocation camps as constitutional. IBM's programmable Automatic Sequence Controlled Calculator; three additions or one multiplication in five seconds, division in fifteen. Log functions take over a minute. Smokey Bear (the one who says "Don't play with matches"). *Pippi Longstocking.* William "Smokin' Joe" Frazier is born.

1944, July 6, just after 3:00pm: Location: Meadville, "residential section of Chestnut." Victim: Mrs. Arch M. Wooley (wife, 54). Suspect: Mr. Arch M. Wooley (husband, 70). Act: gunshot to the head. Notes: Married only 14 months ago. Quarreled badly and had separated. Victim is returning from work and is shot in the head as she walks along Chestnut. Outcome: Husband goes to his home on Pine Street where he shoots himself in the head. Lives hours before dying at Meadville's City Hospital.

1945: Germany surrenders after Hitler kills himself. President Franklin Roosevelt dies of a brain hemorrhage. Vice President Harry S Truman takes over. Japan surrenders after being bombed, atomically, twice. The Slinky® goes on sale.

1946: Future Presidents Bill Clinton and George W. Bush are born. Laborers across the U.S. begin striking for better wages and improved working conditions. The microwave oven is invented by Percy Spencer. Sony is founded with fewer than two-dozen employees. The bikini is introduced. Crawford County experiences six suicides over a six-week period. Irving Berlin's *Annie Get Your Gun*.

1946, January 29: Location: Meadville, 200-block of Arch Street. Victim: Bess Beal (56). Suspect: Lee R. Ackley (54). Act: Struck in head with a hammer and then strangled with a necktie. Notes: Victim and suspect are common-law partners. Outcome: Suspect commits suicide by gunshot. The couple's collie dog, "Queenie," is mournfully howling. Neighbors peek in the windows and hurriedly call for police.

1946, SEPTEMBER 24: Location: Meadville. Victim: Rose Davidio (wife, 40). Suspect: Luigi Davidio (husband, 52). Act: Gunshot to the head with .32 caliber revolver. Notes: Their son, Joseph (26), rushes downstairs to find the victim on the dining room floor and the perpetrator sitting up on the living room davenport. Suspect worked at Erie Railroad shop as a machinist's helper for 23 years. Has been ill and acting strangely. Outcome: Suspect commits suicide by gunshot.

1947: The sound barrier is broken by Chuck Yeager. Mahalia Jackson sings like nobody before, or since. Mobile phones are created but don't go on to become the murderers of peace and quiet until after 1983. Earl Silas Tupper invents his wares. Henry Ford dies in Dearborn Michigan from bleeding on the brain. WMGW, the first radio station in Crawford County, goes on the air. The call letters are the initials of founder Dr. Harry C. Winslow's daughter: Mary Gene Winslow.

1948 – 1964

THE HONORABLE HERBERT A. MOOK

O. Clare Kent retires. President Judge Herbert A. Mook is elected.

At first glance, Herbert Mook's portrait presents a somber face with a good head of silver-gray hair combed back and away from his broad forehead. He has a furrowed brow and dark eyes behind tortoise-shell-frame glasses propped on a generous nose. He seems to be frowning. But, look a little longer. The portrait will reward you with a light-hearted aspect.

Herbert Mook is born in Saegertown on November 22, 1908 (the first President Judge born in that century). He graduates as the valedictorian of Saegertown High's class of 1925. He enters Allegheny College, graduates in 1929, and goes on to receive his law degree from the University of Pennsylvania in 1932. He is the first President Judge to possess a "formal education" in jurisprudence.

He is elected to two, four-year terms as Crawford County District Attorney before his 1947 election to his initial term as President Judge at the age of 39. His second election sees him unopposed in both the primary and general elections—another first in the county's history.

A religious man, he attends Meadville's Stone Methodist Church and, for a while, is the Sunday School Superintendent.

Judge Mook displays a deep sympathy for youth and their problems. During his time on the bench, he insists that names of juvenile offenders not be made public.

The judge is a hard worker but chafes under his increasingly heavy case load. He repeatedly calls for the creation of a second judgeship in Crawford County. His efforts are rewarded in December 1963, when then District Attorney P. Richard Thomas is named to that position. It is worth noting that P. Richard is the grandson of 1898's President Judge Frank J. Thomas.

Herbert Mook is not able to share the burden for long. He becomes seriously ill the next summer. He is treated at Pittsburgh's Shadyside and Meadville's City hospitals and, at first, seems to respond. Taking a rapid turn for the worse, Judge Mook dies while in office on September 4, 1964.

1948: Truman defeats Dewey. Individuals and organizations begin to alter the *Pledge of Allegiance:* "I pledge allegiance to the Flag of the United States of America and to the Republic for which it stands, one nation, *under God,* indivisible, with liberty and justice for all." The Frisbee®, Velcro®, and the Wurlitzer Jukebox®. Columbia Records introduces the "long playing vinyl album." The Berlin Airlift. Segregation "officially ends" in the U.S. Armed Forces. Israel (the modern one) is founded. Its Arab neighbors are not very enthusiastic about the idea.

1949: The term "Big Bang" is first used to refer to the abrupt beginning of the known universe by English astronomer Fred Hoyle during a BBC radio show. George Orwell's book *1984* is published. Have you read it? Former President Judge Thomas J. Prather dies.

1950: The Korean War begins. A handful of American military advisors are sent to South Vietnam—it takes a quarter-century to leave. The first "Peanuts" cartoon is published. McCarthy begin his hunt for communists. It takes almost a decade before the U.S. Supreme Court shuts him down. The credit card. Crawford County's population rises 10% to 79,948.

"A Plain Backwoods Kid"

On the pleasant evening of the 15th of May, 1950, Harry M. DeForce, of East Main Street, Titusville, is strolling along the tracks of the New York Central Railroad. South of the Cities Service Refinery, he sees a large object tangled in some brush washed across a small sandbar about ten feet out into Oil Creek. He's not sure what it is, at first. His sense of dread increases as he draws near. DeForce pokes at the mass with a broken limb of a tree and is convinced to call the police when the stick comes back covered with hair.

Deputy Coroner, Dr. C.M. Sonne is there when the body is dragged from the creek. The victim wears a pullover army sweater, tan shirt, union suit underwear, overalls that look like fatigues, hunting socks, and a new pair of ankle-high boots. The corpse has been in the water long enough that "the skin slipped from one hand like a glove."

The pants pockets hold a little more than two bucks in change plus social security and selective service cards. It is twenty-four-year-old Robert LaRue Loop.

This is confirmed by a cousin of the victim, Lloyd Young, 46, of Daytown (near the intersection of Fish Flats and Fink Roads in northern Rome Township). Young describes his cousin Robert as "a plain backwoods kid" who never had an enemy in the world. He thinks Loop fell in the creek by accident. If it was suicide, the victim never gave any sign or inclination.

The young man's immediate family describes him as "afraid of the water because he could not swim" and maintains he had to have been pushed into the fast-flowing Oil Creek. He never would've gone near it on his own.

Loop's many relatives thought him a lonely fellow who did not care for his home life. He was something of a drifter, moving about but never going too far. He left Erie County after graduating high school and stayed with many of his numerous cousins in Pennsylvania and Ohio, all of whom liked him. He once had a serious girlfriend but split up with her three years ago and since paid little attention to women.

Loop enjoyed music, bought records, and liked listening to the radio. He whistled and sang while he worked. His younger cousins liked being with him, and he was their willing and popular babysitter. He was generous, always paying his way with money or work. He enjoyed working hard but had a temper. He disliked criticism and would fly off the handle when what he was doing was called into question.

The young man was in Daytown, around Easter, when he had walked off a logging job. From there he had had gone on to his several cousins scattered around Rome Township. One, Alvin White, drove Loop to Titusville in late March and gave him a new pair of boots.

As might be imagined, the condition of the body makes the autopsy an ordeal. Helping are Drs. H.S. Anderson and C.M. Hazen, both wearing gas masks against the "fearful stench." Going old-school, Dr. Sonne puffs furiously on a cigar, instead. Following their work, the doctors "lost no time in heading for the showers." Sonne says he suffered no ill effects but admits, "he could not face all of his favorite dessert, strawberry shortcake."

The examination shows considerable hemorrhaging under the scalp in the region of the right ear. The lungs are not what would be expected in a drowning. The Coroner concludes the victim was dead of a blow to the head before he hit the water. This is no accident or suicide, it's murder. Police theorize that Loop fell into a gang that blackjacked, robbed him, and dumped his body into Oil Creek.

Mantford Vroman of Windfall Road reports seeing the man, drunk, in the South Franklin Street Dinor [*sic*] about 11:00 at night on April 8. Loop ordered food, then asked for nickels for the jukebox, and when told to "sit still or leave," began to cry, saying "Nobody wants me. Nobody seems to understand me or wants me around. I'm going to get out of here." Vroman says Loop was like a "farm boy who had taken his first drink."

Police have few other clues. There was the drunk they picked up a few weeks ago with bruises on his face. That doesn't pan out. Robert Wakefield (of the 400-block of West Spring Street) finds the victim's cap at the Oil Creek end of Monroe Street, some distance from where the body was discovered. It holds several gray hairs in the band but provides no other help. Old offenders are questioned as to their whereabouts. There are no leads.

The investigation continues on to the end of May when Titusville Police travel to Warrensville, Ohio to question a Robert Knapp, being held in jail on other charges. Police think he may know something about Loop's death. The interview takes them nowhere. The investigation stalls.

The murder of Robert LaRue Loop remains unsolved.

1951: Color televisions are being sold. *The Tennessee Waltz* is at the top of the charts when Cleveland disk jockey Alan Freed starts using the term "rock n' roll" to help give white kids an excuse to listen to the "rhythm and blues" of black artists—a rose by any other name. Atomic-bomb testing begins in Nevada making Midwest sunsets particularly beautiful. The United Nations building opens in New York City. One of the best science fiction movies ever, *The Thing (From Another World)*. Also, one of Gramma Esau's favorite soaps, the *Search for Tomorrow*.

1952: Mr. Potato Head®, diet soft drinks, the hydrogen bomb. Queen Elizabeth II. First passenger jet route between Johannesburg, South Africa and London, England. The word "smog" is coined, a combination of smoke and fog. The occasion? London's "Great Fog of 1952" that kills, it's figured, 4,000 people. The barcode and barcode reader are patented by inventors Joseph Woodland and Bernard Silver in response to a request by a food-store chain for an automatic checkout system. We'll have to wait fourteen more years before their first commercial use.

1952, FEBRUARY 17: Location: Meadville, 1200-block of South Main Street. Victim: Mrs. Minnie Thrash (61). Suspect: Eugene Lilly (33). Act: Bludgeoning. Multiple depressed fractures of the skull. Notes: Husband, Homer Thrash, says suspect was visiting while the victim was out of the house. After playing cards, shooting craps, and drinking beer, suspect asks for a $2 loan. When Homer refuses, suspect chokes him unconscious. Homer later awakes on a bed, discovers he's been bashed in the head, and stumbles over his wife's body. Suspect is arrested shortly after and questioned for more than two hours during which he says he met the victim on the front porch when he was leaving the house but continued on his way. Police find an old-fashioned flat-iron that carries traces of blood and hair. District Attorney Raymond Shafer charges Lilly with murder in the first degree. Lilly pleads innocent with attorneys John and Robert Kent defending him. Husband Homer, from his bed in Spencer Hospital says: "My head hurts so. Lilly didn't do it. I don't know who did." Judge Mook charges the jury, telling them they can find for any degree of murder, anything below that, or acquit. The jury's out about four hours and decides to set Lilly free. Courtroom spectators cheer. Lilly is mobbed by well-wishers. As he steps into a car outside the courthouse he's quoted as saying "That's a lot off my head." No one else is ever charged.

1952, OCTOBER: The cornerstone is laid for the "new" Crawford County Courthouse on the site of the old one.

1952, DECEMBER: The song *I saw Mommy Kissing Santa Claus* is banned from radio in Huntington, West Virginia. It is "an insult to Santa Claus and the sacred occasion of Christmas." As a sign of the times, Crawford County District Attorney, Republican Raymond P. Shafer takes "Girlie Magazines" to task as "mindless filth and pornography."

Preacher's son Shafer, born in 1917, is an Eagle Scout, graduate of Allegheny and Yale, and is awarded the Bronze Star and Purple Heart while serving on World War II PT boats in the Pacific in and around the Philippines. Following his stint as Crawford County District Attorney, he serves in the Pennsylvania State Senate and, from there, goes on to be the 1962 Lieutenant Governor under Yale classmate Bill Scranton. Shafer wins the Governorship in 1966. He's popular for his expansion of the Commonwealth's highway system. He isn't so well-liked when he proposes Pennsylvania start collecting income tax. He isn't the first governor to call for such action, but the mere suggestion of the idea is blamed for the subsequent sweep of state-wide elections by Democrats. Ironically, it is Governor Milton Shapp, himself a Democrat, who signs the commonwealth's income tax into law during his first term (1971-1975).

Shafer backs Rockefeller instead of Nixon in 1968. Despite the snub, President Nixon give Shafer the lead of what becomes known as the "Shafer Commission" that studies the use and abuse of marijuana and other drugs. Pennsylvania's ex-governor rubs conservatives of all parties the wrong way when his commission recommends marijuana be "decriminalized." Shafer serves as special council to Vice President Rockefeller in 1974, and pulls a one-year stint as President of Allegheny

College (1985-86). He dies in December of 2006 and is buried in St. John's Cemetery, Union Township.

It's Why The Papers Call it "Spa"

Cambridgeboro was incorporated in 1866 and is located smack-dab in the middle of Crawford County's north-central township of Cambridge. The town owed its existence to water. It was founded where French Creek was easily crossed. A break in topography slowed the creek upstream to a series of flat meanders that created rich farmland. Downstream, the more rapidly flowing water provided a useful source of power.

The growth of Cambridgeboro was steady but slow until the coming of the railroads allowed it to take better advantage of its surrounding hardwood forests. But it wasn't lumber that brought the town fame.

In 1860, a local doctor, John H. Gray, discovered an artesian spring on his property. This wasn't all that unusual, and the good doctor pretty much forgot about it—until he happened to visit the thriving city of Hot Springs, Arkansas. Back home in Cambridgeboro, Dr. Gray started to promote the springs on his farm as a fix for all kinds of ailments. He built a relatively modest pavilion and began selling his curative mineral waters.

With time (and savvy advertising by a variety of entrepreneurs) Cambridgeboro was filled with people from around the world hoping that "taking the waters" would cure what ailed them. In 1897 citizens renamed their town "Cambridge Springs."

By the very early 1900s the area was bustling with health spas, hotels, businesses, and amusements that catered to the needs of each and every guest. The spas were so popular that railroads routed tracks through the region to boost their passenger traffic.

But, as they say, all good things must come to an end. The number of visitors began to wane as an ever-more sophisticated scientific community disproved the medical effectiveness of water cures. Hotels and spas closed, were abandoned, and condemned.

The Riverside Inn still operates in Cambridge Springs, a reminder of days gone by. When you stop, be sure to ask if you might take the waters.

"Number One Suspect"

Twenty-two-year-old Doris Hatch leaves for lunch from her job at the First National Bank of Cambridge Springs. With her is a brown paper bag containing a pair of shoes that she's told co-workers she plans on getting repaired. Along her way to the cobbler's, she stops at Park Hardware, where she works part-time as a bookkeeper for William Turner. She's there to help find an invoice that has turned up missing.

Doris leaves the hardware and steps down the street in a dark orange summer dress and white, open-toed shoes. She visits a nearby grocery, buys some cookies and candy bars, and… vanishes.

The plain, young woman, "a quiet girl who spends much of her time at home," is reported missing on July 27, 1953. Her mother, Mrs. Lucy Hatch, many friends, and employers can think of no reason for her disappearance. The cops, including County Detective John O'Laughlin, tell the public they don't necessarily figure foul play is involved.

What's kept from everyone is that 38-year-old William Turner, Doris' boss at Park Hardware, is a suspect from the start. A native of Cambridge Springs, Turner is a graduate of both the University of Pittsburgh and the University of Pennsylvania School of Law. He failed his bar exam, then hoped to join the FBI, but that didn't pan out. Turner served in the Philippines as a lieutenant in the military police during World War II, worked as a personnel investigator at the Keystone Ordinance Plant in

Greenwood Township, and was a former police reporter and Sunday editor for the *Erie (Pennsylvania) Dispatch* newspaper.

Police know that the afternoon Doris Hatch vanished, William Turner had driven to Erie on what he called a "business trip." Four days later, he traveled to Magnolia, on the coast of Massachusetts where his wife and daughter were visiting his in-laws.

Upon his return, Turner trades his car for a new one. The interior of his old car has new seat covers and is stained in several places with what looks like human blood. The man voluntarily submits to questioning. Calling himself the "Number One Suspect," he explains that the blood came from accident victims he'd picked up and a bad cut on his hand that he had suffered some time ago. Police cannot confirm these stories. Forensics provide no extra clues.

A week after the woman goes missing, police ask anyone with information to come forward. By the end of September, reports are distributed to officials across the country. In mid-October the State Police asks hunters going out for the start of the waterfowl season to be alert for any signs of Hatch, whether she might be a victim of accident or crime.

Still holding their cards close, investigators convince themselves that Hatch was in love with Turner and extremely jealous of his relationship with his wife. They are certain this triangle, somehow, played a part in Hatch's disappearance. The trouble is, their evidence is circumstantial.

Turner denies dating the missing woman, though he admits people might have thought he was. He disavows knowing where Hatch went after she left the hardware store. The suspect refuses to submit to a lie-detector test because there has been no charge of a crime.

In mid-November the First National Bank of Cambridge Springs offers a $500 reward to anyone with information as to the whereabouts of Doris Hatch. A week later it's raised to $700 when two local men, J.C. Allee, bank president, and George

Klandatos, restaurant owner, add a hundred bucks each. The total eventually reaches a grand ($8,500 modern), thanks to a donation by the *Erie Daily News*.

That same month, the Pennsylvania State Police assign PFC Lewis P. Penman of the Lawrence Park Station as a Special Investigator to the case.

William Turner is admitted for a long stay at Warren State Hospital for treatment of what the papers call "a nervous breakdown." Following his release, Turner, his wife, and daughter move to Manchester, Massachusetts where he takes a job preparing advertising copy for the Jet Spray Company.

The months drag on. A small article appears every few weeks in area papers saying the same thing: she's still missing. The reward remains in place. Police have not abandoned hope.

Special Investigator Penman spends the spring of the next year checking out rumors that circulate about the location of the victim's body: it's in the swamp north of town or somewhere along Woodcock Creek.

Almost a year to the day that Hatch went missing, Penman watches as Park Hardware is renovated. He wants to be sure no clues exist in the walls, under the floor, or in the ceiling. He also hopes to prevent having to pull the building apart should future investigations warrant.

Fruitless attempts are made to match the missing woman to bodies of unidentified females found across the United States. Lucy Hatch continues paying on her daughter's insurance. The policy cannot be cashed without proof of death until seven years pass from the date of her daughter's disappearance.

It's been two years. The reward expires in March of 1955. Police figure Doris is dead and her body buried in the swampland north of Cambridge Springs. They also figure a complete and thorough search of the marsh is impossible.

~~~~~

The first of November, 1955. Fifty-year-old Raymond

Genholt is out training his hunting dogs. Some distance away from a secluded "lover's lane" he comes across a well-hidden and badly decomposed body. Scattered about are bones, torn fragments of a orange summer dress, a pair of white, open-toed shoes and, most significantly, a gold Bulova® watch.

Each Bulova carries a serial number traceable to the store that sold it. This particular serial number matches a watch purchased in Cambridge Springs by one Doris Hatch. That, and a close match of dental records, convince authorities they've finally located their missing woman.

But the location of the body isn't the hometown swamp. It's along State Line Pond Road, near Stafford Springs, Connecticut, a small town northeast of Hartford, and less than a mile from the Massachusetts state line. The pond is along a likely driving route from, say, northwest Pennsylvania to Magnolia, Massachusetts. It's also close to the town where Turner arranged to have his old car's upholstery replaced.

Before the news hits the papers, Connecticut Coroner Bernard J. Ackerman begins an investigation that determines the body has been in place at least a year. He eventually decides that the victim had been hacked to death. First from the back, then to the throat, possibly with a machete.

Pennsylvania State Police withhold information while obtaining a warrant for the arrest of William Turner. But, on November 3, before authorities can act, the suspect is called at his Massachusetts home by the *Erie Times* newspaper. Turner sounds astonished that a body has been found and swears he has nothing to do with what is now murder.

William Turner discusses the matter with his wife, Diane. He tells her he plans to return to Crawford County and clear his name, for once and for all. He leaves for a stroll along the ocean's shore. He wants to clear his head.

Office Penman arrives that day to take his man into custody, but he's too late. A Manchester policeman, out walking his dog, has already found William Turner, propped up against a seawall, dead, shot through the heart with a .45 automatic. Connecticut Medical Examiner Winfred G. Stickney rules it a suicide.

Diane Turner finds two brief notes from her husband. Both apologize for his suicide. Both say things are better with him gone. Neither note refers to the death of Doris Hatch.

Cambridge Springs is stunned; from the victim's mother, still holding out hope her daughter is alive, to Turner's immediate family, reluctant to believe their suddenly-dead relative had anything to do with the crime. There have been so many rumors about Doris Hatch over the past couple years that many townspeople flat-out refuse to accept the truth that her body has been found.

Turner is buried in Rosedale Cemetery in Manchester, Massachusetts. Doris Hatch is returned home to be buried in the Venango Cemetery beside her father and grandparents.

~~~~~

One of the notes William Turner leaves behind tells his wife to "write to George McGaffick and tell him he has some letters for you." Police immediately begin a search for McGaffick, who was Turner's former partner at the hardware store and also a former patient at the Warren State Hospital. He is eventually found in Texas and cleared of suspicion.

Ten days after William Turner's suicide, a letter arrives for Will Rose, publisher of the *Cambridge Enterprise-News*. It was written by the now-dead man on November 3, the date of his death. The airmail postmark is eight days later, stamped in Houston, Texas. The letter was first sent to McGaffick who forwarded it to the paper.

The text is Turner's explanation for the suicide: not wanting to drag his family through a trial, his own poor physical and mental health, a lack of money for his defense, his death providing a new start for his family. It ends with a declaration of innocence.

Published along with Turner's letter is one from his sister.

In it, she refers to Turner's days of delirium in the hospital with no admission of guilt; of his battle with alcoholism, made worse by the persistent questioning of police and the constant pain of a war injury received while serving in the Philippines; how Turner had rebuilt his life and then, tragically, decided to end it when he saw his ordeal beginning all over again. Turner's sister seems certain of her brother's innocence in the disappearance and murder.

Stafford Connecticut Coroner Bernard Ackerman states all evidence points to Turner. Special Investigator Lewis Penman concurs, as does Crawford County District Attorney Raymond Shafer.

The authorities close the case of Doris Hatch.

~~~~~

Prior to his civilian career in law enforcement, PFC Lewis Penman served during World War II as an investigator in the European theater with U.S. Army Intelligence. He obtained the rank of lieutenant in his 37 years with the Pennsylvania State Police. Penman passed away in August, 2008 at the age of 88.

THE SCIENCE OF CRIME

It may seem incredible that the 1953 authorities in charge of the Doris Hatch murder possessed so many clues but still waited more than two-and-a-half years until her body was found before moving on William Turner. The situation isn't puzzling, once you understand a little of the past.

For hundreds of years, western courts followed the legal maxim of "no body, no murder." This concept was rooted in English Common Law and partially based on the 1660 case known as "The Campden Wonder" in which a mother and two sons, were found guilty and executed for the murder of one William Harrison, who later showed up alive. Oops.

The specter of that triply-fatal mistake haunted lawyers,

judges, and juries for the next three centuries. The idea of "corpus delicti" (body of crime) referring to the actual body of a murdered person was hard for the courts to shake. Prosecutors always waited for a dead body, or substantial parts thereof, before pursuing a charge of murder. This put them at a real disadvantage since clever criminals knew suspicion and circumstantial evidence were not enough in cases where there was no corpse to be had. Law school graduate William Turner, of our previous story, knew as much, challenging and taunting police when questioned, "Well, if I am guilty—and I am not—where is the body?"

Why was a corpse so critical? Forensic science was inadequate. For much of our history, we were unable to distinguish dried blood from other stains. Microscopic and chemical tests began, through the early part of the 20th century, to differentiate between animal and human blood. But it wasn't until the 1950s that non-destructive tests for blood and its full typing were readily available. Even then, the information was useful only in ruling out a suspect. Such simple results could suggest, but never prove guilt.

Doris Hatch was killed seven years before it was clearly established in United States courts that circumstantial evidence alone could prove guilt of murder when the victim's body could not be found (1960, People v. Scott, 176 Cal. App. 2d 458, wealthy husband convicted of murdering his wealthy wife with the body never found). The first court case in the United States that used DNA to gain a conviction took place in 1987 (Tommy Lee Andrews, of a series of sexual assaults in Orlando, Florida). It took more than a full generation for science to catch up with the needs of the Commonwealth in the murder of Doris Hatch.

1953: Dwight D. Eisenhower is President of the United States. Korean War ends. Inmates riot in Pennsylvania's Western State Penitentiary and Rockview Prison. This leads to the creation of the Pennsylvania Department of Correction. Bill Haley and the Comets *Rock Around the Clock*. Radial tires and Texas Instrument's "transistor radio." DNA is figured out by Crick and Watson. Stalin dies. The United States Central Intelligence Agency helps overthrow the government of Iran, and how well did that little adventure pan out?

"By the Lapels of His Coat"

1953. December 27, just past midnight, conductor E.H. Earley and engineer Harry Mitchell take their train slowly past the rail yards at Meadville. The multitude of crossings and dozens of switches warrant caution, even on the quietest of nights.

Erie Railroad Patrolman M.R. Craig stands a respectful distance from the east side of the track, opposite and a little south of the Mercer Street Bridge. In the gaps between the cars of the screeching freight he sees the outline of two people struggling. The train moves past. Craig hurries to the spot and finds a woman's head and body cleanly separated by the action of steel wheels and track.

He spots a man a short distance away, stumbling slowly in the direction of French Creek. Craig calls him to a stop. The man is confused, as if he cannot understand what's happening around him. Police are called.

Moses Terrell (43) is arrested for the murder of Miss Lora Belle Starr (31). When questioned by City Police Captain John Holt and Erie Railroad Detective Roger V. O'Dea, Terrell gives the following story:

He and Starr had left her home on Williams Street, Kerrtown, shortly after 6:00 the evening before (Saturday). They had a few drinks at a Meadville hotel and continued to imbibe at a private home. They then started out for a club, but began to argue and decided to head home.

Their path took them along the tracks. While the freight

was passing, he stood with his back to it. Lora was facing him, holding onto the lapels of his coat. In Terrell's own words, he "got tired or something and shoved her away." That action might've thrown her beneath the wheels of the freight, but he never meant for it to happen.

Their argument, he said, was over his girl's jealousy of the attention paid to him by her own mother, Mrs. Agnes Starr. He'd been boarding with the two women since coming to Meadville in August 1953 from Muse, in Washington County, southwest of Pittsburgh, Pennsylvania.

Terrell shows no emotion when he pleads guilty at his arraignment. But Judge Mook cannot receive a guilty plea for murder without the case first being considered by the Grand Jury. Only after it returns a true bill, and the degree of murder is established by either the jury or judge, can Mook sentence the guilty man.

In the meantime, Lora Starr, former employee of the Meadville Laundry, Central Dry Cleaning Co., and the Oakland Beach Hotel at Conneaut Lake, is buried in Greendale Cemetery from the Byham Funeral Home.

The February 1954 Grand Jury indicts Terrell for first degree murder. They find he "willfully and with malice aforethought did kill and murder the said Laura Belle Starr." Terrell is expected to go in front of Judge Mook and plead guilty that same day for a sentence of either life in prison or death by electrocution.

Instead, the destitute Terrell asks for counsel and gets it in the form of court-appointed attorneys Paul E. Allen and Vincent J. Pepicelli. The rumor-mill starts. The scuttlebutt is that Terrell will change his plea to innocent and, in so doing, force a criminal trial.

The scuttlebutt is absolutely true. Thirty-five jurors are examined to seat the fourteen required (twelve active plus two alternates). The trial is held in the "basement assembly room" of the courthouse because of construction work in the main court rooms. The venue is filled to capacity and Judge Mook has his hands full controlling the constant flow of spectators anxious to hear to the testimony.

District Attorney Shafer starts with a bang. The Commonwealth's first witness, Mrs. Alberta Vactor of French Street, testifies that on "the Saturday before Thanksgiving" Terrell had taken Starr "down to the railroad tracks, slapped her around, and threatened to throw her under the train." Defense strenuously objects to this as "hearsay" but Judge Mook allows it.

Mrs. Vactor continues that she and her husband, James, had been drinking with Terrell and Starr at the Triple City Elks Club the night of the murder where the victim and accused were ordered to leave because they had grown "too boisterous." They left for a short time, then returned. It was then that Starr told Vactor about the previous threats. On cross exam, defense lawyers are able to get Vactor to admit Terrell had been "saying bad things about her." The witness denies it shapes her testimony.

Mrs. Agnes Starr, the victim's mother, wanders from questioning with inflammatory statements and is stopped several times by Judge Mook who instructs the jury to disregard her testimony. The mother does describe numerous arguments between her daughter and Terrell. How the deceased had ordered the man from the house "around Thanksgiving time." But that Terrell had asked to be allowed back in and Lora had agreed.

City Police Captain John Holt tells how Terrell exclaimed, "something just snapped in my mind. I done committed the crime. Now it's up to the judge and jury!" And "I'm the one who threw her over against that train, that's all there is to it." And, also, "I wouldn't have wanted to kill her. I threw her before and she seemed to hang up on me—I was juiced up!"

Holt admits that Terrell was "very emotional, shed tears, said he was sorry for what he did" when he viewed Lora's remains at Byham's Funeral Home. The defendant had told Holt that he would've jumped under a train himself, but for Patrolman Craig stopping him.

Howard C. Caldwell, part-time driver for Lafayette Taxi, says Starr and Terrell had ridden in his cab from French Street to the Elks Club around 12:21am on December 27 and that there was "a scuffle" in the back over who would pay the tab. Terrell paid, but when the two left the cab, the man slapped the woman whereupon the woman grabbed Terrell by the coat lapels and shook him.

Terrell takes the stand in his own defense. He denies any intent to kill: "I just pushed her away from me and I wasn't trying to hurt her. It never came to my mind to kill her or anybody else and I didn't intend to push her under the train." He stops during his testimony to wipe tears from his eyes. He relates how they had known each other for ten years when both were living near Canonsburg, Pennsylvania, and that he had taken her out once there.

Terrell, who admits to a prior criminal record of breaking and entering, says he was persuaded to come to Meadville by one James Fields whom he describes as "Agnes Starr's boyfriend." Terrell testifies he started dating Lora in September of 1953 and moved into the Starr home soon after. At first he gave Mrs. Starr fifteen dollars a week for room and board. Later, he turned his laborer's pay from the American Brakeshoe Corporation over to Lora. The accused says once they were ready, he and Lora had planned to leave for Maryland to get married but that Agnes objected to that idea, saying the distance was too great.

The accused corroborates the earlier testimony about his whereabouts the evening of Lora's death and admits he had far too much to drink. He says they'd argued by the tracks because he threatened to leave Meadville, get a job elsewhere, and then send for her. She said she would go with him and began to shake him by the lapels of his coat. He pushed her hands away, then turned and walked off without looking back.

When stopped by Patrolman Craig and shown the body,

Terrell explains, he didn't even know what it was. He claims he didn't know Lora was dead until told by a prisoner in an adjoining cell. He admits he was jealous when she gave attention to other men, but that would not cause him to kill her.

D.A. Shafer pushes for murder in the first degree but says the Commonwealth is "not going to recommend execution unless you, the jury, feel that way." Defense attorney Pepicelli maintains that Terrell never denied responsibility for the death, but that he does deny the intent to murder. Judge Mook defines the varying degrees of murders and manslaughters and charges the jury with deciding the severity of the crime.

After more than 8 hours of deliberation the jury comes in at 11:50 pm on February 18, finding Terrell guilty of murder in second degree. The next week Judge Mook sentences him to not less than ten and not more than twenty years, saying "It's rather fortunate you are not facing life imprisonment or the electric chair."

1954: Englishman Robert Bannister becomes the first human being to officially run a mile under four minutes. He holds the record for about seven weeks. Runners peel another 15 seconds from Bannister's time over the next half-century. Polio injections. The rest of the United States begins to start catching up with the 1881 school ruling by Crawford County President Judge Pearson Church. United States President Dwight Eisenhower signs a bill that makes the "under God" in the *Pledge of Allegiance* official. It has stood, since: "I pledge allegiance to the Flag of the United States of America and to the Republic for which it stands, one nation, under God, indivisible, with liberty and justice for all." Once almost compulsory across the nation (along with a Bible reading and the Lord's Prayer), by the end of the 20th century, only half of the 50 United States will "encourage" their public schools to recite the pledge. The religious activities are long gone.

1954, JULY: The new Crawford County Courthouse opens for business.

1954, AUGUST 27: Location: Meadville, West Street. Victim: Clifford L. Decker (61, white). Suspect: Robert Brinkley (24, black). Act: Death due to loss of blood from a stab wound in leg. Notes: Brinkley claims Decker turned on him with a knife when he tried to stop a fight between the dead man and Percy Powell, also from Meadville. Brinkley maintains that, at no time, did he knowingly cut Decker and that any stabbing was purely accidental. Jury evenly split between men and women. Police Captain Holt testifies there was no direct evidence that the stabbing was intentional. The Commonwealth pushes for second degree murder. Over the objections of defense attorney Kenneth W. Rice, District Attorney Raymond P. Shafer plays the race card, asking the Police Captain "Do white persons go down to West Street to find prostitutes from time to time? Isn't it a fact that colored persons resent this?" Brinkley is acquitted by the jury after eight hours. He weeps and sobs "Thank you, thank you." Brinkley is re-arrested on charges of involuntary manslaughter and larceny of the knife police say was used in the stabbing. He pleads not guilty. The jury disagrees, finding him guilty of those crimes.

1955: Chuck Berry hits it big with *Maybelline,* but Elvis Presley finds acceptance easier with *Baby, Let's Play House.* Disneyland opens. McDonald's® (you want fries with that?) is incorporated. Black teenager Claudette Colvin is arrested and carried from a bus in Montgomery, Alabama for refusing to give up her seat to a white woman when the driver demands. Colvin receives no press. Nine months later, Rosa Parks does the same and sparks the Montgomery Bus Boycott. Why didn't Colvin galvanize the black community into action? Most say it's because she was pregnant but unmarried.

1955, JULY 17: Location: Titusville, Hancock Place. Victim: Thomas G. Prody (43). Suspect: Lewis D. Brown (29, of Youngstown, OH). Act: Death due to skull fracture. Notes: Fight occurs when suspect loses his temper during a drunken argument with the victim's daughter, the woman he is living with. Suspect rips the aerial from his car and begins striking her and their two-and-a-half year-old daughter. The victim intervenes. Brown fights Prody back against a small wooden fence over which he trips and strikes his head on the cement sidewalk. The suspect jumps on him to continue the beating and also stabs him with a screwdriver, inflicting four puncture wounds. The victim dies while in transport from Titusville to Hamot Hospital in Erie, Pennsylvania. Witnesses say Brown showed no mercy, continuing the beating once the victim was down. Suspect is charged with murder. Outcome: Murder charges are dropped when Brown pleads guilty to voluntary manslaughter (the first plea-bargain I found). Jury convicts on involuntary manslaughter. Judge Mook's sentence: not more than 4 nor less that 10 years in prison because, despite the severe beating, the "intent to kill was not present."

ONE LAST STORY

We've been around the block, and back, with killings, haven't we? We've looked beneath all of the rocks and left no stone unturned. Well, not really. There's something we've not hit quite yet...

"Just Off the Road"

July, 1955. Lawrence Gilbert, of Meadville, is driving along the Smock Memorial Highway when he comes across a petite, but pregnant woman wandering alongside the road. She's bloodied, with wounds to her abdomen and one of her arms. Gilbert takes her to Spencer Hospital.

Police are called. Brown-haired, blue-eyed Donna Green confesses to killing her husband, Lawrence, with a high-powered hunting rifle after a savage beating at his hands. When told things would go easy on her because she shot her husband in self-defense, she replies, "I wouldn't care if I got the electric chair, I just want to die."

She and her husband had arrived in Meadville only a couple months earlier from Coral Gables, Florida. He had found work in an area factory, and they were happy, at first. Since her pregnancy, Donna explains, things had gone steadily downhill between the two of them. Her husband had grown increasingly violent. The beatings had escalated to the point that she was constantly frightened for her safety and the health of the baby inside her.

She tells a minister that she is an only child and that her parents are dead. She had nowhere to turn. She had no choice.

Donna is steadfast in her refusal to give an address. "If I tell you where I live," she says, "you'll find his body." She describes her home as a yellow, four-room house "just off the road" somewhere south of Meadville. Police take the woman on a three-hour ride through the countryside, trying to convince her to identify her home.

A request is sent to Florida for more information on the couple. The Coral Gables authorities come up blank. Local police have trouble finding her mailing address. An unsuccessful attempt is made to track the dead husband through the 1951 Chevy she says they own.

Once the papers get a hold of the story, Reverend George Harvey, of Pilgrim Holiness Church in Geneva, Greenwood Township, steps forward to identify the woman as Mrs. Verla Brest of Sharon, Mercer County, Pennsylvania. Reverend Harvey, who used to live in that city, says the woman is ill and has made similar excursions in the past, telling much the same story to authorities.

Mrs. Brest had been admitted to the Greenville Hospital in Mercer County on June 28 and discharged July 3. Readmitted for observation, she left on her own six days later. She'd tried to walk the substantial distance from Greenville to Geneva to visit Reverend Harvey, became lost, and ended up in Meadville nearly 30 miles away.

Verla is taken to Sharon and released into the custody of her very much alive and worried husband. His first name, incidentally, *is* Lawrence.

1956: Albert Woolson (born 1847) dies as the last Union veteran of the Civil War. The last verifiable Confederate veteran, Pleasant Crump, also born in 1847, passed away five years back. President Eisenhower is re-elected. Pakistan is the first "Islamic Republic." Great Britain tries, and fails, to abolish the death penalty, but they'll succeed in 1998, for civilians, at least. *Peter Pan* comes to television, as does *The Wizard of Oz*. Lewis and Martin split up. Huntley and Brinkley start up. Asian Flu debuts in China. Sabin develops the oral polio vaccine—many of us take it dropped on sugar cubes.

IBM debuts the 305 RAMAC (Random Access Method of Accounting and Control). These 6-foot square, 3-foot thick computers weigh more than a ton and use the first commercially available hard drives to store data; 50, 24-inch disks with a total capacity of about 5 megabytes. The machines are too costly for companies to buy. IBM leases 1,000 of them, each for $3,200 a month ($25,500 modern). You do the math.

The first snooze alarm is marketed—we've been late ever since.

AND THERE YOU HAVE IT

One hundred and fifty-six years of murder and mayhem, all within the seemingly calm and quiet borders of Crawford County, Pennsylvania.

It's up to you what lessons (if any) you choose to take away from this book. As for me, I learned the following, in no particular order:

- Folks wishing they could live in the past should read the newspapers of the era before they build their time machines.

- Murder trials used to take less time—on average. Still, trials that take years to complete are nothing new.

- When you read about the courts, they work as they should. It doesn't always seem that way when you sit in a court.

- It's the combination of judges and lawyers that gives the court its flavor. But they shouldn't get all puffed up about it because that taste is flat without the spice everyone else adds.

- A group of 12 people can't agree what to have on a

pizza. It may be odd to think you can trust them with a murder case, but they seem to do okay.

- The county's legal history would be different without Meadville's Allegheny College. It's tough for a Thiel graduate to admit, but I suppose Allegheny has a right to brag. Maybe. A little.

- People haven't changed in the last 250 years, and they won't change in the next 250, either (actually, I knew that *before* I started this book, but it's always good to be reminded).

- There are fatally good reasons for laws and the requisite funding to protect women and children from angry men. Anybody who thinks such services are a waste is dead wrong.

- If you want to get away with killing somebody, it's best if you're young, pretty, female, and have an all-male jury.

- Pressures of society are a contributing cause of death for unwed mothers and their babies. Making a choice illegal and dangerous doesn't keep desperate people from making it, even when there are safer and more socially-acceptable alternatives readily available.

- Likewise, prohibition of a thing people desire never, ever makes it go away. It does organize criminals who make money, spread terror, and cause heartbreak while supplying exactly what has been forbidden in the first place.

- It's easy to see how people correlate the availability

of firearms and the occurrence of murder. *People kill people,* it's true, but a gun sure as heck *does help.*

- Surveyors are very brave people.

- Murders are solved by a combination of hard work, clear thinking, and dumb luck. They become a mystery when any of those three things are missing.

- People are murdered for things many of us have done, for things they know nothing about, and for no good reason other than being in the wrong place at the wrong time.

- Providing legal protection and due process to the suspect of a crime is a mark of a civilized society. Those thinking it's a bad idea should hold their tongues until they have been arrested.

- There are occasions when a killer deserves pity. Whether the courts will see it that way is another matter entirely.

- Given the correct set of circumstances anybody, *anybody,* is capable of killing somebody else.

- Men often kill because they cannot control basic emotions like greed, jealousy, and fury. A large number of these fellows are stupid-drunk at the time. For me, the biggest lesson of this book could be its subtitle:

Don't hang out with angry drunk men!

By The Numbers
Even if You Don't Like Math

When and Where

Townships and Years
(Plus Meadville and Titusville)

Here's a list of the general locations of the 135 killings, along with the year in which they were committed. One thing that jumps out of this chart right off the bat: the number of murders is led by the cities of Meadville and Titusville. This makes sense since they were the county's largest centers of population through the period covered. Generally speaking, more people cause more trouble.

A location listing "None found" is not, necessarily, murder-free. All it means is that I didn't find any. That's a very different thing.

<u>Location (# found):</u>	<u>In the Years:</u>
Athens (0)	*None found.*
Beaver (1)	1869.
Bloomfield (2)	1912, 1934.
Cambridge (5)	1878, 1900, 1913, 1943, 1953.
Conneaut (3)	1822, 1889, 1924.
Cussewago (1)	1880.

East Fairfield (3)	1833, 1904, 1918.
East Fallowfield (2)	1908, 1921.
East Mead (1)	1932.
Fairfield (0)	*None found.*
Greenwood (2)	1902, 1925.
Hayfield (1)	1891.
Meadville (47)	1805, 1881, 1884, 1886, 1896, 1904, 1908, 1910, 1911, 1911, 1911, 1914, 1914, 1915, 1915, 1916, 1918, 1918, 1919, 1920, 1920, 1920, 1922, 1922, 1923, 1923, 1924, 1925, 1926, 1929, 1929, 1931, 1932, 1932, 1934, 1934, 1935, 1937, 1937, 1941, 1941, 1944, 1946, 1946, 1952, 1953, 1954.
North Shenango (0)	*None found.*
Oil Creek (3)	1866, 1870, 1917.
Pine (2)	1928, 1932.
Randolph (2)	1864, 1930.
Richmond (1)	1941.
Rockdale (1)	1908.
Rome (0)	*None found.*
Sadsbury (2)	1924, 1927.
South Shenango (0)	*None found.*
Sparta (3)	1817, 1878, 1923.
Spring (1)	1916.
Steuben (0)	*None found.*
Summerhill (1)	1943.
Summit (2)	1923, 1924.
Titusville (23)	1866, 1870, 1871, 1873, 1878, 1881, 1884, 1885, 1893, 1894, 1899, 1902, 1907, 1912, 1912, 1917, 1921, 1923, 1925, 1926, 1943, 1950, 1955.
Troy (2)	1879, 1915.
Union (1)	1926.
Venango (1)	1875.
Vernon (7)	1870, 1908, 1919, 1921, 1925, 1927, 1935.
Wayne (0)	*None found.*
West Fallowfield (2)	1910, 1925.

West Mead (0)	*None found.*
West Shenango (0)	*None found.*
Woodcock (5)	1860, 1912, 1913, 1926, 1929.
Unknown Location (8)	1853, 1853, 1858, 1868, 1878, 1889, 1899, 1942.

Killings in Titusville occurred mostly within an eight-block residential area. Interestingly, homes that hosted a murder are gone, even though their neighbors might remain standing. Murder sites outside this residential district, in the "less desirable" areas of town, have been obliterated by urban renewal.

Meadville's murders, while slightly more widespread, were concentrated in the southwestern "4th Ward" in an area bordered by West, French, and Dock Streets. Close by the railroad, these neighborhoods were destroyed in 1974 when the "French Creek Parkway" was built to carry state highways 6 and 19 around, instead of though, the city.

Cochranton, located near where French Creek exits southern Crawford County, is curiously absent from our charts. I suspect it's because the town was founded fairly late (1855) and its growth was slow and steady, allowing city services to "keep up." Cochranton may have been relatively peaceful during the period covered by this book, but the town eventually goes on to gain some notoriety in the county's criminal courts.

Location, Location, Location

Let's take the dates from above and stack them this way:

Population:	Years:	Murders Found:		
2,346	1800 – 1809	1		
6,178	1810 – 1819	1		
9,397	1820 – 1829	1		
16,030	1830 – 1839	0		
31,724	1840 – 1849	0		
37,849	1850 – 1859	3		
48,755	1860 – 1869	5	*Titusville 1*	/ Meadville 0
63,832	1870 – 1879	11	*Titusville 4*	/ Meadville 0
68,607	1880 – 1889	11	Titusville 3	/ Meadville 3
65,324	1890 – 1899	6	*Titusville 3*	/ Meadville 1
63,643	1900 – 1909	10	Titusville 2	/ Meadville 2
61,565	1910 – 1919	25	Titusville 3	/ *Meadville 12*
60,667	1920 – 1929	32	Titusville 4	/ *Meadville 12*
62,980	1930 – 1939	13	Titusville 0	/ *Meadville 8*
74,644	1940 – 1949	10	Titusville 1	/ *Meadville 5*
79,948	1950 – 1955	6	Titusville 2	/ *Meadville 3*

There are clear differences in the rate and timing of murders in the county's two major cities.

Titusville experienced explosive, oil-fueled growth from the late 1850s until the early 1900s, and more people generally cause more trouble, remember? These early killings gave Titusville a rough-and-tumble reputation that has, deserved or not, tended to stick to the Queen City.

Any notions of gentility felt by the County Seat should certainly have been wiped away by the years of booze- and prohibition-fueled mayhem that followed. But people don't always respond logically. Do they?

In Titusville, murders were most often a mix of at least two of the following: liquor, money, and love.

As for Meadville... The causes of capital crime were rapid growth, the influx of unattached male immigrants, booze, prostitution, and the failure of the city to deal with the situation.

Note, also, how the population of the county has to reach a certain point before killings become more common. The relationship between population and the number of murders is not a solid one, however. The county's most violent decades were ones in which the population was decreasing.

The single, most violent ten-year period was 1920-1929—during Prohibition—when the population was at a relative minimum.

A LITTLE MORE DETAIL, PLEASE

It's interesting how killings increase as the months warm up. This trend, which didn't appear until after 1900, matches modern stats: More people out and about in nicer weather results in more crime. The big exception to this trend is November with lots of murders around the start of hunting season and, then again, at Thanksgiving. *Almost all of the killings in the months of March and December occurred prior to 1900.* Cabin fever?

It's hard to tell in this chart, but the most likely date to be killed—with almost twice the murders of other days— is the 13th of any month. How's that for bad luck? Days with no murders? The 1st, 14th, and the 21st.

Month of Year:	Days of Month:
January (8)	5, 6, 6, 8, 16, 18, 28, 29
February (5)	5, 5, 8, 8, 17
March (7)	2, 10, 13, 18, 24, 30, ud (unknown date)
April (13)	3, 4, 6, 11, 13, 13, 15, 16, 19, 23, 24, 26, 28
May (11)	6, 9, 9, 23, 25, 25, 26, 26, 28, 30, ud
June (12)	9, 11, 11, 13, 13, 16, 19, 20, 28, 28, ud, ud
July (13)	2, 4, 6, 9, 12, 12, 16, 17, 17, 18, 23, 25, 30
August (10)	5, 6, 7, 13, 15, 19, 22, 23, 27, 31
September (9)	13, 13, 13, 17, 19, 19, 24, 26, 30
October (8)	2, 6, 8, 10, 10, 12, 23, ud
November (14)	3, 3, 4, 8, 9, 9, 9, 11, 13, 16, 27, 28, 29, ud
December (10)	2, 8, 19, 24, 24, 26, 27, 29, ud, ud

Day of Week:	Murders Found:
Monday	12
Tuesday	18 (paydays, maybe?)
Wednesday	12
Thursday	14
Friday	19 (party-Party-PARTY!)
Saturday	19 (ditto)
Sunday	16 (most are Saturday night drunks)

WHO AND WHAT

WHO WAS SUSPECTED OF KILLING WHOM?

The answers can be found in this chart, at least for crimes listing such data. *The numbers won't add up because of gaps in the information:*

Of the 135 Killings:	Murders Found:

Male suspects:
96 killings, total: Male Victims – 60 deaths
      45 Acquaintances
      3 Strangers
      3 During Arrest
      2 Fathers-in-Law
      1 Father
      1 Brother
      1 Brother-in-Law
      1 Newborn
    Female Victims – 33 deaths
      18 Wives
      5 Acquaintances
      3 Lovers
      2 Mothers-in-Law
      2 Patients
      1 Mother
      1 Sister-in-Law

Female Suspects:
10 killings, total: Female Victims
    None found
    Male Victims – 8 deaths
      3 Husbands
      2 Acquaintances
      2 "Customers"
      1 Newborn

Why and How

It Goes to Motive, if You've got the Guts

The old saw says: "Men kill out of anger. Women kill out of fear." That is generally true, but not always the case.

Of the 135 Killings:

Motive Described:	Number Found – Victim *killed by*:
Anger	53 – mostly male *kb* male
Fear/Self Defense	20 – mostly male *kb* female
Jealousy	11 – both sexes *kb* both
Greed	8 – mostly male *kb* male
"Accidental"	5 – both *kb* both
"Insanity"	3 – both *kb* both
During Arrest	4 – male *kb* male

Death Occurred by:	
Shooting	59 – both *kb* both
Blunt Trauma	24 – both *kb* male
Stab/Hack/Cut	13 – mostly female *kb* male
Abortion	8 – female & viable infants *kb* both
Drowning	9 – always unsolved
Run Over by Auto	2 – both *kb* male
"Neglect"	2 – infant *kb* female
Choking	1 – female *kb* male
Decapitation	1 – female *kb* male
"Misuse"	1 – female *kb* male
Poison	1 – male *kb* male/female couple

Booze involved:	
Yes	48 – mostly drunken, male killers
No	71

A Little Bit More on
Victims and Suspects

Murder Isn't Just for the Young

Age data is mostly missing from many of the earlier murders. That being said, there really isn't much difference between the ages of victims and suspects, or ages of men and women involved in Crawford County murders.

There are two exceptions: The first is the large number of infants, all of whom, no doubt, had a much older killer. The second is the slightly higher number of suspects in the upper age range. These are all men who finally wigged out when pushed too far by some neighbor or relative.

The sole 81 – 90 year-old victim is an aged mother-in-law who happened to be in the wrong place at the wrong time. So much of being murdered is nothing but simple bad luck.

Of the 135 Killings:

Age Range in Years:	Victims:	Suspects:
1 – 10	13	0
11 – 20	3	4
21 – 30	18	18
31 – 40	10	9
41 – 50	12	7
51 – 60	3	4
61 – 70	3	3
71 – 80	0	2
81 – 90	1	0

PAYING THE PIPER

A SUMMATION OF SENTENCES

Doing the crime *may* add up to doing the time. You'll notice a lack of women in the punishment chart. That's because they were almost always forgiven by the courts, even when they confessed their crimes.

Of the 135 Killings:

Charged With:	Number Found – Suspect:
Murder in the First	19 – 17 male, 2 female
Murder in the Second	19
"Murder"	24

Outcomes:	Number Found – Suspect:
Guilty	39 – mostly male
Not Guilty	32 – mostly male
	2 – cases "thrown out" by judge
No Trial	45 – 21 – suicides of which 19 were males who killed females
	2 – escapes, both male
	22 – unsolved

Sentences/Punishments:	Number Found:
Murder in the First	5 – to be hanged (4 completed)
	4 – to be electrocuted (2 completed)
	3 – death commuted to life
	4 – retried to lesser charges
	4 – acquitted (male and female)
"Treatment"	5 – both sexes
0 – 10 Years	4 – male and female
11 – 20 Years	13 – male
More than 20 Years	2 – male (both paroled)
Life	2 – male (commuted)

Sources and Sundries

Newspapers

The "facts" of these murders were taken almost entirely from printed articles. Sometimes, just one article. Now, I don't to want aggravate any newspaper folks (they can be a mean bunch), but relying on a single news piece is a dicey proposition.

A single article always made me uncomfortable because I regularly saw pieces in different papers at complete odds with each other. I also found subsequent articles in the same newspaper disagreeing with what was printed the day before, or the same article with a couple of different spellings of the same name. But, you have to take what you can find.

The newspapers used most were:

The *(Greenville) (Record) (Advance) Argus* (starting 1880) was an excellent source. Its home was (and is) Greenville, Mercer County, Pennsylvania, south of Crawford. The *Argus* always reported major crimes in the western portion of Crawford County, drawing apparent delight in taking editorial pot-shots at what they seemed to consider their violent, hick, backwards neighbors to the north.

The *Titusville (Morning) Herald*, first published in 1865, was outspoken, combative, somewhat rough-edged, and tended towards over-heated prose. They reported world, national, regional, and local news along with (of course) a wealth of information on the early years of the oil industry. Most political shading was of a local, or county-wide color. Though, during the late 1800s, when Titusville was trying to peel itself apart from Crawford, it was difficult to find *any* references to the rest of the county—sometimes to the point of ignoring the Meadville court sessions unless somebody local to the paper was involved in the trial.

A variety of Meadville papers were available starting in the early 1800s. Many ran their news through some sort of strong political filter, Democrat, Republican, and otherwise. *The (Meadville) Tribune (Republican)* grew to consider itself Crawford County's newspaper of record. Care to guess what the *Herald* thought about that?

The *Tribune* reported world, national, regional, and local news, with a sometimes snooty, superior, and condescending tone. Through the late 1800s and early 1900s, it showed a propensity towards racism that was mostly lacking in other county papers. That might have been the result of the others ignoring the news that concerned immigrants and those of color.

The *Trib* always included a synopsis of court proceedings. Its regular readers included the judges and many of the lawyers involved in those cases, so the paper seemed fairly careful in its reporting on such topics.

Newspapers were my most common source of information. I used nearly 1,400 articles from the *Titusville Herald* alone. There were at least half again as many from the *Meadville Tribune* employed as cross-references. There's no telling how many total newspaper articles I read to find the ones I eventually used.

I probably don't want to know.

Court Records

Nearly every death in the county was attended to by a Coroner's Jury. The findings were always recorded in the Civil Court Dockets.

Never seen a docket? Imagine a huge, cloth-covered, hard-back book about two feet long and a half-foot thick. Filled with several hundred pages of heavy parchment or paper, they're about three feet wide when opened, dense, cumbersome, and usually pretty dusty. I spent hours sitting in a corner at the Recorder's Office in the Crawford County Courthouse, docket on my lap, leafing through thousands of pages looking for coroner's reports. It was enjoyable, if sneezy work. But, not all dockets were available to the public. Some were buried in basement storage.

Surprisingly, these most official of records were not always accurate. Dates were usually correct, but the names of the dead were sometimes misspelled—or simply wrong. This was hard for me to accept, at first, but I grew convinced after finding a number of cases where the courts spelled a name one way and other sources spelled it another.

One extreme example: Crawford County Quarter Sessions Civil Docket 2, p.20, no.50 listed a dead woman as "Millie Henderson." The newspapers referred to her as "Nellie Dennison." Her gravestone had the last name "Denison"—with one "n"—I used that. Another example of official records gone wrong was the death certificate issued for the man hanged for the murder of Daniel McGrath. The name on the certificate was "Frank Major" even though everyone knew it actually was "Daniel Kehoe."

During the period covered by this book, almost all court records were handwritten. Some recorders possessed extremely legible writing. Others weren't so hot. When "a" looked like "e" looked like "o," and "b" looked like "k" looked like "l," things got confusing pretty doggone fast. Considering the multitude of records that were written by hand, I suppose I shouldn't complain—too much.

Finding a Murder

Start with the Civil Dockets, if they are available. Read the findings of every Coroner's Jury—they always list a cause of death. Make note of all that are not attributable to age or illness. Get all the information: dates, names, ages, the works.

Go to the newspapers. The *Argus* and *Herald* are available online and can be searched with keywords. Theoretically, entering a word into a search engine pulls up relevant results. But it doesn't work that way. The software doesn't "read" the text. Instead, it takes the pattern of letters it receives and tries to match it to a similar pattern in the digital facsimile of a sheet of faded newsprint that might be more than a hundred years old. Often, the facsimile is a digitized image of faded newsprint taken from a hunk of microfilm that's also carrying a half-century of scratches.

Trial and error shows the best keywords contain low and round letters: "killing" doesn't work, but "murder" does. The name of the deceased might help, but remember, it might be wrong.

Plug in the year and month taken from the Coroner's Jury and try the word "murder." No valid results? Then, slog through the on-line papers one page at a time, starting a week ahead of the Coroner's Jury and proceeding to about a week after.

The entire edition of the paper must be examined, especially if the murder took place early in the county's history. The front page of the early *Titusville Morning Herald,* for example, is nothing but ads—no matter the story. Plus, there may be more than one article on the same story, perhaps an editorial, or sidebar. Good thing most early newspapers are only a few pages long.

Once a murder is found, hope the article refers to an earlier date that can be used to find previous news that describes the crime. Early newspapers, particularly the weeklies, are self-referential because there's no room to reprint news already published. The phrase "as described previously" means a long journey through earlier editions until what was already printed can be found.

Also be sure to work forward through the papers to find the trial, verdict, and sentence. Use the knowledge that Grand Juries meet on a quarterly basis. Grand Jury decisions are *almost* always reported within a few days of their dissolution. A person going to criminal trial is assigned a court date within a few days and that might be published. Depending on the circumstances, the criminal trial might net a only a column-inch, or two. The verdict is usually reported. Sentencing follows within the next couple of weeks, or months but doesn't always hit the papers. Readers are interested in crime and guilt, but not punishment.

No Court Dockets? Now the fun begins. Start with the online papers and examine every article found with the keyword "murder." A smart person might include the last name of the presiding judge, since one has to hear the case when it went to trial.

Trouble is papers love to print murder stories, local or not. Many older papers carry serialized stories, and many of them are murder mysteries. Once sports pages become common, one team is always being murdered by another. Be prepared for an over-abundance of "false positives."

No electronic versions of the paper to be searched? Now, the *real* fun begins. Get thee to a microfilm reader and start scanning one newspaper reel after another. Hopefully, there's no strong tendency toward motion-sickness, but if there is, close one eye while zooming through those rolls of film. That little trick really helped me.

As before, once a murder is found, work back to its origin and forward to its conclusion.

With a little good luck, the murder might be something sensational, say a policeman is involved, or the victim or suspect is a woman, or rich, or both. In these cases, there will be a large number of easy-to-find articles.

With a little bad luck, the murder might involve nobody of general interest. In these cases, consider it good fortune to find a description of the crime and a notation of the verdict some months later.

Articles on one crime sometimes refer to another with something like "similar to the _____ murder in April of '40." This gives a clue to cross-check. "End of the year" news summations printed in the last edition of one year's paper, or the first edition of the next, provide an excellent synopsis of the major crimes. "In the past" sections that list stories from that day over the last 5, 10, 15, and 20 years are also a great source for double-checking for murders that might otherwise be missed.

Murders, like suicides, seem to "cluster"—meaning when one happens it apparently increases the chance of another. Many murders can be found by paying attention to information close by what's being looked for. Take care to examine the obituaries printed near a known murder victim, and look at the previous and next edition of the newspaper.

After a few thousand look-ups, what kind of news is where in which newspaper becomes second nature. Want to see the verdicts of the third quarter-session's Grand Jury? Then, skip directly to that week and scan the appropriate page in that particular paper. Don't get over-confident. Newspaper formats change over time, sometimes suddenly.

Was I able to find every murder using these techniques? *No. Definitely not.* During my last session at the microfilm reader, I stumbled upon a murder that occurred in 1860. Finding yet another killing so close to the end of my active research produced a strongly mixed emotion: equal parts "Cool!" and "Crap!"

Sources of History

Information on general history was collected, as needed, from sources old and new. Some of it was found in the entertaining, wonderfully biased, and sometimes inaccurate *History of Crawford County, Pennsylvania: containing a history of the county; its townships, towns, villages, schools, churches, industries, etc. etc, etc.* by Samuel P. Bates (1885).

Biographical information on the judges was found in newspaper pieces leading up to elections (arguably one of the least trustworthy sources) and obituaries (arguably the most scrutinized articles printed). There was also excellent biographical information to be had in speeches given when one courthouse was replaced by the next. That is, except for the county's first judge, the Honorable Alexander Addison, who turned out to be a well-known example of the mistreatment of the judiciary by the legislative branch of government.

Most other information was gleaned from the plethora of ".gov" and "pa.us" web sites. It takes some digging, but given enough time, a persistent (stubborn?) researcher can find almost anything. Stuff from a ".gov" or "pa.us" site isn't necessarily more accurate, but it is more legitimate. That seems to be important.

FACT CHECKING

I always tried to cross-reference what I found with at least one other source. If the *Tribune* and the *Herald* agreed, I figured I was good to go. I couldn't do this in all cases because, as mentioned, there were times when all I had was a single newspaper article or an entry in a Civil Docket. That's why a number of listings include question marks—information wasn't there to be found.

LAST NOTES

I've been asked if anything "creepy" happened to me during the course of working this definitely morbid subject.

I've had a number of dreams on the topic. Some nightmares, but mostly, more like documentaries. The cases involving abused women and dead infants definitely bothered me the most.

I visited many of the murder sites and, at each one, felt a little thrill of excitement knowing what had happened there. I wanted to stop people on the street, point out the location, and describe the crime and its results. I never did, of course, but it might've been fun to try.

Likewise, I visited a number of gravesites of those involved. It was odd, knowing exactly how some forgotten person ended up in that small plot of ground. It made me wonder about the life-stories of those resting nearby.

One day, I was busy at one of the microfilm readers at the Crawford County Historical Society (please support your local organization). I had, after a long search, found a story describing the 1869 murder of Clarence Curtis. As I was reading the article, I was distracted by a middle-aged man visiting from another state. He was doing genealogical research and mentioned the surname Curtis. I asked if he had an ancestor named "Clarence Curtis." He did, and knew the man had died at a young age, but didn't have a cause of death. I printed the article I was reading and handed it to him.

A few months later I was sitting at a table in the Crawford County Historical Society compiling notes. I struck up a conversation with a young man reading microfilm. When I told him what I was working on, he looked at me strangely and said his own family had suffered such a tragedy. He gave me the names of the people involved. I had information that he did not. He shared his family's version of the story and how the killing had changed the lives of three generations.

ONE FINAL STORY

On a lark, I asked a person in a new building that occupies the old location of the home of a murdered man, if she ever heard anything "go bump in the night."

Her eyes widened. "Anybody who ever spent the night here will tell you this place is haunted. There are noises all the time.

Doors opening and closing, the sound of foot-steps, things being dropped."

I told her the story behind the property. She smiled and said, "Next time, I'll use his name when I tell him to cut it out!"

Indexes of Crime

Year – Victim – Suspect

1805 – ? – ?
1817 – Fitzpatrick – Van Holland
1822 – Smith – Lamphier
1833 – Hickenbottom – Gosnell
1853 – ? – Brecoev
1853 – ? – Breeder
1858 – Shellito – Shellito
1860 – Hope – Garvey
1864 – Shoemaker – Rouchlander
1866 – Doyle – ?
1866 – Hickey – Hickey
1868 – ? – Mook
1868 – ? – Work
1869 – Curtis – Varnes
1870 – Infant – ?
1870 – Kightlinger – Brown
1870 – Kightlinger – Turner
1870 – Richards – ?
1871 – Wisner – ?
1873 – Nielson – Hallingreen
1875 – Infant Boy – ?
1878 – ? – Snyder
1878 – Infant Girl – Fairchild
1878 – Miller – Miller
1878 – Miller – Minimum
1879 – Winters – Winters
1880 – Hattie – ?

1881 – Childs – ?
1881 – Howard – Bork
1884 – Campbell – Schultz
1884 – Infant Girl – ?
1885 – Kepler – Keck
1886 – Powers – Fairchild
1889 – Turner – Turner
1891 – Hotchkiss – Hites
1891 – Hotchkiss – Peelman
1891 – Hotchkiss – Skeel
1893 – Crecraft – Crecraft
1893 – Crecraft – Newton
1894 – McAndrew – McDonnel
1896 – Karleskind – Karleskind
1899 – Infant – Chamberlain
1899 – Infant – Havaty
1899 – Kelly – Chamberlain
1899 – Kelly – Havaty
1899 – McGrath – Kehoe
1899 – McGrath – Woodard
1900 – Infant – ?
1902 – Goodwill – Peer
1902 – Riley – ?
1904 – ? Man – ?
1904 – Infant Boy – ?
1907 – Infant Boy – ?
1908 – Hover – Hover
1908 – Petrole – Nosti
1908 – Sheldon – Hall

1908 – Winters – Cronin
1910 – Falcet – Dandren
1910 – Tartaglion – Del Curto
1911 – Gulick – ?
1911 – Orner – Orner
1911 – Rosse – Polliquay
1912 – Infant – ?
1912 – Infant – ?
1912 – Russe – Senenlillo
1912 – Wellmon – Wellmon
1913 – Terna – Nuncite
1913 – Tino – Nuncite
1913 – Wonich – Cooklin
1914 – Constatino – ?
1914 – Raucci – Dimmaggio
1915 – ? – ?
1915 – Henry – Henry
1915 – Smith – Henry
1916 – Covell – McHugh
1916 – Haymer – Burgess
1917 – Denison – Haley
1917 – Gerson – Wood
1918 – Mickle – Smith
1918 – Oxley – Smith
1918 – Schnepp – Waters
1919 – Dernfanger – Dernfanger
1919 – Munno – Mastrovito
1919 – Munno – Vardarno
1920 – Kulich – Cullen
1920 – Morneweck – ?
1920 – Schultz – Smock
1921 – ? Man – ?
1921 – Sieczka – Pendolino
1921 – Tropksi – Toms
1922 – Breed – Larosa
1922 – Roberts – Kudrian
1923 – Crawford – Ewing
1923 – Infant Girl – ?
1923 – Petrolia – ?
1923 – Sterling – Weatherbee
1923 – Weber – ?

1924 – McGowan – Platt
1924 – Plummer – Shorts
1924 – Tedesco – ?
1924 – Terril – Hotchkiss
1925 – Hill – Kuhn
1925 – Krenz – Flanders
1925 – Krenz – Moran
1925 – Locke – ?
1925 – Malek – Levinsky
1925 – Malek – Patterson
1925 – Williams – Ogram
1926 – Dawley – Stitt
1926 – Infant Dow – Dow
1926 – Mariarz – DeMaio
1926 – Muztuck – Muztuck
1927 – Schroedel – Peterman
1927 – Waitschis – ?
1928 – Wallace – Wallace
1929 – Brown – Boulton
1929 – Brown – Dewey
1929 – Brown – Stainbrook
1929 – Jones – Gilbert
1929 – Toppo – Trotto
1930 – Infant Boy – ?
1931 – Holt – Wade
1932 – ? Woman – ?
1932 – Boush – Boush
1932 – Kinley – Kinley
1932 – Slingluff – Hamilton
1934 – Cardinale – Belifore
1934 – Richards – Richards
1934 – Sugar – ?
1935 – Johnston – ?
1935 – Shellenberger –
         Shellenberger
1937 – Catalino – Dellario
1937 – Strickland – Walls
1941 – DePascale – DePascale
1941 – Miller – DePascale
1941 – Reuchart – Ikenburg
1942 – Johnson – Johnson

1943 – Allen – Russell
1943 – Muir – Marvin
1943 – Phelps – Kinch
1944 – Wooley – Wooley
1946 – Beal – Ackley
1946 – Davidio – Davidio
1950 – Loop – ?
1952 – Thrash – Lilly
1953 – Hatch – Turner
1953 – Starr – Terrell
1954 – Decker – Brinkley
1955 – Prody – Brown

Victim – Suspect – Year

? – ? – 1805
? – ? – 1915
? – Brecoev – 1853
? – Breeder – 1853
? – Mook – 1868
? – Snyder – 1878
? – Work – 1868
? Man – ? – 1904
? Man – ? – 1921
? Woman – ? – 1932
Allen – Russell – 1943
Beal – Ackley – 1946
Boush – Boush – 1932
Breed – Larosa – 1922
Brown – Boulton – 1929
Brown – Dewey – 1929
Brown – Stainbrook – 1929
Campbell – Schultz – 1884
Cardinale – Belifore – 1934
Catalino – Dellario – 1937
Childs – ? – 1881
Constatino – ? – 1914
Covell – McHugh – 1916
Crawford – Ewing – 1923
Crecraft – Crecraft – 1893
Crecraft – Newton – 1893
Curtis – Varnes – 1869

Davidio – Davidio – 1946
Dawley – Stitt – 1926
Decker – Brinkley – 1954
Denison – Haley – 1917
DePascale – DePascale – 1941
Dernfanger – Dernfanger – 1919
Doyle – ? – 1866
Falcet – Dandren – 1910
Fitzpatrick – Van Holland – 1817
Gerson – Wood – 1917
Goodwill – Peer – 1902
Gulick – ? – 1911
Hatch – Turner – 1953
Hattie – ? – 1880
Haymer – Burgess – 1916
Henry – Henry – 1915
Hickenbottom – Gosnell – 1833
Hickey – Hickey – 1866
Hill – Kuhn – 1925
Holt – Wade – 1931
Hope – Garvey – 1860
Hotchkiss – Hites – 1891
Hotchkiss – Peelman – 1891
Hotchkiss – Skeel – 1891
Hover – Hover – 1908
Howard – Bork – 1881
Infant – ? – 1870
Infant – ? – 1900
Infant – ? – 1912
Infant – ? – 1912
Infant – Chamberlain – 1899
Infant – Havaty – 1899
Infant Boy – ? – 1875
Infant Boy – ? – 1904
Infant Boy – ? – 1907
Infant Boy – ? – 1930
Infant Dow – Dow – 1926
Infant Girl – ? – 1884
Infant Girl – ? – 1923
Infant Girl – Fairchild – 1878
Johnson – Johnson – 1942

Johnston – ? – 1935
Jones – Gilbert – 1929
Karleskind – Karleskind – 1896
Kelly – Chamberlain – 1899
Kelly – Havaty – 1899
Kepler – Keck – 1885
Kightlinger – Brown – 1870
Kightlinger – Turner – 1870
Kinley – Kinley – 1932
Krenz – Flanders – 1925
Krenz – Moran – 1925
Kulich – Cullen – 1920
Locke – ? – 1925
Loop – ? – 1950
Malek – Levinsky – 1925
Malek – Patterson – 1925
Mariarz – DeMaio – 1926
McAndrew – McDonnel – 1894
McGowan – Platt – 1924
McGrath – Kehoe – 1899
McGrath – Woodard – 1899
Mickle – Smith – 1918
Miller – DePascale – 1941
Miller – Miller – 1878
Miller – Minimum – 1878
Morneweck – ? – 1920
Muir – Marvin – 1943
Munno – Mastrovito – 1919
Munno – Vardarno – 1919
Muztuck – Muztuck – 1926
Nielson – Hallingreen – 1873
Orner – Orner – 1911
Oxley – Smith – 1918
Petrole – Nosti – 1908
Petrolia – ? – 1923
Phelps – Kinch – 1943
Plummer – Shorts – 1924
Powers – Fairchild – 1886
Prody – Brown – 1955
Raucci – Dimmaggio – 1914
Reuchart – Ikenburg – 1941

Richards – ? – 1870
Richards – Richards – 1934
Riley – ? – 1902
Roberts – Kudrian – 1922
Rosse – Polliquay – 1911
Russe – Senenlillo – 1912
Schnepp – Waters – 1918
Schroedel – Peterman – 1927
Schultz – Smock – 1920
Sheldon – Hall – 1908
Shellenberger – Shellenberger – 1935
Shellito – Shellito – 1858
Shoemaker – Rouchlander – 1864
Sieczka – Pendolino – 1921
Slingluff – Hamilton – 1932
Smith – Henry – 1915
Smith – Lamphier – 1822
Starr – Terrell – 1953
Sterling – Weatherbee – 1923
Strickland – Walls – 1937
Sugar – ? – 1934
Tartaglion – Del Curto – 1910
Tedesco – ? – 1924
Terna – Nuncite – 1913
Terril – Hotchkiss – 1924
Thrash – Lilly – 1952
Tino – Nuncite – 1913
Toppo – Trotto – 1929
Tropksi – Toms – 1921
Turner – Turner – 1889
Waitschis – ? – 1927
Wallace – Wallace – 1928
Weber – ? – 1923
Wellmon – Wellmon – 1912
Williams – Ogram – 1925
Winters – Cronin – 1908
Winters – Winters – 1879
Wisner – ? – 1871
Wonich – Cooklin – 1913
Wooley – Wooley – 1944

Suspect – Victim – Year

? – ? – 1805
? – ? – 1915
? – ? Man – 1904
? – ? Man – 1921
? – ? Woman – 1932
? – Childs – 1881
? – Constatino – 1914
? – Doyle – 1866
? – Gulick – 1911
? – Hattie – 1880
? – Infant – 1870
? – Infant – 1900
? – Infant – 1912
? – Infant – 1912
? – Infant Boy – 1875
? – Infant Boy – 1904
? – Infant Boy – 1907
? – Infant Boy – 1930
? – Infant Girl – 1884
? – Infant Girl – 1923
? – Johnston – 1935
? – Locke – 1925
? – Loop – 1950
? – Morneweck – 1920
? – Petrolia – 1923
? – Richards – 1870
? – Riley – 1902
? – Sugar – 1934
? – Tedesco – 1924
? – Waitschis – 1927
? – Weber – 1923
? – Wisner – 1871
Ackley – Beal – 1946
Belifore – Cardinale – 1934
Bork – Howard – 1881
Boulton – Brown – 1929
Boush – Boush – 1932
Brecoev – ? – 1853
Breeder – ? – 1853

Brinkley – Decker – 1954
Brown – Kightlinger – 1870
Brown – Prody – 1955
Burgess – Haymer – 1916
Chamberlain – Infant – 1899
Chamberlain – Kelly – 1899
Cooklin – Wonich – 1913
Crecraft – Crecraft – 1893
Cronin – Winters – 1908
Cullen – Kulich – 1920
Dandren – Falcet – 1910
Davidio – Davidio – 1946
Del Curto – Tartaglion – 1910
Dellario – Catalino – 1937
DeMaio – Mariarz – 1926
DePascale – DePascale – 1941
Dernfanger – Dernfanger – 1919
Dewey – Brown – 1929
Dimmaggio – Raucci – 1914
Dow – Infant Dow – 1926
Ewing – Crawford – 1923
Fairchild – Infant Girl – 1878
Fairchild – Powers – 1886
Flanders – Krenz – 1925
Garvey – Hope – 1860
Gilbert – Jones – 1929
Gosnell – Hickenbottom – 1833
Haley – Denison – 1917
Hall – Sheldon – 1908
Hallingreen – Nielson – 1873
Hamilton – Slingluff – 1932
Havaty – Infant – 1899
Havaty – Kelly – 1899
Henry – Henry – 1915
Henry – Smith – 1915
Hickey – Hickey – 1866
Hites – Hotchkiss – 1891
Hotchkiss – Terril – 1924
Hover – Hover – 1908
Ikenburg – Reuchart – 1941
Johnson – Johnson – 1942

Karleskind – Karleskind – 1896
Keck – Kepler – 1885
Kehoe – McGrath – 1899
Kinch – Phelps – 1943
Kinley – Kinley – 1932
Kudrian – Roberts – 1922
Kuhn – Hill – 1925
Lamphier – Smith – 1822
Larosa – Breed – 1922
Levinsky – Malek – 1925
Lilly – Thrash – 1952
Marvin – Muir – 1943
Mastrovito – Munno – 1919
McDonnel – McAndrew – 1894
McHugh – Covell – 1916
Miller – Miller – 1878
Minimum – Miller – 1878
Mook – ? – 1868
Moran – Krenz – 1925
Muztuck – Muztuck – 1926
Newton – Crecraft – 1893
Nosti – Petrole – 1908
Nuncite – Terna – 1913
Nuncite – Tino – 1913
Ogram – Williams – 1925
Orner – Orner – 1911
Patterson – Malek – 1925
Peelman – Hotchkiss – 1891
Peer – Goodwill – 1902
Pendolino – Sieczka – 1921
Peterman – Schroedel – 1927
Platt – McGowan – 1924
Polliquay – Rosse – 1911
Richards – Richards – 1934
Rouchlander – Shoemaker – 1864
Russell – Allen – 1943
Schultz – Campbell – 1884
Senenlillo – Russe – 1912
Shellenberger – Shellenberger – 1935
Shellito – Shellito – 1858
Shorts – Plummer – 1924

Skeel – Hotchkiss – 1891
Smith – Mickle – 1918
Smith – Oxley – 1918
Smock – Schultz – 1920
Snyder – ? – 1878
Stainbrook – Brown – 1929
Stitt – Dawley – 1926
Terrell – Starr – 1953
Toms – Tropksi – 1921
Trotto – Toppo – 1929
Turner – Hatch – 1953
Turner – Kightlinger – 1870
Turner – Turner – 1889
Van Holland – Fitzpatrick – 1817
Vardarno – Munno – 1919
Varnes – Curtis – 1869
Wade – Holt – 1931
Wallace – Wallace – 1928
Walls – Strickland – 1937
Waters – Schnepp – 1918
Weatherbee – Sterling – 1923
Wellmon – Wellmon – 1912
Winters – Winters – 1879
Wood – Gerson – 1917
Woodard – McGrath – 1899
Wooley – Wooley – 1944
Work – ? – 1868

About the Author

The irony is that Don Hilton doesn't care much for history. Neither is he a fan of murder mysteries. But he loves to research and is happy to learn almost anything to tell stories that nobody else remembers. This is his third book based on the past of Crawford County, Pennsylvania.